THE WORLD OF THE EARLY CHURCH
A Companion to the New Testament

THE WORLD OF THE EARLY CHURCH
A Companion to the New Testament

Priscilla and Rebecca Patten

WIPF & STOCK · Eugene, Oregon

Wipf and Stock Publishers
199 W 8th Ave, Suite 3
Eugene, OR 97401

The World of the Early Church
A Companion to the New Testament
By Patten, Priscilla and Patten, Rebecca
Copyright©1991 Skaggs, Rebecca
ISBN 13: 978-1-55635-860-9
Publication date 2/12/2008
Previously published by Edwin Mellen, 1991

*Dedicated to the Memory
of Our Beloved Brother
Tom Patten*

TABLE OF CONTENTS

PART I - BEFORE THE TIMES
Chapter
1. Alexander the Great — 1
   - *The Music of Israel* — 12
2. The Maccabees — 15
   - *Jewish Instruments* — 30
3. The Jews and the Romans — 33
   - *Music in the Bible* — 42
4. The Pharisees and Sadducees — 47
   - *Biblical Instruments* — 67
5. The Essenes — 71
   - *The Scrolls* — 85
   - *Chart of Scrolls* — 100
   - *Wind Instruments* — 102
6. The Samaritans — 107
   - *Percussion (Shaking & Rattling Instruments)* — 115
7. Messianic Expectations — 117
   - *Orchestras of the Temples* — 133
   - *Augustus* — 134

PART II - BIRTH, SURVIVAL, IDENTITY
Chapter
1. The Identity of the Church — 139
   - *Tiberius* — 145
2. Persecution of the Church — 147
   - *Caligula, Claudius, Nero* — 159
3. The Judaizers — 167
   - *Vespasian* — 175

	4.	The Greek Gods	177
		- *Titus, son of Vespasian*	184
	5.	The Mystery Regions	187
	6.	Stoicism	201
	7.	Epicureanism	215
	8.	Gnosticism	225
		- *Domitian*	239

CONCLUSION 243
BIBLIOGRAPHY 245
INDEX 257

PREFACE

To many students of the New Testament the environment into which the Christian gospel was born is an unknown world. They read it only in the light of their own time and interpret it by their own experience. In reality, its several books were written for a culture that has long since passed out of existence and for modes of thought that are not remembered or understood by the modern world, except for professional scholars. That culture, however, bears a remarkable parallelism to our own in many ways; and while its terminology is very different, its basic philosophical principles still survive.

This volume will clarify many obscure allusions and illuminate a number of difficult texts in the New Testament. It will provide a better knowledge of the Palestinian background of the life of Christ and the church of the first century, as well as aid in understanding the struggle of the church as it confronted the complex social and religious world around it. It should assist any reader as he/she attempts to interpret the nature and problems of the present church in light of its past problems.

In organizing the material for this book, it seemed useful to include the information on ancient music in the first half and the church under the Roman Emperors in the second half. In order to make reading more interesting, we have interspersed this material throughout the other chapters.

We want to thank the many people who helped with the editing and typing of this manuscript. Particularly we want to acknowledge our brother Tom Patten who did the research on ancient music, Hannah Harrington who wrote the first draft of the chapter on Alexander, and Beverly Mowrer who contributed some work on the Maccabees.

PART I
BEFORE THE TIMES

Chapter 1

ALEXANDER THE GREAT

ALEXANDER THE GREAT! Great in his impact on world civilization. Great in his vision of a unified world that blended cultural values of the West and East in the most humane and enlightened empire the world has ever known. His policies of cultural assimilation, education and world commerce benefited all the nations comprising his empire. His rule gave new thrust to the concept of the importance of the individual as envisioned by Plato, Aristotle and, later, by the Epicureans and Stoics. This was a world that in language, philosophy and culture became a seedbed for early Christianity and helped to make possible its widespread acceptance and rapid extension in the first century.

Alexander the Great, son of Philip of Macedon, probably made more changes in the world of his time than did any other universal figure, before or since. His influence can still be seen. He gave the world new concepts of armies and of government. He made possible universal world trade, and he successfully blended the Greek and Asiatic cultures. He made education blossom in many fields through his personal discoveries and through exchanges of knowledge made possible by his world empire. Philosophical ideas of his era inspired the minds of men, instilling new thoughts and questions which prepared the world for the message of Christianity.

Alexander was an invincible military genius. He conquered the known world of his day, using a nationalistic army with no mercenaries, relying solely on the ties holding his men to their own land. He knew that the spirit of his fellow Macedonians would be stronger than that of the mercenary armies of the other nations because they were fighting for their own soil. Unlike earlier armies, the Macedonians spent enough time in rigid training to consider soldiering a true profession. Yet at heart they were still farmers. Other armies of the time were either mercenary, caring only for money rather than their homeland, or they were quickly assembled in times of emergency without previous training.

One of Alexander's great contributions was the refinement of this nationalistic army. Founded by his father Philip, the Macedonian phalanx reached its peak under Alexander and lasted beyond the coming of Rome to world power. Alexander introduced the heavy use of cavalry, new organization for the army, and ingenious strategies that enabled him to conquer the world at the age of thirty-two. The army was made up of the phalanx of infantry in the center and two wings, one of infantry and one of cavalry. The phalanx, the army's heart, consisted of 1,000 footmen in rank and sixteen in file – 16,000 men armed with sixteen-foot iron spears and iron shields. Alexander used cavalry of different types, opening and sometimes ending battles with his cavalry. Between the phalanx and his cavalry Alexander's army was almost invincible.

Tracing some of his battles, we can see Alexander's tactical prowess. In the attack on Thrace, in the north, the Macedonians had to climb steep mountains. The Thracians sent loaded wagons over the mountains to roll onto and crush Alexander's army. Alexander had the men lock their shields over their heads so the wagons would roll over the shields. Only a few men were lost. In the siege of Tyre, the Greeks learned how to attack a walled city. Alexander had battering rams made – long, heavy beams headed with iron or brass and suspended by a chain. These were swung into the wall until a breach was made. Alexander taught the men to build a huge causeway from the mainland of what is now Lebanon to the island of Tyre. As they worked on this ramp they erected machines for throwing stones and darts onto the Tyrian galleys that tried to approach them The siege at Tyre with the powerful stone-throwing machines and catapults was made possible because of Alexander's earlier experience at Halicarnassus, where for the first time in world history catapults were used to hurl objects over a city wall.

Alexander built siege sheds to cover the battering rams, thus enabling them to reach the walls of Halicarnassus. Later, at Tyre, the catapults actually threw the objects directly at the walls until they gave way. These machines were tremendously complementary to the battering rams.

In his battle against Darius, Alexander introduced a procedure to defeat the fearsome Persians, who drove their elephants and chariots with scythes attached to the axles straight into the enemy lines. First, Alexander would frighten the elephants; then his footmen would seize the horses of the chariots. After this the Greeks would fall back, let the Persians charge through, then attack them from the rear. Never before had an army been able to defeat the terrible Persians decisively.

Alexander introduced new ideas of government, based partially on his self-concept as a deity. When he marched through Egypt, he established himself as the son of the god Jupiter-Ammon. From his birth it had been rumored that he was the product of his witch-mother and a god. Many believed this, and the public announcement of it in an Egyptian temple appeared to confirm Alexander as monarch-god.

As W. W. Tarn has shown, Alexander set the example for the Ptolemies and Seleucids. Ptolemy I inaugurated official worship of the late Alexander "probably soon after he took the crown in 305. Soon after 290 Ptolemy II instituted at Alexandria a great festival in worship of his father, Ptolemy I, and Antiochus I followed by deifying Seleucus as Zeus Nikator; and therewith established the further principle that the kings, like Alexander, officially became gods after death." Alexander was especially worshiped in Alexandria, Egypt, the greatest of the cities he founded. As might be expected, his army also worshiped him greatly after his death at the age of 33.

Alexander's purpose in deifying himself was not so much to start an official cult for his personal glorification as it was to unify his subjects under him. The political advantage of this policy, along with the personal excesses which Alexander apparently never intended, were seized upon by his successors, and thus the old Hellenic democratic city-states were quickly formed into monarchies headed by power-hungry despots claiming divinity for themselves.

The military colony was established under Alexander; before his time the Greeks had known only the *polis* (city), or the *kome* (village). Alexander personally founded more than seventy cities; all of the "Alexandrias" were of his making. But these cities were not as formally structured as the Greek *polis*, each of which was characterized by the division of citizens into tribes, a council chosen from the tribes, magistrates, separate city-lands belonging only to its citizens, laws, a budget, an assembly, and city subdivisions. Only a king could found a true city in the Greek sense. The king would have to find land and settlers, build the walls and supply food and livestock for the people. Taxation would not be enforced at the beginning. It was the king's responsibility to provide housing and a city code, and to establish the political and social life of the city. Although many of Alexander's military colonies eventually became cities under the Seleucids and Ptolemies, they were not founded for that purpose. Neither was the military colony like a *kome*, or village. These were simply collections of houses without the orders of the city; the *kome* could be very large or very small. To the Greeks, even cities as large as Jerusalem, Babylon and Memphis were only villages because they did not have the systematized government of the Greek *polis*.

In keeping with Alexander's policy, the purposes of the military colony were to infiltrate the newly conquered Asian peoples with Greeks to spread Greek culture, to provide military defense, and to establish reserves for Alexander's army. It was not necessary to set up the military colony as the king would set up the *polis*; it could be founded by the monarch and then given to subordinate governors to finish.

Alexander appointed a commander of troops, a tax collector and a general administrator with orders to make Greek centers out of the Asian settlements. He imposed Greek law on the colonies and encouraged Greeks to settle in them. This idea was taken up by the Seleucids, the dynasty which succeeded Alexander in much of Asia Minor.

The main purpose of the military colony was to provide defense. Alexander set up some colonies in Bactria-Sogdiana (Asia Minor) for protection against the nomads, and in Media to defend his land from attack by native tribes. Later the Seleucids made a chain of such settlements across Asia Minor to protect their costal area from the Galatians.

Reserves for the Macedonian army were organized in the colonies. Each colonist was given a *kleros*, a piece of land, in return for military service. Colonists were to be available any time they were needed, as the obligation to serve went along with the property. If the land was sold, the obligation to serve was transferred to the buyer. In this way, the Macedonians increased their ranks. The *kleros* system originated with Alexander and was widely used after his death to augment the Seleucid armies. One could find military colonies beside any city or village.

Alexander's policies opened up world trade. Merchants from the Far East could exchange goods with those of the ports of Corinth, Tyre and Alexandria without fear of crossing hostile territorial boundaries along the trade routes. Now that the whole world was under one regent, no nation could interrupt the flow of commerce. Opportunities opened up and money flowed more freely, encouraging the growth of interesting new trade developments.

Before Alexander, the Persians had excluded the Greeks from trading with inner Asia, but now the territories of Asia and Egypt flourished with new wealth. New cities and towns had sprung up, primitive forms of credit and banking were introduced, and the standard of living was improved for the upper classes. Contracts were signed, and usually the demand for products was greater than supply.

To accommodate the increase in world trade, new ports and bigger ships had to be built. Merchant ships were built with a capacity of 4,200 tons, and a new method of sailing was introduced enabling ships to sail directly from one point to another instead of hugging the coast from point to point – one could, for example, now sail directly from Tyre to Alexandria in Egypt without following the Palestinian coastline. As international trade grew, Alexander's empire set precedents for the efficient Roman road system to come.

Alexander's own currency became international, and the amount of money in circulation increased tremendously. Fortunately, the Alexander-drachma was equivalent to the Attic currency which had been used over a wide area. The Romans later made their denarii equal to the Attic drachma, and during the third century B.C. the Alexander-drachma was still used and persisted even beyond the coming of Rome to world power.

The role of the city in the economic system changed with Alexander. Instead of concentrating only on small-scale production, cities now began to trade and compete on a larger basis. In former days one city could provide most of its own needs and be relatively independent, but this was only because trade laws with surrounding countries were never certain and relations were often strained. With the opening of trade, however, cities specialized and depended on other cities to supply the rest of their needs. From Alexandria came papyrus, glass, linens and perfumes, to trade with Antioch for textiles, with Corinth for bronze, with Miletus for wool, with Rhodes for pottery, while Delos was a major trading center for slaves. Since most Hellenistic cities lay in fertile lands that produced their own food, trade was mostly in manufactured goods and raw materials. Trade and economic developments were vast and were constantly expanding.

As stated, Alexander encouraged the blending of Asiatic and Greek cultures. He did this, in part, by instigating marriages between his own soldiers and Oriental women and by combining in various ways the luxury and more relaxed life of the East with the simplicity and energetic life of the West.

From his childhood Alexander had been enchanted by the East. He believed that the true gods dwelt in the East (as suggested by the sunrise). As a student of Aristotle, Alexander studied for hours, reading stories of the East after completing Aristotle's endless projects and experiments. He would question ambassadors from the East who visited his father concerning the habits of their kings and the geography of their land.

When Alexander finally conquered the East he took a wife from the barbarian Bactrian tribe, Rushanak (Roxana), a girl who knew no Greek and had no education. He encouraged his soldiers to marry Oriental brides also. At Susa he invited his officers to a mass wedding where he took another wife, Darius' eldest daughter. Eighty of his officers followed his example.

One writer says that perhaps as many as 10,000 soldiers followed Alexander's example, for he gave each of them dowries and listed them in a special roster. These marriages between Greeks and Asiatics produced an influential upper class in the Hellenized areas and were continued during the fourth and third centuries B.C., because few woman immigrated to the East during or after Alexander's lifetime.

The sensuous life of the East was in direct contrast to the hard life of the Macedonians. Asia seemed to be made up of splendid palaces, vast cities, and enormous armies. The Greeks led disciplined lives, encouraging hard work, courage, genius and skill. They built strong citadels and compact towns. In conquering Persia and becoming the owner of these elegant luxuries, Alexander's habits changed drastically, and a large part of his army followed his example. The old, simple, Hellenic life was soon tainted with the corruptions and the ostentatious gaudiness of the East. The wealth of the East was sent back to Greece. As Edward Burns states, "The Hellenic devotion to simplicity and the golden mean gave way to extravagance in art and to a love of luxury and riotous excess" (Burns, 188).

But an educational revolution occurred as a result of Alexander's success in blending East and West. He supported private and community educational institutions everywhere and was responsible for the development of Alexandria, the great learning center of the ancient world, with its vast library and university, where Jews and Greeks were brought together in the first translation of the Old Testament into Greek.

Alexander's study under Aristotle was marked by a great interest in science, an interest that led him to take along with his army two surveyors, a mineralogist, a weather expert, scientists of animal and plant life, physicians and musicians. The discoveries made on his Asian campaigns opened the way to further discovery and advancement. Alexander's surveyors formed a geography of Asia, and laid the foundations for Dicaearchus' map of the world, drawn in 300 B.C., a time in which the heights of Greek mountains, and even the earth's circumference, were calculated. His scientists proved that India was not connected to Africa. Eratosthenes of Cyrene (275-200 B.C.) deduced that all the oceans were one and one could sail eastward from Spain around Africa and arrive in India. Theophrastus (372-287 B.C.) compiled the discoveries of Alexander's expeditions in his famous *History of Plants*. Alexander's conquests supplied scientists with information on botany, zoology, geography, ethnography and hydrography, and because of the new political unity in the world Chaldeans, Egyptians and Greeks were able to exchange their knowledge.

Alexander financed Aristotle's work in Greece. Aristotle has been credited with establishing the first library of any means, a library made possible by Alexander. As a result of Alexander's help, libraries began forming in cities everywhere, including Antioch, Pergamus, Rhodes and Smyrna, and he established theatres and temples in the new cities he built.

Of all the cities built by Alexander and his successors, Alexandria, in Egypt, is the most famous. This city was responsible for the preservation of much valuable research. Ptolemy I, one of Alexander's generals, established a museum or school there, with a library that grew to more than 500,000 manuscripts. Alexandria rivaled Athens in knowledge and was far more cosmopolitan racially and culturally. Alexandria was important not only for the preservation of highly valued manuscripts, but for the diffusion of Hellenic literature throughout the world. W. H. McNeill comments that although no explicit records exist, that there must have been some regular permission to copy books in the library. Slaves probably copied them by hand, before dispersing them by way of trade all over the Greek-speaking world. The Alexandrian scholars also systematized Greek grammar and edited and preserved the famous literary works of the Greeks.

The Eastern contribution to world knowledge included records and traditions dating back to pre-Hellenic times, and their scientific observations added much to the knowledge of the Greeks. In exchange Greece gave the East her art, literature, games and philosophy. Technological inventions of the fourth and third centuries are so numerous that a separate study would be needed to enumerate them. The sciences of mechanics and astronomy were completely revamped; geometry and trigonometry were introduced; steam power was discovered (in an experimental sense) and hundreds of new theories and products were invented.

Alexander's policy of promoting a unified world based on Hellenistic philosophy and culture profoundly influenced the development of the pre-Christian world. He sought to establish one *lingua franca*, one fusion of the gods, one empire, one monarch-god, and one blend of culture.

With the expansion of culture, two major philosophies began to develop in about the year 300 B.C.—Stoicism and Epicureanism. Man stopped thinking of himself as merely another stone in the wall of the city. He began to realize his own emotional and intellectual needs as an individual. He was no longer merely an instrument of the city or state. The Stoics enlarged upon Alexander's idea of human brotherhood and the ideal state. Before Alexander, the Greeks had looked upon the barbarians as inferior, but Alexander rejected this view. The Stoics too believed that the souls of barbarians were not inferior. Tarn well describes the situation:

> Man as a political animal, a fraction of the *polis* or self-governing city-state, had ended with Aristotle; with Alexander begins man as an individual....At a banquet at Opis, Alexander prayed for a union of hearts (*homonoia*) among all peoples and a joint commonwealth of Macedonians and Persians; he was the first to transcend national boundaries and to envisage, however imperfectly, a brotherhood of man in which there should be neither Greek nor barbarian. (Tarn, 79)

The Stoics also rejected the idea of separate city-states. They wanted one great city, or world state, under one law. All citizens would be willingly bound together.

Epicurus (342-270 B.C.), father of Epicureanism, adopted Alexander's concept of individualism in another way. He said that man was not just a political being, that he had intellectual and practical needs as well. The major aim of Epicureanism was to avoid pain. The type of pleasure he advocated was not sensual but intellectual, one in which the mind is quiet and free from all anxiety. Happiness is the goal, and it is achieved by friendship, virtue, and living apart from the world. With the development of a world empire in which the emphasis shifted from the city-state to the individual, Epicureanism became popular.

In the third century B.C. education became more widespread and many private philosophies developed. Foreigners established various clubs among the Greeks with the purpose of promoting their special philosophies or religions.

By opening men's minds through the diffusion of education and culture, Alexander in no small way prepared the world for the coming of Christianity. As we have seen, he stressed unity, attempting to unite everyone under himself as a god. This policy was followed up by the Roman Caesars of the New Testament era.

Philosophical discussions in Alexander's time often centered on such questions as, "How many gods are there?" "How were the world and man formed?" "Why are we here?" "Is there a second life?" "Are souls immortal?" Various philosophers tried to answer these questions. Thus, when Christianity began to develop, many of the concepts that defined it were already being discussed by the non-Christian world, giving the early Christians a responsive audience. Many found it to be the answer to their mental struggle as well as to their soul's salvation. Plato had said that souls are immortal, and the Stoics stressed virtue as a means of achieving happiness. These truths are found in Christianity. Of course, there were ethical limits to the foundational supports provided by pre-Christian philosophies: None of them, for example, stressed the Christian message, "Love thy neighbor as thyself."

With Alexander promoting Oriental ideas, many mystery religions of the East came into the Western world. To some extent at least, such cults met personal needs that many began to realize. People were becoming dissatisfied with the remoteness of the old Greek pantheon. They could no longer relate to a carved god or goddess of stone. It is probable that the decline of the Greek gods came about with the decline of the Greek city-states. Mystery religions like the cults of Isis and Serapis, Attis, and the Great Mother Goddess of Asia Minor provided personal involvement for the individual.

While the educated upper classes were impressed with the new philosophies, the mystery religions, featuring many licentious rites, appealed to the lower classes. Christianity supplied answers to both classes: a religion with strong ethics *and* truths that provided a personal experience with a deity. As we will discuss in later chapters, the idea held by some that Christianity evolved from the ethical philosophies and mystery religions has no support in fact. These ideas merely paved the way, and in one way or another made the world receptive to the message of Christ and the Church.

Hellenistic educational developments also aided the spread of Christianity. Ptolemy II (Philadelphus, 284-247 B.C.) asked Jewish rabbis to come to Alexandria from Palestine to translate their sacred scriptures into Greek. This was probably a unifying measure, for theirs was a powerful Jewish sect in his kingdom. Thus, through the translation of the Greek Septuagint, men were provided with a Jewish Bible in the Greek tongue long before Christianity came into being.

Certainly, the systematization of the Greek language into specific declensions, along with other developments, provided a basis for the writings of the New Testament authors. All of the New Testament was written in Greek–the universal language of the first century–because of the Hellenistic influence. The expansion of human ideas and the development of the Greek language following Alexander set the scene for the mission of Jesus and the establishment of the Church.

THE MUSICAL STORY *of Israel can be traced back to Lamech's son, Jubal, the "father of all those who play the lyre and pipe." It next appears in Ur where Abraham first lived. In that country it was the custom that upon the king's death the court musicians and attendants were slain and buried with him. From this point onward, music has been attached in some way or other to the children of Israel. Later in history they were commanded to make no "graven images" of their deity and because of this, music, among other things, became very important and took on a deeper meaning. It united them as a congregation in singing and faith in God who at least would hear them, they felt, even if they could not see Him. It also united them in one of the deepest and oldest impulses of the human spirit: "To give songful expression to a sense of awe before the terror and the glory of creation."*

With time, different types of songs evolved from the physical rhythms of daily work and from chants by which tribal elders passed on to younger members the lore and teachings of their clan. In this way personal passions came to be expressed in song. Hebrew shepherds following the nomadic pattern of the Near East made primitive instruments similar to those that almost all herdsmen used. Some of these were most likely a reed with holes (flute); a ram's horn with the tip cut away; a hollow gourd and a bit of sheep gut (crude stringed instrument); and dried gourds filled with seeds and pebbles (percussion instruments).

The next incident significant to the progression of Hebrew musical history is the episode in which Laban asked Jacob: "Wherefore didst thou flee away secretly, and steal away from me; and didst not tell me, that I might have sent thee away with mirth, and with songs, with tabret, and with harp?" (Gen. 31:17).

Evidently by this time certain types of instruments were used and accepted in the daily life of the ancient Semitic peoples. When the Israelites submitted to Egypt's high culture they were able to develop and refine their gift of music very rapidly. Four hundred years later when they left they were a people uniquely given to song. Moses taught them to preserve their songs, proverbs and the musical instruments they had brought from Egypt. He can even be regarded*

---

*Alfred Sendrey and Mildred Norton, *David's Harp*.

as their first music teacher. This most likely took place during the forty years of wandering.

Israelites, in their zealous desire to please God, turned their creative powers full force into the making of music, dances, poetry and songs. Songs at times welled up spontaneously. All a leader had to do was strike up a tune and all would join in. This often became a kind of free prose-poetry. The song found in Exodus 15:1-19 might have come about in such a way.

The women also took an active part. An example of this was Miriam when she took the timbrel in hand and led the women in a dance of joy, caroling to one another the verses that men sang with Moses (Exod. 15:20-21).

Aron M. Rothmüller points out that songs of the past became encoded into the national life:

> In their exile, all the past achievements of Jewish national and religious life came to be regarded as a cultural heritage which was their one spiritual surety, their one rallying-point in defense of national solidarity....On the return from exile they rallied still more strongly around their traditions, and probably only a few psalms or hymns were written in the ensuing period. Psalms were generally appreciated and sung or recited in public after 500 B.C., but their poetic quality was already declining. The writing of psalms probably came to an end in the days of the Maccabees, in the middle of the second century B.C. (Rothmüller, 73)

Chapter 2

THE MACCABEES

SOME OF THE changes brought about by Alexander's conquests eventually led to desperate conflict. When agents of Hellenism began to interfere with Hebrew religion and culture, the Jews revolted to defend their religious and political freedom. The revolt was led by the courageous and intensely dedicated Maccabees. Their religious zeal and heroic self-sacrifice were the determining factors in the Jewish defeat of Hellenic-Syrian monarchs such as Antiochus Epiphanes who sought to destroy Judaism and impose idolatrous worship on the Jews. The heroic faith of a father and his five sons united a divided and seemingly defeated people and led them to religious and political independence and the restoration of their Temple worship. Their faith and courage were keys to the recovery and strengthening of Jewish religious identity and unity. Without the exploits of the Maccabees, Judaism would surely have perished and the foundation of Christianity would have been destroyed.

From the death of Alexander the Great in 323 B.C. until 198 B.C. the Jewish state of Judea was a vassal of Egypt. Fortunes of war, however, then made it part of the Syrian Empire – not the Syria of today, of course, or the Assyria of antiquity, but the Greek Seleucid empire which embraced the Syrian region. An "empire" in those days was composed of any number of petty kingdoms and principalities which paid tribute to an overlord and owed him loyalty. In exchange for tribute money they often were allowed to set up their own local governments and were seldom interfered with, politically or religiously. Usually, however, vassals of this sort were commanded to worship the pagan gods of their overlords, and in most cases the subjugated peoples never minded adding a few more gods to their list of local deities.

The Jews were different: they worshiped one god – the God of Israel – refusing to recognize any others. As a vassal nation they were willing to pay taxes and work as government officials and so on, but they would not burn incense to the king's image. This could have been taken to suggest treason, but as long as the Jews were allowed freedom of religion they were submissive to their rulers. Indeed, this was the situation under Antiochus III, of the Seleucid Empire, 223-187 B.C. The Jews were permitted to establish their own community and govern themselves with their own officials. Their high priest could act as their natural ruler.

Under Antiochus III the Jews were favored; they were exempted from taxes for three years, supplied with timber from Lebanon for the rebuilding of the walls of Jerusalem, given money for temple sacrifices, and given political freedom as already mentioned (Jos., *Ant.* xxi, 3,3). Thus for a number of years the Jews lived in relative peace and prosperity. They even accepted certain elements of Greek culture (I Macc. 1:10-15). Even the most liberal of the Jews, however, would never be ready to throw out their laws and traditions, especially those concerning eating unclean food or desecrating the Sabbath day.

As the Greek culture began to permeate the Jewish way of life, their government also changed. What had once been a spiritual leadership by the high priest was combined with civil leadership, which carried with it the more democratic Greek notions of government. Thus the office of the high priest became increasingly subject to venal competition and dispute. Just how embroiled the high priest became in worldly intrigues was demonstrated by the actions of one Heliodorus.

In 190 B.C. Antiochus was defeated by the Romans at the Battle of Magnesium and was forced to give twenty hostages to Rome, including his son, Antiochus IV (Epiphanes). After this, Antiochus III was a broken man, dying three years later. He was succeeded by another son, Seleucus IV, who after an uneventful reign was murdered by his high priest Heliodorus. Heliodorus then proclaimed Seleucus' young son king of Syria. Antiochus

Epiphanes, hearing the news, returned from Rome, murdered his nephew and set himself up as king (175 B.C.). With Epiphanes began the period that was to culminate in the Maccabean revolt.

Antiochus Epiphanes was a controversial figure, whom Polybius (a pagan writer who lived during 205-125 B.C.) called a "madman." He associated with the common people in their festivals and baths, yet loved pomp and glory and spent much time in erecting statues and temples. The latter practice culminated in his proclamation of himself as a god, and his demand for worship from the people. The Syrians complied but Jews resisted, and thus began an era of turmoil between Hellenistic and anti-Hellenistic factions.

Had Antiochus IV left the Jews to choose their own leaders and run their own affairs they might never have given him any trouble, despite their revulsion at Hellenism and Greek culture. To most Jews, the Greek culture was odious since it involved worship of foreign deities, eating of food regarded as unclean, and participation in games considered indecent. At the same time, under the Seleucids the Greek language prevailed and Greek architecture, ideas and customs had become common.

Antiochus Epiphanes deposed the high priest Onias, successor to Heliodorus, and appointed in his stead Jason, brother of Onias, who had turned his back on religious orthodoxy and supported the aims of Antiochus, offering a higher tribute to the coffers of his Majesty. The Jews were shocked by the deposition of their high priest. They rejected this royal ascendancy over their priesthood, bitterly resenting interference with their leaders and their religion. Having their leaders selected for them was galling enough, but Antiochus chose those who were essentially Hellenist. Committing further outrages against the Jews, he outlined a program, to be carried out under Jason, that would turn Jerusalem into a Hellenistic city. The name of the city was changed to Antioch. A gymnasium was built in the city for Greek games in which the participants appeared naked. Sacrificial offerings to the gods preceded the games. Since gymnasiums of this type exerted a powerful attraction on the young men of the subject people, they were a major force for the promotion of Hellenism. The introduction of the gymnasium to Jerusalem – with its naked exercises and association with pagan worship – shocked the Jews most of all. The Jews looked upon these heathen practices with gross repugnance.

Although Jason had greatly intensified the Hellenistic influence in Jerusalem he still showed compassion for Jewish traditionalists, permitted religious separation, respected the sanctity of the Temple, made no bans on Jewish laws and customs, and did not coerce the community to adopt Hellenism. But Jason's policy proved too moderate to satisfy Antiochus, who dismissed Jason and appointed Menelaus, an extreme Hellenist, to the office of high priest in Jerusalem.

Under Menelaus, Hellenism became a plague against Judaism. Whereas Jason did not force or coerce the traditional Jews, Menelaus actively sought to impose Hellenistic practices on them. He would not tolerate religious separation. He subjected Jews to taunts and flagrant acts of contempt for their customs. He persuaded young Jews, including priests, to enter the Greek games. Since they had to appear naked, some of these young men sought to eradicate the sign of circumcision by undergoing a painful operation.

Menelaus committed other outrages against the Jews. He was implicated in the murder of Onias, who had been in hiding since his removal from office. Onias was still regarded as the true high priest by traditional Jews who, when they heard of his murder, rose up in angry demonstration against the ruling group. An additional reason for their uprising was a raid by Menelaus on the precious vessels of the Temple to help pay the heavy tribute he had promised to the king. Menelaus had gone too far. The Jews discovered the violation of the Temple treasury at the same time they heard the news of Onias' murder.

A rift was now developing among the Jews. Some were pious and refused to accept Hellenism, others grudgingly gave in to it, and still others accepted it willingly. For the most part, the Jews were God-fearing, following the Torah and the customs and traditions of their religion. They spurned the material benefits of Hellenism when the price was religious abdication. Still, a few wealthy Jews were attracted by commercial opportunities offered by the Greeks and succumbed to the new fashions and worldly ideals of Hellenism, while some of the younger Jews were attracted to the Greek games. These few adopted the characteristics of the conquerors – their diversions, social and domestic habits, costumes, architecture and language.

To this point Hellenism still had not been forced on the Jews; Menelaus had taken no overt action against the traditionalists, made no mandatory laws regarding the acceptance of Hellenism. Although under great social pressure, the Jews were allowed to accept or refuse, and many left the city, going out to the villages and towns that were as yet untouched by the abhorred Hellenism. One of the exiles was Mattathias who took his family back to his native village, Modin, where they could worship and live as Jews (II Macc. 3:1-6; I Macc. 2:1-5, 15-31). The Hellenization of Jerusalem under Menelaus may have seemed severe enough to warrant rebellion, but the real explosion was yet to come.

During this time of stress in Judea, Antiochus invaded Egypt, trying to unite Syria and Egypt, and was rebuffed by the Romans. His unification scheme collapsed, leaving him angry and frustrated. Word spread in Judea that Antiochus had been killed, and immediately there was armed conflict between Hellenistic and anti-Hellenistic Jews. Many Hellenistic Jews were killed, some thrown from the more than 100-foot-high wall of the Temple. Antiochus, hearing of the revolt, rushed back from Egypt, now doubly incensed and, according to contemporary sources, slaughtered 10,000 Jews. It was a terrible time of butchery and plunder; the Syrian army that he sent in behaved as though they were in a rebellious country.

But Antiochus went even farther. He issued an edict forbidding the keeping of the Sabbath, religious festivals, and the rite of circumcision. He forbade Jews to offer sacrifices to God and compelled them to worship idols. He entered Jerusalem and plundered the Temple, setting up a statue of Jupiter in the Holy of Holies, the most sacred part of the Temple. Pigs, which were abominable to the Jews, were sacrificed on the Temple altars and their blood sprinkled on the Holy Scriptures. He compelled the priests to eat unclean flesh and burned the Books of the Law.

All Jews were ordered to renounce the laws of their God and to offer sacrifices to the Greek deities. Under penalty of death it was prohibited for Jews to congregate in prayer, to observe the Sabbath and the religious festivals, to have sacred writings in their possession, to be circumcised or to follow the dietary laws. Death was also the penalty for refusing to follow idolatrous practices, to eat the flesh of a pig, or to join in sacrificial pagan rituals. Cruel forms of torture and execution were devised to serve as examples of the price to be paid by all who refused to conform. An example is seen in Eleazar, a learned, warm-hearted, 90-year-old man who was loved by the Jewish community and respected even by the Seleucids. Antiochus chose to use him as an example, knowing full well that Eleazar would not comply with his orders. He ordered him to eat swine's flesh; when he refused the guards seized him, stripped him, bound his arms, and scourged him with whips. He was then broken on the rack and his maimed body was taken to the flames. They burned him with wickedly devised instruments and poured into his nostrils a hot, strong fluid. In the midst of these torments, he died. Never before the death of Eleazar – and perhaps never since – has the spiritual existence of Israel been so imperiled.

The sudden persecution was almost too much for the Jews. Small groups of them gathered together to try to resist, but were unequal to their oppressors, and many were martyred. One group hid in caves, where they continued to observe the dietary laws, the Sabbath, and the law of circumcision. Their hiding place was discovered, however, and Phillip, the Phrygian, led a group against them. It being the Sabbath, the people offered no resistance, and most were killed when soldiers threw firebrands into their caves. This led to the decree by Jewish leaders that in extreme necessity the Holy Day might be broken to resist the enemy.

The persecution culminated in the revolt of the Maccabees (c. 168 B.C.). According to I Maccabees 2:1ff., the elderly priest Mattathias first raised the flag of revolt. During a meeting of Jews a commissioner of the king compelled a priest to offer a sacrifice at a local altar. This was too much for Mattathias, who slew both the apostate Jew and the commissioner. "Whosoever is zealous for the Law and maintaineth the covenant," he said, "Let him come forth after me!" (I Macc. 2:27; Jos., *Ant.* xii, 6,2). As he was speaking, his five sons attacked the rest of the troops. The sons, led by Judas, then went throughout the towns and cities, inciting the people to revolt. They would attack suddenly, destroying temples and altars. Though small in number, they had such a thorough knowledge of the terrain that they were almost impossible to defeat.

Seen through the eyes of worldly power, Mattathias' deed was an act of political terrorism. He and his five sons, John, Simon, Judas, Eleazar and Jonathan, fled from punishment, accompanied by the people of Modin. They took essential belongings, food, and the uniforms and weapons of the slain troops, and headed for the hills above Gophna, just beyond the Judean border in southern Samaria, thirteen miles northeast of Modin. The band numbered 200 in all, of which forty or fifty were men.

For whatever reason, the Seleucid authorities left the group unmolested for about a year. In that year, the rebels trained Jews in guerrilla warfare; roused the spirit of resistance among the Jews of Judea, recruiting as many as possible to their ranks; restored respect for the Law of Moses and "maintenance of the covenant" where this had been weakened by the Hellenizing process; and gave battle when they encountered the enemy, but did not initiate military action until they were ready. From their base in the hills of Gophna they organized an intelligence network, supply system and messenger service through friends in the villages; they arranged for reliable contacts throughout the villages to gather information on Seleucid troops; they spread the news by relay from village to village of what had happened at Modin; and reported on their resistance aims. Young villagers volunteered to join the rebels, and Jews hiding in the hills and wilderness of Judea, mostly Hasidim, made their way to the rebels' base at Gophna.

Mattathias anticipated that the Seleucid troops would attack on the Sabbath, thinking that the Jews would not fight on that day. Therefore, having seen and heard of massacres of pious Jews on the Sabbath, he rallied his followers to defend themselves, saying, "If we all do as our brethren have done, and do not fight against the Gentiles for our lives and our ordinances, they will soon destroy us from off the earth" (Bickerman, 18-20). They resolved not to attack, but to defend themselves on the Sabbath. Thus they prepared themselves to violate the Torah for the sake of the Torah.

In 166 B.C. Mattathias died, and his place as leader was taken by his third son, Judas, described as "a mighty warrior from his youth" (I Macc. 2:66) "like a lion in his deed, like a lion's cub roaring for a prey" (I Macc.

3:4). He was given the nickname "Maccabee," meaning "hammer" or "hammer-headed," in token of his military exploits. The name was continued by his brothers, who escalated the revolt. Under Judas' leadership the struggle turned into a full-scale war, with well-planned battles.

The first two battles were fought northwest of Jerusalem, in Modin. In the first, Apollonius, general of the Samaritan forces, attacked the Jews and was defeated. In the second, when Seron, the "strategus" of Coele-Syria, came, Judas exhorted his people to remember that God could save them. And, suddenly attacking the Syrians, they drove them down the pass at Bethhoron, where Joshua had destroyed the army of the five kings.

Antiochus Epiphanes, who was in Syria while these battles were being fought, proclaimed that decisive action was necessary and sent out 40,000 infantry and 7,000 cavalry troops. But Judas and his band of 3,000 surprised and defeated them, pursuing them into the plains of Philistia. By this time more Jews were being recruited, and soon their army numbered 10,000. Judas was then able to defeat the Syrian general Lysias in Beth-Zur so that the Syrian had to return home.

Judas proved to be a great leader of his people. He embodied piety, valor, resourcefulness and good sense. By making the best use of these attributes, with God's help he was able to defeat the Syrians with a small army of untrained warriors.

Now that their enemies were in disarray, the Maccabees' task was to purify the Temple and rededicate the Sanctuary. In 164 B.C. Judas marched on Jerusalem and occupied Mt. Zion, shutting up the Syrian troops and their sympathizers, including Jewish collaborators, in the Akra, the citadel near the Temple. Then he chose new priests and set up the altar, once again dedicating it to the God of Israel. In the month of Kislev (i.e., December) 164 B.C., exactly three years after its desecration by Antiochus, the Temple was restored to its former service. (The day is still commemorated at the Feast of Hanukkah, or "Dedication.") To ensure the Temple's future safety, the Jews built high walls and strong towers around Jerusalem and stationed a garrison there to defend it. They took similar measures also at Beth-Zur on the borders of Idumea to the south (I Macc. 4:60-61).

The Jews were now in a relatively secure position, and Judas carried out a series of successful campaigns against the Idumaeans in the south, the Baenites in Trans-Jordan, and the Ammonites northeast of the Dead Sea. With the help of his brothers Simon and Jonathan, he also engaged in a campaign in Galilee and Gilead, bringing many Jewish inhabitants back to Judea. Subsequently he captured Hebron and Ashdod and returned home with much plunder (I Macc. 5:1-8, 63-65).

Another great task remained: The Akra, still in the hands of the Syrians, had to be liberated. Judas attacked it in 163 B.C. Some Syrians managed to escape, making their way to Antioch to the king. Antiochus IV (Epiphanes) had died the previous year, about two months before the rededication of the Temple, and was succeeded by his eight-year-old son, Antiochus V (Eupator). Philip had been appointed guardian of the young king, but Lysias (Antiochus' regent) saw his opportunity, marched toward Judea with a strong army, forced Judas to retreat, and besieged Jerusalem. The Jews were saved, however, when Lysias heard that Philip was going to take over the government in his absence. Generous terms were offered to Judas, who agreed to surrender the fortifications around the Temple. In return, he was granted a general amnesty, rescinding the orders of Antiochus IV made in 167 B.C., and so basic freedom of religious practice of the Jews was at last won.

The Maccabees now moved toward a further goal—political independence. At this time the Seleucid throne was shaky, beset by a bitter and bloody struggle for power. The victor was Demetrius, brother of Antiochus IV, who appointed a new high priest in Jerusalem, Alcimus. Alcimus put to death sixty Hasidim, and a Syrian general, Bacchides, killed many Jews in a village not far from Gophna. This stirred Judas and the Maccabees to renewed action. They now used the same guerrilla tactics that they had used at the beginning of the struggle. Soon the Syrians appealed to Demetrius for help, and he dispatched a force, headed by Nicanor, to dispose of the Maccabees. Fighting with their original tactics, the Jews drove Nicanor back to Jerusalem to appeal for reinforcements. Nicanor tried once more, flushing some of the Maccabees out of the hills. Once again the

Maccabees attacked in guerrilla style, killing Nicanor and annihilating his army.

Judas, desiring the support of a powerful ally, appealed to Rome, sending two ambassadors to the Roman Senate to establish a treaty of friendship. The Romans accepted, agreeing to aid the Jews as allies in case of war and to warn Demetrius to cease oppressing the Jews. In return, the Jews agreed to fight for Rome in case of war and to withhold economic support from the enemy.

Demetrius ignored the warning from Rome, and in 161 B.C. his generals Bacchides and Alcimus again attacked the Jews of Judea. They marched toward Jerusalem with 22,000 men, slaughtering the Jews of Arbela on the way. Judas had only 3,000 men, and now desertions quickly reduced his army to 800. He attacked anyway, and succeeded in driving back the right flank of the army. While pursuing the Syrians' right flank, Judas' forces were pursued by their left and the Maccabees were sandwiched between the two. Many were killed on both sides, including Judas himself (I Macc. 9:1-22; Jos., *Ant.* xii. 11,2). Bacchides tracked down friends and followers of Judas and executed them. The remaining Maccabees fled to the wilderness where they built fortresses and gathered their forces, trying to keep the Jews calm.

Jonathan was chosen leader in Judas' place. The Maccabees regrouped, and reverted to the tactics that they had used so successfully at the beginning of the revolt – guerilla training and the use of underground contacts, messengers, spies and recruits. Once again they confined the Seleucid troops in Jerusalem, and Judea soon came under Maccabean rule once again.

Bacchides was sent to defeat the Maccabees and to free the garrison in Jerusalem, but Jonathan drove him back with a surprise attack. Jonathan then made a treaty with the Syrian general, stipulating that all Jewish prisoners would soon be released and that peace would be established. The Maccabees had achieved a partial independence and were now free for a time from Hellenistic domination.

In 150 B.C., Alexander Balas, claiming to be the son of Antiochus IV, and his rightful heir, took possession of Ptolemais and proclaimed himself king. He was backed by Rome, Egypt, Cappadocia and Pergamum.

Demetrius was the ruler at the time, but was unpopular with his subjects because he was harsh and negligent, and he had no allies or support. Both king and claimant, recognizing that the Jewish rulers held the balance of power, sought to secure the active support of the Jews of Judea. The Jewish resistance of the Seleucid army had proved that the Jews were a potent factor in the affairs of Palestine. They courted the favor of the Jews with bounteous offers, appealing to Jonathan for his friendship and military help.

Demetrius acted first. He ordered that all Jewish hostages in the Citadel be returned to Jonathan and he conferred on Jonathan the title of "ally," giving him authority to raise and equip an army. Jonathan took advantage of this and established himself in Jerusalem. He refortified the Temple Mount and rebuilt the walls of Jerusalem. The Hellenistic party fled Antioch. Only Beth-Zur (on the borders of Idumea in the south) and the Citadel remained refuge for Hellenists. Judea, now virtually free, though without formal independence, came under the operational control of Jonathan. Alexander Balas then made *his* offer to Jonathan; he ordained him as high priest of the Jews and sent him a purple robe and a gold crown (Jos., *Ant*. xiii. 4,2f.).

Demetrius, seeking to outbid Alexander, exempted Judea from a wide range of taxes, tributes, imposts, and levies, such as the tax on salt, one-third of the grain harvest, and one-half of the fruit harvest; restored to Judea three districts of Jewish population; evacuated the Citadel of Seleucid troops, assigning the city of Jerusalem to Jonathan; and granted 15,000 silver shekels annually for the cost of repair to the Temple, the wall of Jerusalem, and all Judean fortresses.

In the final battle between the two rivals, Demetrius was killed and Alexander became ruler. Alexander treated Jonathan with great respect, calling him friend. Alexander appointed Jonathan high priest, commander and governor of Judea.

After three years of peace, there was another struggle for the throne—this time between Alexander and Demetrius II (Nicator). In the ensuing battle, Macedonian mercenaries and refugee Hellenists again inhabited the Citadel in Jerusalem. Alexander was killed and Demetrius II became king.

Jonathan laid siege to the Citadel, trying once more to rid the land of the Seleucid presence. Demetrius demanded that Jonathan lift the siege and summoned him to his presence. Jonathan bribed Demetrius with 300 talents of gold and received a full guarantee of the concessions that Demetrius I had granted Jonathan. These concessions set Judea free from all tribute and gave the Jews additional territory. Judea was now close to national independence.

The Seleucid kingdom was split. Demetrius ruled one half, and Antiochus VI the other, the latter giving Jonathan control and authority over the territory of Judea. The territory Jonathan now controlled was approximately the size of the original land of Israel. The Maccabees were reaching their goal. Simon was appointed military commander of the whole of Coele-Syria, and the two brothers made the most of their new powers. Simon captured the fortress of Beth-Zur and replaced the Seleucid garrison with his own men. Jonathan marched north though the entire country to Damascus and then toward Galilee, securing cooperation and friendship along the way. He sent an embassy to Rome and renewed the friendship established under Judas. His brother built fortresses in Judea, heightened the walls of Jerusalem, and erected a barrier separating the Citadel from the city.

Another fight for the throne followed between Antiochus VI and Trypho (Jos., *Ant.* xiii. 5). Trypho sought to remove Jonathan, who supported Antiochus, and persuaded Jonathan to visit him on the pretense of peace. When Jonathan came with 1,000 men, Jonathan was taken prisoner, and his men were slaughtered. Trypho eventually executed Jonathan.

Simon, last surviving son of Mattathias, assumed command and became high priest. He conquered Jaffa, Gezer, and Jamnia. When Trypho dethroned Antiochus and became ruler of his half of the Seleucid empire, Simon transferred his support back to Demetrius, who once again granted Judea freedom from all taxation and tribute. This action in the year 142 B.C. was hailed by the Jews as marking the lifting of "the yoke of the heathen from Israel," and the people began to write on their contracts and agreements "In the first year of Simon the great high-priest captain and leader of the Jews" (I Macc. 13:41-42). This also marked the beginning of the Hasmonean dynasty, the name "Hasmonean" being derived from Hasmon, great-great-grandfather of Mattathias.

After imperial troops of the Citadel had surrendered to Simon, he leveled the Citadel and later built the Hasmonean palace on its ruins.

The whole of Jerusalem was at last under Maccabean control, and Judea was again an independent Jewish state. As Seleucid authority in the divided empire grew weaker, Simon continued to advance the strength, size and welfare of Judea. In addition to religious freedom the Maccabees had now achieved political freedom and independence. Antiochus VII, heir to the throne of Demetrius, wrote to Simon:

> Now therefore I confirm all the tax remissions which my royal predecessors granted you, and all their other remission of tribute. I permit you to mint your own coinage as currency for your country. Jerusalem and the Temple shall be free. All the armies you have prepared, and the fortifications which you have built and now hold, shall remain yours. When we have reestablished our kingdom, we shall confer the highest honors upon you, your nation, and Temple, to make your country's greatness apparent to the whole world. (I Macc. 15:3-9)

No endorsement of Judean independence could have been more explicit.

The Maccabean revolt had the most profound effects upon the Jewish nation. Through it the Jews were able to win their independence, religiously and politically. The work of the Maccabees thus also helped to set the scene for the time of Jesus.

One effect of their work was the cleansing and restoration of the Temple in Jerusalem, and the reestablishment of Temple worship and sacrifices. As mentioned, this led to the observance of Hanukkah, the Feast of Dedication. To this day, Jews have celebrated Hanukkah eight days of every year. All other great feasts celebrated by the Jews are prescribed by the Torah. Hanukkah alone has survived through the centuries without justification in the Bible.

Josephus shows that from the time this festival was first instituted by the Maccabees until his own day (A.D. 37-A.D. 100) there had been no interruption in its annual observance.

> So much pleasure did they find in the renewal of their customs and in unexpectedly obtaining the right to have their own service after so long a time, that they made a law that their

descendants should celebrate the restoration of the temple service for eight days. And from that time to the present we observe this festival, which we call the Festival of Lights, giving this name to it, I think, from the fact that the right to worship appeared to us at a time when we hardly dared hope for it. (Jos., *Ant.* xii. 7,7)

The New Testament provides evidence that Hanukkah was observed by the Jews during the first century A. D. Unlike the other three Gospels, the fourth refers to journeys of Jesus to Jerusalem other than the final one. On one occasion Jesus is spoken of as being in Jerusalem during the Feast of Dedication (John 10:22). Since there is no other festival with such name or description, this reference is undoubtedly to Hanukkah. Jesus himself knew and honored the festival. Even if one should doubt the authenticity of the journey of Jesus to observe Hanukkah, we still must admit that the New Testament witnesses to the fact that He knew something about the Feast of Dedication, and places the feast in the correct season of the year.

The Maccabean revolt not only saved and preserved Judaism, it established and strengthened the religious identity of the Jews and bound them together within a religious unity. Before the revolt, Jews were separated—some conforming to the Hellenists out of fear, some running and hiding, some simply avoiding and not participating in the Hellenistic culture, some standing against Hellenism and dying for their beliefs. After gaining religious freedom, the Jews were able to establish themselves and be known as Jews. United in religious identity, all could worship as Jews. They could once more follow the Laws of Moses and offer sacrifices. They could worship God in their own way. And they worship today the same way they did after the Maccabees gained religious freedom, except for the offering of sacrifices in the Temple. They observe the Torah, the Sabbath, the same festivals and holidays, and still refrain from eating swine's flesh.

The Maccabean revolt also established a national unity of the Jews, when political freedom was obtained and the Hasmonean state was established. Jews were unified by zeal for the Torah—the set of rules, provisions, hopes and promises of God that Jews live by, and the very strength of their existence—the rededication and reestablishment of the Temple, and the establishment of Jonathan as high priest.

The Maccabean revolt preserved the Judaism which existed in New Testament times and which was the foundation of Jesus' life and ministry, and of Christianity itself. Jesus addressed people with the heritage we have here described. He argued with Jewish religion leaders, and He threatened the religious-political system which developed in the century and a half following Jonathan's triumph.

A PROBLEM IN *determining shapes and characteristics of Jewish instruments was brought about because the Hebrews could not make any graven images, and thus left no pictorial records of them. Therefore, to understand the music that was developed by the Hebrews one must sometimes look to the musical development in surrounding countries. Trade brought about a continuous exchange of goods and articles of luxury. In this way instruments from different countries and cultures were interchanged and knowledge of their use was disseminated. In Oriental life the finer instruments were considered "objects de luxe" and were among the most desirable articles of trade. The religions of that day also played an important role. "Through the mushrooming of religious groups and sects," Alfred Sendrey writes, "all types of hymns, litanies and other sacred songs were created, which eventually were transplanted from one people to another." Undoubtedly, the instruments used in playing these religious songs were also exchanged among different peoples (Sendrey, 35).*

The oldest records of musical organization and system in nations of antiquity are from Sumeria and Egypt. There are many close resemblances between the music of Sumeria and the music of ancient Israel, and at first it was thought that Israel had taken much of its musical art from Sumeria, but in recent times this was found to be erroneous. Although most of the records found in Sumeria concerning musical activities are connected with religious rites and ceremonies, it is also known that they had a vigorous folk music in their culture. Another parallel between Sumeria and ancient Israel is that musicians were employed by the court and nobility in both cultures, though in Israel this occurred much later.

A catalog has been found of Sumerian and Assyrian hymns and secular songs containing poems and songs of all varieties, i.e., liturgies, royal psalms, festival songs, lamentation, poems of victory and heroic acts, popular songs for workmen and shepherds, and numerous love songs for both sexes. Also, as in Israel, they had schools of music at the largest temples in which the young clergy were systemically trained in musical liturgy.

The musical service at these temples was performed by "liturgists" and "psalmists," who administered the daily sacred ceremonies and provided a vocal background for them. In these temples the most prominent object was the temple tower or ziggurat, *crowned by a small room or chapel containing a bed* and a gold table. Galpin describes it, "Here, in the meeting place of earth and heaven, the chosen priestess by night received the revelation of the god" (Galpin, 53). This oracle was delivered by the priest accompanied by the sounds of "cross-strung" harp (zag-sal) or of the lyre (al-gar). This custom was continued by the Hebrew prophets and psalmists who "opened their dark sayings upon the harp."

The prime example of the importance of music in these temples is found in the Temple of Ningirsu at Lagash where a special officer was in charge of the singers. Another had the function of supervising the preparation of a choir made up of both male and female singers. Sacred singers had their own guilds. "...they became at last a learned community, a kind of college, which studied and edited the official liturgical literature....We have...considerable liturgical literature of the learned college attached to the Temple of Bel in Babylon" (Sendrey, 37).

When Sumeria was invaded by foreign conquerors who burned the houses and the Temples of Lagash and carried the inhabitants into captivity, the laments that were composed were very similar to some of the Hebrew psalms also written in times of national disaster.

Prior to the occupation of the Hebrews, the land of Canaan had no distinct civilization of its own, most likely because this narrow strip of land was too much a crossroad of the ancient world. Most of the music used in this area was for pagan ceremonies in the form of worship. We are informed about the character of these ceremonies in the description of the incident at Mt. Carmel – I Kings 18:26-28. Sendrey writes:

> The delirious ecstacy, the invocations (i.e., "singing") accompanied by savage dances and noisy music, were the outstanding features of the ceremonies of the priests of Ba'al. They give us a vivid picture of the orgiastic character of this kind of ritual music. (Sendrey, 37)

As the Israelites became more and more developed in their music, their spirituality and ethically higher religion also took effect and prevailed over the pagan worship of Canaan. These qualities carried them into a victory over the crude forms of the heathen cults. This was the start of the transformation of music of pagan rites into the spiritually loftier music of the Hebrews. They were able to create their own music and withstand the surrounding pagan musical influence which so encompassed them at the beginning of their quest for what *would later become the land of Israel. Israel brought from Egypt and the desert the joy of singing, a vivid fantasy in music, as well as wealth of old songs. The Hebrew music prevailed despite its undeveloped form. Hebrew musical culture came into bloom relatively soon after the conquest of Canaan, approximately in Samuel's time. Its development was rapid, for by the time of David and Solomon there were highly organized musical institutions. Israel learned to preserve and develop its musical culture.*

Chapter 3

THE JEWS AND ROMANS

THE FREEDOM BROUGHT by the Maccabean revolt existed until the Herodian times, when the Romans took over and Judea again became part of a larger empire. This was the world into which Jesus was born. The history of the Jews had been long and tragic to the time of the Romans, but now there was to be even more oppression and bloodshed; it would not end until after the destruction of the Temple in A.D. 70.

Between 350 and 50 B.C. Rome, through a series of wars, grew from a small nation to become world ruler. What once was the Empire of Greece became the Empire of Rome. Greece and Rome shared a peculiar relationship: Greece was beautiful, cultured, haughty and intellectual, while Rome was strong, rich, uncouth and practical. The saying, "To the glory that was Greece and the grandeur that was Rome" implies their differences. Rome depended on Greece for culture, so that the Jews were not culturally affected by Rome as they had been by Greece. But the Jewish nation felt the Roman impact in other, equally intense ways.

Pompey's conquest of the Hasmonean Kingdom came about because, while contending for the throne of the Hasmonean Kingdom, Hyrcanus II and Aristobulus II (Hasmoneans) came before Pompey to settle their dispute. The people of Jerusalem, disliking both of them, sent their own delegation to Pompey, but Pompey ignored them all, marched on Jerusalem, and took the defended and fortified Temple. He entered the Holy of Holies, but was so struck with awe because there were no representations of a deity within that he left the sacred treasures alone and reinstated Hyrcanus II as both high priest and the ruler of Judea. In this way, the Hasmonean Kingdom became a Roman province. The area was of the utmost importance to Rome because it formed a line of defense against the continuous Parthian invasions from the East. This new province could be used to full advantage only if there was complete unity within it, and if it was controlled by a central government. So, administrative reforms took place; some Hasmonean areas were given to the Governor of Syria – Samaria and the Jordan Valley (the Decapolis of ten cities) – while other areas were put under Jewish control: Judea, Galilee, Idumea and Perea. The Jews were no longer independent: They were a religious community with their center of worship in Jerusalem but the high priest was responsible to the Roman governor and levied annual tax upon the people.

Six years of outward peace followed; yet the people were resentful against Hyrcanus II because he was personally responsible to the Roman government to whom they had to pay their tax. Revolt began to brew, although Hyrcanus II was not entirely to blame for his actions against the Jews as he was influenced and supported by Antipater, his political advisor, a crafty, self-seeking Edomite (from Idumea). Antipater was not a Hasmonean but was of the Idumeans, who had been forcibly converted to Judaism eighty years earlier by John Hyrcanus, son of Simon.

In 57 B.C. the pent-up emotions of the people erupted with Alexander, son of Aristobulus II, leading the revolt. He captured the fortresses Alexandreion, Hyrcania, and Machaerus. Gabinius, governor of Syria, requested Anitpater's aid in trying to win the confidence of the Jews, but Antipater refused. Then Gabinius appealed to Mark Antony, who responded and helped to defeat Alexander near Jerusalem. Alexander was captured at Alexandreion, but was later freed. Political and territorial changes resulted from this revolt: Government control was tightened over the Jews, and as Antipater wished, the territory was divided into five independent districts. These districts were responsible to the provincial governor for government and taxation. But this caused further revolts and uprisings.

In 54 B.C., Crassus replaced Gabinius as governor of Syria. He was even more severe with the Jews: He ransacked the Temple, taking the sacred treasures to finance his planned campaign against the Parthians. A year later he was killed by the Parthians near Carrhae.

Civil war broke out in 49 B.C. between Julius Caesar and Pompey, resulting in Caesar's becoming the master of Rome. Pompey withdrew, leaving Antipater open to invaders. Antipater, seeking Caesar's friendship, aided Caesar's campaign in Egypt. Hyrcanus II also supported Caesar, urging the Egyptian Jews to join his side. For this help, Antipater was made procurator of Judea, with all the rights of Roman citizenship, including exemption from taxes. Hyrcanus was also rewarded—he was made high priest and the five districts were abolished and united under his leadership.

The arrangement with Rome benefited not only Antipater and Hyrcanus personally, but also the Jews. No Roman troops were billeted in Judea during the winter and no money was exacted from the people for their maintenance. Permission was granted to rebuild the walls of Jerusalem, and the seaport of Joppa was restored, along with other sites. The Jews of the dispersion in Alexandria and Asia Minor also enjoyed these privileges, including possibly the best privilege of all—the freedom to worship in the place and manner that pleased them. It is no wonder that the Jews so deeply mourned the death of Julius Caesar a few years later.

In 47-46 B.C., Antipater appointed his eldest son, Phasael, governor of Jerusalem, over Judea and Perea, and his second son, to become known as Herod the Great, governor of Galilee. Soon afterward, Herod decided to take things into his own hands—he routed Ezekias and his men, Jewish revolutionaries, who had been troubling Galilee with their crimes, and executed them. This enhanced Herod's reputation, causing Hyrcanus II to become jealous. He summoned Herod before the Sanhedrin, which so insulted Herod that for a while he planned vengeance on Jerusalem. Fortunately, his father, Antipater, persuaded him against the use of violence. Upon returning to Galilee, Herod was appointed governor of Coele-Syria and Samaria by Julius Caesar.

After the death of Julius Caesar in 44 B.C. Cassius became governor of Syria. He exacted large sums from the people for support of the army, an action that soon brought upon him the hatred of the Jews. This hatred was also aimed at Antipater and Herod, for they had again shifted their allegiance, offering to collect these sums from the Jews. For this, Herod was confirmed by the Romans as governor of Judea. Antipater was poisoned soon after (43 B.C.) by his rival, Malichus, whom Herod later put to death.

Not long after, Cassius joined Brutus in the struggle for control of Rome. Herod strengthened his position with them by becoming engaged to Mariamne, the daughter of Alexander and Hyrcanus' daughter Alexandra, (Jos., *Ant*. xiv. 12,1). But Cassius and Brutus were defeated at the Battle of Philippi by Mark Antony, who took over Syria. Herod changed sides once again, winning the approval of Antony despite the charges the Jews had brought against him; Antony appointed him and Phasael joint tetrarchs over Judea. A tetrarch literally means 'ruler of the fourth part,' but is loosely applied to any subordinate prince. Hyrcanus II again lost his power over Judea.

In 40 B.C., Antigonus (one of the last Hasmoneans) attempted to gain the throne. He bribed the Parthians to help him, and to their own astonishment they defeated Jerusalem's Roman overlords and took Jerusalem itself. Antigonus set himself up as high priest and king. He captured and mutilated Hyrcanus II and also took Phasael prisoner, who later committed suicide from despair. Antigonus reigned for three years.

Herod had escaped from the revolt to Masada, the fortress near the Dead Sea. He left his family there and went to see Octavian and Antony (*cf.* Jos., *Ant*. xiv. 14,3-6). Josephus says that Herod met Octavian at Rhodes "dressed as a private person with the demeanor of a king." Octavian was so impressed by Herod that he and the Roman Senate unanimously elected Herod king of Judea (39 B.C.). Now the problem was to possess the throne, and Herod still lacked an army. He therefore went to Galilee to rid the land of robbers and insurrectionists, for which service Antony gave him the military support he needed. He made himself master of Galilee and the surrounding country, and with Antony's Roman force besieged Jerusalem. In 37 B.C. Herod and the Roman army prevailed, capturing Jerusalem; Antigonus and 45 members of the Sanhedrin were put to death, and Herod married Mariamne. Thus, possessing the throne, he ended the Hasmonean dynasty. There is great irony here, since the Idumeans now ruled the people who had converted them.

Herod was now king of the Jews. In religion he was a Jew, in race an Idumean, in cultural sympathies a Greek, in political allegiance a Roman. To his inferiors he was ruthless, to his own family he was sometimes cruel, if affectionate, and to his superiors he was an opportunist. He "played along" with whoever was in power; he was always ready to change sides. Emperor Augustus said of him, "I had sooner be Herod's swine than his son," a reference to Herod's murders of his own sons (Roth, 95). From most accounts, one pictures Herod as a hideous madman, almost inhumanly evil, but in Josephus' report he does not appear quite so terrible. While he was not virtuous, and was often ruthlessly cruel, in comparison to other rulers of his age (the Seleucids, Ptolemies, Romans and previous priest-kings) Herod did accomplish some good. In his day harem intrigues, jealousies between royal brothers and murderous conspiracies were common factors in the life of any Eastern monarch. Looking at Herod from this angle, he seems more to be pitied than scorned.

Herod was one of the most competent rulers of his day. During his reign he regained almost the entire area that had been the Hasmonean Kingdom. In 37 B.C. his kingdom consisted of Judea, Idumea, Perea, Galilee, the port of Joppa, and the villages of Jezreel. In 34 B.C. Octavian restored to him the coastal cities of Phoenicia and Philistia, which had been Cleopatra's; and when Cleopatra died in 30 B.C. he received the whole of Palestine minus Decapolis and north Caesarea. The fact that he kept this extensive kingdom until his death speaks well of his powers of diplomacy. He had three policies in maintaining this state of affairs: one, to encourage good relations with Octavian and to promote the Hellenistic culture, of which Rome was now champion; two, to cultivate the confidence of his own people by reducing taxes and avoiding offenses to their religion; and, three, to suppress nationalism. To defend the country from enemies he maintained a standing, mostly mercenary army; established military settlements on the north and east borders; and erected impregnable fortresses which also served as palaces for his own family members.

With the reign of Herod the Great came the end of the hereditary aristocracy. There arose instead a new aristocracy of service—those who were given their positions by Herod—a bureaucracy structured along Hellenistic lines. This signaled the end of the authority and influence of the Sanhedrin—a 70-member ecclesiastical council including both Pharisees and Saduccees and presided over by the high priest—in any but religious and academic matters. Secular affairs were handled by the royal council. Herod was protective of the Pharisees, however, as the result of a favor two of them had done for him during the siege of Jerusalem; Herod felt he had a better chance of securing the people's approval if he were favorably inclined toward the Pharisees.

Though Herod's reign was one of inner strife and bloodshed, it was outwardly peaceful and prosperous. His reign marked the peak of peace and prosperity for the Jewish nation. There were lavish expenditures made on buildings and gifts to foreign leaders, but the coffers were always full. The royal revenue was increased, the lower Jordan valley was irrigated, and a new city and port were built on the site of Straton's Tower. This new harbor, called Caesarea, encouraged overseas trade with the western world. Herod also began an extensive building program in the middle period of his reign: He erected fortresses, magnificent buildings, and cities in the Hellenistic style; he instituted quinquennial games (athletic and gladitorial contests) in honor of the Emperor, supported and managed the Olympic games, built hippodromes, gymnasiums, public baths, colonnaded streets and marketplaces with elegant statues and temples. In Jerusalem he erected a hippodrome, a theatre, and an amphitheatre; and in other cities he dedicated altars, shrines and temples to Octavian and to pagan deities. His most notable work was the reconstruction of the Temple at Jerusalem, begun in 20 B.C. It took eighteen months to complete the main edifice and eight years more to finish the outer courts and porches. It was built according to Jewish scruples: He was careful not to enter the Temple; he did not erect statues in the Temple area or stamp his image on the coins. (The Jewish law forbade images on coins.) He even had the workmen build silently, as the Old Testament had instructed (I Kings 6:7). But Herod did permit the Roman eagle to be placed over the great gate of the Temple, an act which later was to lead to violent reaction from the Pharisees. The Temple was not fully completed until A.D. 65, just five years before it was destroyed.

In spite of all this activity and prosperity, the people disliked Herod: The Greeks did not like a Jew ruling them and the Jews did not accept an Idumean. Besides, everything Herod did showed his devotion to Hellenistic culture: The classical architecture, the urban centers, the games – everything spoke of the Greek and Roman influence and of his utter neglect of the Jewish culture. Taxes grew heavy, Roman legionnaires were always in Jerusalem, and Roman institutions prevailed. The old constitution of the country had been overruled, the Sanhedrin had lost its power except in religious affairs, and the high priests were changed so frequently that it was impossible to establish a way of life as had been done before. The Jews even suspected Herod's reason for reconstructing the Temple. Foakes Jackson comments, "In demolishing the ancient Temple and entirely rebuilding it, Herod doubtless hoped to gain immortal fame and to conciliate his Jewish subjects" (Jackson, 43). The Jews marginally accepted Herod only because one of his wives, Mariamne, was a Maccabean princess. They hoped that eventually one of her sons would inherit the throne and bring back the Maccabean lineage. But Herod grew suspicious of these sons and in 7 B.C. had them put to death (*cf.* Jos., *Ant.* xvi. 11,1-7).

Herod's personal life flowed with blood. Josephus says that the evil influences behind Herod were his sister Salome and his first-born son by another wife, Antipater. Salome convinced him of a plot by his (and Mariamne's) sons to take the throne, and of Mariamne's infidelity, and this led to their execution by Herod. Herod was driven by "unscrupulous ambition" and "fierce jealousy," which led him to murder several other of his wives and children, other relatives, members of the Sanhedrin and other Jews. Josephus lends a tragic note to the murders of Mariamne and her two sons. He tells of Herod's undying love for them, even when Mariamne was unfaithful. Only when he was persuaded of her infidelity did he order her death, and then he went almost mad with remorse.

After Herod had disposed of his two sons by Mariamne, he named Antipater as heir-apparent; but when Herod was dying of an excruciatingly painful disease, he was told of Antipater's part in a plot against him. He then condemned Antipater to death and unceremonial burial. Josephus says that although Herod's career had been otherwise successful, Herod put to death the wife he loved, and her two sons, as well as his first-born whom he had designated heir to his vast dominions (Jos., *Ant*. xvii. 6,7). Again he altered his will, making another son, Archelaus, king of Judea, and Antipas tetrarch of Gaulonitis, Trachonitis, and Paneas. Five days later, in 4 B.C., Herod died and was buried with elaborate ceremony at the fortress of Herodium.

Josephus tells of an event that shows us something of the man: Herod assembled the chief men of his kingdom and locked them in the hippodrome in Jericho, giving express orders to Salome that they were to be massacred as soon as he himself expired, so that the time of his death would be marked by national mourning (Jos., *Ant*. xvii. 6,5). But tradition holds that these "intended victims were released, and the city of Jerusalem, which the tyrant had both beautified and cursed, was filled with rejoicing instead of lamentation."

Thus, the 34-year reign of Herod, called the Great, came to a close. He brought peace and prosperity to Judea, yet he was the most hated ruler of his day. He left behind him the greatest expansion of the kingdom, prosperity unknown since Solomon, freedom from the elements of disorder, an increasing population, an entirely Jewish Galilee of teeming villages, and a prosperous Jerusalem. These blessings came at the expense of liberty, but, in the true sense, what liberty had the Jews enjoyed since the Captivity? The main blot of Herod's reign was the lack of religious advancement; there was always an undercurrent of piety, but during his reign the Jewish religion had been somewhat diluted by the Hellenistic culture.

The contribution of the Romans to the scene of Jesus can be seen through the Herods: The atmosphere was peaceful and prosperous but also suspicious, cruel and politically tense. Such a situation enabled the growth of Christianity and heightened the longing of the coming of the Messiah.

The peaceful and prosperous atmosphere created by Herod the Great was continued by his sons, Herod Antipas (tetrarch of Galilee) and Herod Agrippa (King of Judea). Into this setting Jesus was born and carried out His ministry. The suspicion and cruelty of the Herods also touched Jesus' life as seen in the killing of the children (Matt. 2:16), the beheading of John the

Baptist by Herod Antipas (Matt. 14:1ff.), and the mockery at Jesus' trial (Luke 23:8ff.).

The death of Herod the Great did not end the bloody history of the Jews. Worse was to follow: Jewish persecution by Vespasian and other Roman rulers, and the destruction of Jerusalem in A.D. 70. The study of their history makes one ask with Raskin (*cf.* Levinger, title page):

The Eternal Riddle

Hated and hunted,
Ever thou wand 'rest,
Bearing a message:
God is but One!

Israel, my people,
God's greatest riddle;
Will thy solution
Ever be told?

THE INFORMATION ON *music in the Bible is far more eloquent and meaningful than all other records of antiquity concerning music, except those of the Greeks.* Sendrey explains:

> The musical references of the Bible are almost the first records in the history of mankind that afford a comprehensive insight into the musical culture of a people of high Antiquity....
>
> In Israel's early history, music has been mostly an implement for superstition and magic. In the intermediate stage it was the necessary background for religious rites. Only in its further development it became a possession of the entire people. At this stage, it was deeply rooted in the people's consciousness, it was no more a mere accessory of religion, or the privilege of a single class, but the common property of a whole nation. Music became a people's art, in the broadest sense of the word. (Sendrey, 60)

Because music was a people's art the authors who wrote about it took for granted that their readers had a genuine knowledge of and were thoroughly familiar with all the musical matters of that day; therefore, they considered it unnecessary to give long descriptions and minute details of the instruments about which they wrote.

For musicological research the value of the early rabbinic literature is rather uneven. They tried to clarify obscure passages of biblical text and explain obsolete musical terms. Some of these expressions are rather useful, even if others are of little help. The aim of the rabbinic writers was to preserve and expound tradition and in this way their work was very helpful. Many musical terms, notions, and much musical tradition would be lost without their retrospective care. A good example of this is the rabbinical literature of the early Diaspora which is very important. It shows that the Israelites never entirely gave up their music after the destruction of the Temple in spite of all the severe religious prohibitions.

> As a sign of mourning for the ravaged sanctuary (Sendrey writes), all musical activity was supposed to be abandoned. This interdiction was carried out in one field only, where the spiritual leaders of the dispersed people retained their full sway: in the religious service. Instrumental music, as part of the ceremony, ceased to exist with the downfall of Jerusalem. Singing, however, as practiced in the Synagogue, never was seriously threatened by rabbinic prohibitions. (Sendrey, 63)

The Jews of the Diaspora saved their secular music, especially its intimate forms: the music at home, and the singing of zemirot in the family.

Besides religion, music was the major stimulus for the Jew's inner life. History has proven that he never gave up this comfort to his soul even for a short period.

Another source concerning Jewish music is the writings of the early Church Fathers. All music referred to by the patristic literature is related (directly or indirectly) to Israel. The early Christian church, of course, was the immediate successor to the Jewish religion and, therefore, incorporated the sacred ceremonies of the Temple or Synagogue without change. Vocal music was also an important element in the sacred service of the Temple and continued to be important later during the time of the Apostolic Christians, as in the singing of the psalms, hymns, spiritual songs, and responses, with or without instrumental accompaniment.

Written sources provide good information, but authentic reproductions concerning Jewish music are very scarce. Following are two good examples of visual illustrations, cited by Sendrey:

> On the Arch of Triumph in Rome, erected to the glory of the emperor Titus after the destruction of the Temple of Jerusalem, are shown the sacred silver trumpets (hazoerot), together with the sacred vessels of the sanctuary, which Titus carried away as booty in his triumphal procession.
>
> A coin of Bar Kochba issued during the war of liberation against the emperor Hadrian (132-135 C.E.), shows a pair of trumpets; they are designed in such a shortened and clumsy fashion that it is somewhat difficult to reconstruct their original shape.... (Sendrey)

The importance of the coin is that it was issued by a victorious national hero and had a sacred symbol of the Jewish religion on it. Bar Kochba's revolt was the first successful revolt of Judaism against a powerful oppressor after the destruction of their national existence. Stamping of the coins was a visible sign of the urge for national survival. On the coins, two instruments were represented, an unmistakable sign that they are sacred trumpets.

Other coins of Bar Kochba show the biblical kinnor or lyre in several varieties. The design depicted is crude, the strings are represented by thick lines showing mostly three, five or six strings. The stringed instruments reproduced on the coins show great similarity to the Greek lyra or kithara – which might be later forms of the Israelite instruments designed from Greek patterns.

Depicted on a vase (about 1025 B.C.E.) found at Megiddo, is an early form of the kinnor, probably that of David's time. It shows curved side-arms, a straight, horizontal cross bar, protruding on both sides, to which four strings are attached. The kinnor originally had ten strings, but the vase, like the coins, shows it with fewer. This instrument is very much like a lyre on a wall-painting found in Tomb 38 at Thebes (c. 1420 B.C.E.). Both have a square sounding board, curved side-arms and the same cross bar protruding on both ends. The only difference is that the Egyptian one shows seven strings.

The instrument on the vase at Megiddo is a reproduction of the Egyptian lyre. There is no absolute way of knowing whether the lyre was brought along by the Israelites from Egypt or whether it was imported earlier by the Canaanites and found by the Israelites. There is even a chance that the Egyptian lyre might have served as a model for the Jewish kinnor or even have been used by David himself and introduced by him into the Temple music.

There is also in a fresco of a sepulchural grotto at Beni-Hassan, in the tomb of a prince named Nehera-si-num-hotep, who lived in the epoch of the Pharaoh Amenemhnet II of the 12th Dynasty (1938-1904 B.C.E.), a mural in which a prince is approached by a procession of nomads asking permission to settle in Egypt. In the mural is depicted a Semitic lyre-player holding an instrument of eight strings under his right arm. He manipulated them partly with his bare left hand while his right hand plucks the strings with the aid of a plectrum. There is a chance that his left hand is perhaps "stopping" the strings. "The body of the instrument," Sendrey observes, "is a square board, having an opening at the upper part, which apparently serves as a hole in the resonance body." This instrument was considered to be the prototype of the Hebrew kinnor (Sendrey, 69-70).

Depicted on an ivory from Megiddo, dated approximately 1200 B.C.E., is what might also be a possible model of the Jewish kinnor. Pictured on the ivory is a Canaanite king sitting on a throne drinking from a bowl while one of his musicians entertains him by playing on a lyre. The instrument has nine strings strung horizontally and is plucked with the fingers of the left hand. The large resonant body is held under the left arm of the player. There is no way of finding out what the right hand is doing because it is hidden behind the corpus of the instrument. This is undoubtedly a pre-Israelitic instrument and, therefore, might *have been copied by the Israelites or have been an influence on the form of the Jewish lyre that was to come.*

The last discovery of the pictorial reproductions of ancient Israel recovered so far was at Megiddo. It was a bronze figure (33 cm. high), most likely representing a Jewish flute-girl. The above-mentioned examples are the only known findings to date.

Chapter 4

THE PHARISEES AND SADDUCEES

> The Jews had for a great while three sects of philosophy peculiar to themselves; the sect of the Essens, and the sect of the Sadducees, and the third sort of opinions was that of those called Pharisees....

SO WRITES JOSEPHUS in his *Antiquities*. We know about the Pharisees from Josephus and just a few other primary sources. The New Testament, of course, also tells us something of the Pharisees, but for the most part it discusses them with a negative bias; that is, they stood in opposition to Jesus and thus may seem to be merely "the bad guys." There are also the rabbinic documents, but these are mostly of late composition so they do not shed much light on the early Pharisees.

The problem of the origin of the Pharisees is complicated. George F. Moore states the problem clearly when he says, "Of the origin and the antecedents of the Pharisees there is no record" (More, 59). That is exactly the problem; even Josephus does not mention where they came from. It is commonly surmised among scholars, however, as Moore says, that they succeeded those who earlier called themselves Hasidim "to distinguish themselves as what we call religious men from their worldly and indifferent countrymen" (More, 59).

D. S. Russell takes the view that the Pharisees were spiritual rather than literal descendants of the Hasidim. "It is perhaps more accurate to say that their origin is to be traced to those lay scribes who, from the beginning of the Greek period, did so much to 'democratize' religion through their everyday life" (Russell, 160). The exact relation of the Pharisees to the Hasidim is unclear. I Maccabees 7:12ff. mentions "a company of scribes along with the Hasidim," so the two groups may be linked; but how they are linked cannot now be determined.

Another possible origin of the Pharisees is set forth by Eduard Lohse. He suggests that they began during the Maccabean times, when it was necessary to defend the Jewish faith against Hellenistic influences (Lohse, 77). I Maccabees 2:42 characterizes them as, "a company of pious Jews, brave men from Israel, none but those who willingly submitted themselves to the law." Out of these "Chasidim" who supported the Maccabean revolt came the Pharisees. When the Maccabees became more concerned with the political issue than the religious one, the Chasidim lost interest.

Werner Foerster suggests yet another theory, based on mentions of the Pharisees, or a group presumed to be them, in the Qumran documents of the Essenes (Forester, 65-66). Here there is mention of 'the House of Absalom' and their cronies who kept silent when charges were levelled against the teacher who was expounding the Law aright, and who did not come to their aid against the man of lies when the latter rejected the Torah in the midst of their entire congregation. Other references to the Pharisees in the Qumran documents characterize them as "those who seek after smooth things." Thus the Pharisees are reproached for taking an easier or smoother path in relation to the Law.

In spite of these different theories, the truth as to the origin of the Pharisees cannot definitively be known. Josephus first mentions them by name at the time of John Hyrcanus (135-105 B.C.), when the Hasidim broke with the Hasmoneans. F. F. Bruce suggests that these Hasidim who withdrew from the Hasmoneans were the Pharisees; they withdrew when the Hasmoneans became preoccupied with political rather than religious matters (F. F. Bruce, 72).

The derivation of the name "Pharisee" does not shed much more light on the problem. Lohse says it is derived from the Hebrew *peruschim* or the Aramaic *perischaya* meaning "the separated ones."

T. W. Manson suggests that the name "Pharisee" derives from the Aramaic word "Persian" and indicates innovators in theology, and that they were nicknamed thus because so many of their ideas were derived from Persian (Zoroastrian) sources. Later, it was linked with *paras*, "separate," and became more edifying. This appears to indicate the Pharisees' open attitude in regard to religious innovations, but Russell stresses that too much emphasis should not be put on the idea that the Pharisees' concept of life after death could have Persian origin (Russell, 63).

> The word Pharisee [according to Moore] represents the name in its vernacular form, *Perisha*. The derivation from the verb *përash* (Hebrew *parash*) is plain; not so the significance and occasion of the name. The interpretation that first suggests itself is 'one who is separated, or is separate'; but from whom or from what--a complement which is necessary to give it meaning--the word contains no intimation; nor does either usage or tradition supply the deficiency.
>
> From the peculiar rules and customs of the Pharisees it is commonly inferred that they were so called because they religiously avoided everything that the law branded as unclean, and for fear of contamination kept aloof from persons who were suspected of negligence in such matters. Definitions in this general sense were current among the church fathers. In the 'Aryt' the name is defined: 'A Pharisee is one who separates himself from all uncleanness and from eating anything unclean,' in distinction from the mass of the common people, who were not so particular. In the Tannaite and Amoraic sources the name *Perushim* is used in contrast to 'Am ha-Ares, the ignorant and negligent *vulgus*. (Moore, 60)

Russell explains that the Hebrew word for *Pharisee* (*Perusim*) in the passive form can mean "those who are separated" from the people of the land or from unclean things; thus these "separate ones" are given over to fulfilling the Law (*cf.* Jos., *Ant.* xviii. 1,2-3). Or "separate" may refer to their distinction from the Sadducean Sanhedrin, thus meaning "schismatics." The active form of the word *Parasim* originally meant "expounder" or "interpreter" (of the Law). The verb *paras* can mean "interpret" as well as "separate."

In rabbinic literature, the word means "to separate" and *Pharisee* usually means "one who has been separated." Bo Riecke stresses that it does not mean "dissident" or "separatist." He explains that in rabbinic passages the Pharisees are an "expansive popular party with highly developed social relationships and structures," not an isolated group. In the context where the name is usually found, "puritan" is suggested, one who is a zealous proponent of ritual purity (see Mishna *Hag.* ii. 17; Talmud Yerushalmi *Ber.* ix. 146, 40;

Schwab i. 169). This agrees with the characterization in both Josephus and the New Testament (Jos., *Ant.* xviii. 1,3; Matt. 15:2). Thus, Bo Reicke points out that *Pharisee* as "puritan" would also agree with the Old Testament idea of separation from the pollution of the peoples of the land (Ezra 6:21; 9:1; 10:11; Neh. 9:2; 10:28) and "from the nations of the world with their abominations" (Mekilta, *Exod.* 19. 6,71a) (Bo Reicke, 156).

The Pharisaic sect was composed of priests, laymen, craftsmen, farmers, merchants, those from the city and the country, Judea and Galilee. In other words, they were made up of the middle class. They came together for meals in order to maintain purity (Luke 7:36; 11:37-38), and there were at one time "more than 6,000 members in the Pharisee's fellowship" (Jos., *Ant.* xvii. 2,4 §42). The first Pharisees were law-observing Jews with no political aims. They were filled with zeal for the Law by which Israel led its life (I Macc. 7:13).

The Pharisees can further be defined as "A body of Jews who profess to be more righteous than the rest and to explain the laws more precisely" (*Bell. Jud.* 1,8,14 §162; *cf. Ant.* xvii. 2,4 §41; xviii. 1,3 §12).

Tcherikover points out, however, that the Pharisees were skillful in politics:

> The slogan chosen by the Pharisees testifies to their great skill in political tactics. 'The royal crown is sufficient to you, leave the priestly diadem to the seed of Aaron!' – in these words the Talmud defines the Pharisean demands upon King Jannaeus. At first sight this demand did not detract from the power of the dynasty, for the Pharisees were ready to leave the royal crown – the army, foreign affairs, the court and the administration – in its hands; it was to concede only the Temple.

The Talmud makes an interesting distinction – roughly contemporary with our study – among the Pharisees. It differentiates seven types: the "wait-a-little" – puts off doing a good deed; the "bruised" or "bleeding" – shuts eyes not to look at a woman, and so stumbles against a wall; the "shoulder" – wears good deeds on shoulders for all to see; the "hump-backed" – walks stooped in false humility; the "ever-reckoning" – continually counts up his good deeds to balance the bad; the "God-fearing" – stands in awe and dread of God; and, the "God-loving" or "born" – is a true son of Abraham and a genuine Pharisee

(Metzger, 41-42; *cf.* Kohler, "Pharisees," *Jewish Encyclopedia,* Vol. IX (1905): 665).

Although it is unknown exactly when the Pharisees originated, their antecedents seem to lie in the Jews who were exiled in Babylon in the sixth century B.C. Probably, when the Jews could no longer worship at the Temple (after being carried captive to Babylon), they formed groups to study the Law and the Scriptures in their own homes or in some public place. We see the seeds of these scholars in Ezra and Nehemiah when, as reformers, the Pharisees developed the ideal of Ezra and the Levites (e.g., Neh. 8:7-9,13; 10:29f.).

It is not until the Maccabean revolt (167 B.C.) that a case can be made for the emergence of the Pharisees as such. The writer of I Maccabees states that a group of Hasidim, or pietists ("pious"), pledged to obey the Law and withstand Hellenistic influence (I Macc. 2:42). Of course, we cannot assume that this is the origin of the Pharisees. In 161 B.C. some outstanding scribes were deceived by Alcimus, the Hellenistic high priest (I Macc. 7:12-18). This forced the pious group to become more closely associated with the Maccabees themselves.

In the Hasmonean times (142-37 B.C.), the Pharisees were led by learned scribes and had authority as lay members of the *Gerousia* or *Sanhedrin*. Their religious influence was great in the synagogues and schools in Jerusalem and throughout the Dispersion, where they interpreted and explained the Scriptures. They formed "brotherhoods" and had great influence on Judaism, although they were small in numbers. They did missionary work among the Gentiles (Matt. 23:15).

When the Hasmonean cause became more political than religious, it appears that the Pharisees separated from them. Under Alexander Jannaeus in particular, there arose a bloody conflict in which the high priest gained the upper hand by terror, including execution of dissidents. At this point the Pharisees began to emphasize the task of preparing themselves by pious living, prayer and fasting for the future change which God would bring about. This became their aim rather than seeking a political change by means of violence. Thus, they later refused to join the Zealots to bring in the Messianic age by force.

According to Josephus, John Hyrcanus was a highly esteemed Pharisee until a personal grievance caused him to defect to the Sadducean party (Jos., *Ant.* xiii, 10,5f.). Hyrcanus abrogated the ordinances which the Pharisees had established and punished those who observed them. Because of this, the common people assertedly hated him and his sons.

The next we hear of the Pharisees is during the time of Herod, when they were described as "A Body of Jews who profess to be more religious than the rest and to explain the laws more precisely" (*Bell. Jud.* 1.8, 14 §162; *cf. Ant.* xvii. 2,4 §41; xviii. 1,3 §12).

We also have a wider knowledge of the Pharisaic party at this time because two famous Pharisees, Hillel and Shammai, were then living. Hillel was the liberalizing factor in Pharisaism while Shammai represented a stricter application of the Law. Thus, by this time there were conflicting doctrines within Pharisaism.

Hillel was known for his gentleness, humility and patience of character. He did not accept the rule of Herod, nor did he advocate Messianism and apocalyptic speculation. These aspects were absent since they would lead to political conflict. He saw the future hope as present in the pursuit of peace and love of humanity. David Rhoads quotes him as saying, "He who has acquired for himself words of the Torah has acquired life in the coming world" (Rhoads, 36-37).

In other words, the study of the Torah was the key to eternal life more than the acquisition of information of worldly things. A rule of Hillel was, "What is hateful to yourself, do not to your fellow. That is the whole Torah. All the rest is commentary. Now go forth and learn!"

Jacob Neusner says,

> Hillel taught a methodology of interpreting Scripture which in time revolutionized the intellectual life of Pharisaism. These principles,...included the following: 1. Inference *a minori ad majus*; 2. Inference by analogy; 3. Constructing a family on the basis of one passage (extending a specific regulation of one biblical passage to a number of passages); 4. The same rule as the preceding, constructing a family on the basis of two biblical passages; 5. The General and the Particular, the Particular and the General; 6. Exposition by means of another similar passage; 7. Deduction from the context. (Neusner, 36)

Thus, Hillel made his interpretation as broad and as liberal as possible. He changed many things for the good of the people. For instance, Bruce explains, "To Hillel is assigned a legal innovation which went far to modify, if not to nullify, the ancient law that debts owed by a fellow-Israelite were to be remitted every seventh year (Deut. 15:1-6)" (Bruce, 80). Thus, the Pharisees who followed Hillel could interpret a law so far as to actually change its original meaning. Hillel employed logical argument as the basis for the exposition of the text, and this helped to apply the Law and to take account of the existing social conditions.

Compared to Hillel, Shammai represents strict interpretation of the Law. He seems to have been remembered mainly for his petulance, but accounts of him are most likely prejudiced. Shammai left few sayings and those we do have were written by Hillel's disciples. Bruce observes,

> It is probable that the Lawyers in the Gospels record, who 'load men with burdens hard to bear' but do not themselves lift a finger to ease their weight (Lu. 11:46), are Shammaites. But in the reconstruction of national life that followed the war of A. D. 66-73 it was the school of Hillel, under Yohanan ben Zakkai and his associates, that became dominant. (Bruce, 80)

There are 316 recorded controversies between these two schools, the Shammaites typically taking the stricter side and the Hillelites the milder. Most of the conflicts had to do with ritual and legal matters, although some were more fundamental. For instance, the two schools debated for two-and-one-half years over the question, "Was it good that man had been created?"

A typical example of the differing approaches was in regard to divorce. Shammai held that the only valid reason for divorce was adultery, whereas Hillel acknowledged the problem of incompatibility.[*]

During Jesus' ministry (6-44 C.E.), Josephus tells that the Pharisees staged a passive sit-in before Pilate at Caesarea. Several of these acts of passive resistance evidently took place. One particular event occurred in a later period (44-66 C.E.) when irate Jews protested the burning of the Torah by a Roman soldier (Jos., *Wars* ii. 12,2; *Ant.* xx. 5,4).

During the Apostolic era, the Pharisees had great influence on the High Council and in government (Jos., *Ant.* xviii. 1,4). They were especially

---

[*] For other examples, see Grant, p. 258.

powerful under Agrippa I (A.D. 41-44), who sought to cultivate the Pharisees for political reasons. After A.D. 50, however, their popularity yielded somewhat to the Zealots. Throughout this era the Pharisees remained within the society in accordance with the words of Hilled, "Do not separate yourself from the community" (*Avot* 1.5).

There arose still other differences within Pharisaism. The Zealots among them sought to restore Israel through war, while the others centered on spiritual reform. Josephus wrote of the Pharisees,

> ...on account of which doctrines they are able greatly to persuade the body of the people; and whatsoever they do about divine worship, prayers, and sacrifices, they perform them according to their direction; insomuch that the cities gave great attestations to them on account of their entire virtuous conduct, both in the actions of their lives and their discourses also. (Jos., *Ant.* xviii. 1,3)

Thus the Pharisees fostered their opinions among the people.

At this time, the Pharisees seem to have been more favorable toward the new Christian community, as seen in several accounts in the New Testament: Gamaliel I opposed the arrest of apostles (Acts 5:34); although his disciple Paul persecuted the Church (Acts 9:1f; Phil. 3:5f), Pharisees joined the Church (Acts 15:5); and Pharisaic scribes spoke in Paul's behalf (Acts 23:9).

Gamaliel I followed his father Hillel and his rival Shammai as head of the Pharisaic community. Simeon ben Gamaliel and Yohanan ben Zakkai succeeded him, two decades before the revolt of A.D. 66-70, although it was Zakkai who actually took the lead. (*Avot* 2.9). Zakkai was Hillel's disciple and student and we can see Hillel's teaching reflected in Zakkai's ideas; for example, in his concept of responsibility toward social problems and his devotion to the Torah.

Although Zakkai represented the Pharisees in the disputes with the Sadducees, he attempted to unite the religion of Galilee and Jerusalem. Neusner comments that the two dynamics in religion were united in the experience of the Torah and the act of continuing study and application of Scripture (Neusner, 64).

The book of Acts tells us that the Pharisees had influence in the Sanhedrin (5:34-40; 23:6-8). But when the revolt came, in A.D. 66-70, not even the Pharisees could prevent disaster. Some joined the revolt, others did not. Some survived the war and exerted influence after A.D. 70 on the Synagogue, both spiritually and intellectually. During the revolt, Ben Zakkai preached passivism. When he saw that war was imminent, he escaped while it was still possible. All accounts agree that he met Vespasian and prophesied his imminent rise to power and was thus allowed to go to Yavneh, in Galilee, to take refuge. Here, Ben Zakkai established an Academy that insured the future of Pharisaism, while the other parties met disaster.

Why did the Pharisees survive, while the Sadducees and the Essenes did not? Why did the Romans permit the Pharisees to establish an Academy that preserved the seeds of the later revolt in A.D. 139?

> The Pharisees (Josephus wrote)...have by far the greatest influence with the people. Any government which secures their support is accepted; any government which alienates them has trouble. The Sadducees, it is true, have more following among the Aristocracy...But they have no popular following at all, and even in the old days when they were in power, they were forced by public opinion to follow the Pharisees' orders. (Morton Smith, 76; cf. Jos., *Antiquities*)

Neusner adds that the other parties were ineligible for serious consideration by the Romans: Josephus presents the Essenes as a "Philosophical curiosity," the Zealots as, of course, Anti-Roman, and the Sadducees as an aristocratic minority. "So any Roman government which wants peace in Palestine had better support, and secure the support of, the Pharisees." In addition, the Pharisees actively advanced their own candidacy as Roman supporters; they possibly even negotiated for it (Neusner, 169).

The worst problems faced by the Pharisees after A.D. 70 were liturgical. Yohanan and the Academy eventually claimed "that the Academy held the authority formerly exerted by the Sanhedrin in Jerusalem," Neusner writes. "The Yavneh Academy was now *the* high court capable of issuing authoritative enactments" (Neusner, 196-97).

Ben Zakkai used the method of Hillel – to issue decrees of specific legal problems. By A.D. 75, and again by A.D. 145, Jewish autonomous government was again functioning. The Judaism that survived was different form pre-war Judaism. "It was a Judaism shaped by men who shared a community of interest with Rome." Neusner also says that "What survived in time became a force for peace, not subversion, and its central institutions consistently and, after the Bar Kochba War, effectively worked to secure loyalty to Rome and tranquility in Palestine" (Neusner, 171).

The Pharisees outlived the other religious parties because, when the social structure collapsed, they continued to evolve their own ideas about the proper conduct of society according to the biblical imperative. In contrast to the Sadducees and the Essenes, they pursued their studies and attempted to apply them to public life.

In their beliefs and practices the Pharisees were separatists in the sense that they separated themselves from those who did not know the Law. They were thus disassociated from such people as tax collectors, prostitutes, fallen men and sinners (Mark 2:14-17; par. Luke 15:2). Such separatism was largely to maintain purity. The Pharisees felt that the Old Testament commandments were necessary, not only for priestly purity but also for the purity of all Pharisees in everyday life. For instance, anyone who made contact with a dead corpse or an animal, or anyone who had a bodily discharge had lost his cultic purity. In order to gain it back, one must undergo a bath of purification and sometimes a period of time before he was regarded as clean. For this reason, the Pharisees washed their hands before every meal (Mark 7:3-4). The Pharisees paid attention not only to purity of the person but also to the purity of the vessels that they used. For example, if a mouse ran across a plate or if a bone fell into a cup, the plate or cup were rendered unclean (Matt. 23:25-26; par. Luke 11:39-40). According to Lohse, the Pharisees felt that "God had revealed the norms of purity through holy scriptures, traditions and scribes; the Pharisees sought to develop this revelation and make it applicable to society, so that every Jew could realize the ideal of the covenant people (Neh. 10:29-30)" (Lohse, 78-79).

In order to preserve and develop this purity, the Pharisees analyzed and discussed the books of the Bible. This exegesis was called "midrash," meaning "investigation" (c. 20 B.C.). The resulting material became revered almost above the biblical material itself.

Beyond the Midrash other writings were developed: *halaka* – tradition of observances, based on the legal material of the Bible; *haggada* – tradition of edification, based on narrative material; Talmud – literature of the systematic tradition comprising two collections; the Hebrew Mishna, containing 63 tracts assembled c. A.D. 200 in Tiberias, and the Aramaic Gemara, containing 36 (or 39) tracts of the Mishna, preserved in a Palestinian version dating c. A.D. 400 and a Babylonian version dating c. A.D. 500, Talmud Yerushalmi and Talmud Babli; and, *Tosefta*–like the Mishna but larger, edited c. A.D. 250.

The Pharisees accepted the Prophets Writings as authoritative sacred Scripture, and used them in their interpretation of the Torah. Russell comments, "In the course of time they (Pharisees) declared that this 'tradition of the elders' was as authoritative and binding as the written Torah itself, and so gave it an honoured place alongside Scripture" (Russell, 161).

Josephus comments on the situation that the Pharisees had passed on to the people certain regulations handed down by former generations and not recorded in the Laws of Moses, for which reason they were rejected by the Sadducean group, who held that only those regulations should be considered valid which were written down (in Scripture), and that those which had been handed down by subsequent generations need not be observed. And concerning these matters the two parties came to have serious differences and controversies (Jos., *Ant.* xii, 10,6).

Hence the Pharisees accepted as Law certain legal regulations which had been handed down by the fathers. Bruce explains the purpose of these "traditions": "The 'tradition of the elders' was largely designed to mitigate the rigours which a literal application of the written Law would impose on people living under conditions widely different from those which were obtained when the Law was first promulgated" (Bruce, 79; *cf.* Jos., *Ant.* xviii. 10,6).

At the same time, however, the whole life of the Pharisees was to observe the Law exactly. Josephus sums it up by saying that "The Pharisees are a group of Jews who have the reputation of excelling the rest of their nation in the observance of religion, and as exact exponents of the Laws" (Jos., *Wars* i. 5,2). Again in the *Wars*, Josephus calls the Pharisees the "leading sect" and the "most accurate interpreters of the Laws" (*Wars* ii. 8,14). The Pharisees attempted to *adapt* the written commands to the present and thus discover practicable regulations regarding everyday things; for example, the Sabbath rules. In fact, Rhoads goes so far as to say that the *essence* of Pharisaism was "the attempt to put the whole life under the control of the Law" (Rhoads, 34).

It is interesting to note that even when Pharisaism itself split into the schools of Hillel and Shammai, both groups held to the oral tradition (scribal interpretation of the Scriptures), although Hillel had to learn to do so.

The Pharisees believed in God's predetermination of Israel's destiny. They held that people must contribute to its sanctification and perfection through a precise fulfillment of the law (Jos., *Bell* ii. 162ff.; *Ant*. xiii. 5,9; xviii. 1,3).

The Pharisees taught the resurrection of the dead, the survival of the soul (Acts 23:8; Jos., *Bell* ii. 163; *Ant*. xviii. 1,3), a last judgment (Jos., *ibid*.), and a world to come (*Pirke Aboth*. ii. 8; *Ant*. xviii. 1,1-3). They supported their belief in the resurrection of the dead by their interpretation of the entire Scriptures, as expanded by the oral tradition. (Also see Mark 6:16; Luke 9:9) They developed this expectation of resurrection into a tightly formulated doctrine.

The Pharisees observed voluntary fasting twice a week to show penitence and to pray for Israel and its salvation. They also observed the commandment to give a tenth of the harvest and of one's earnings so that the tribe of Levi could be supported and the sacrificial service in the Temple could be maintained (Lev. 27:30-33; Num. 18:21-24). The Pharisees not only tithed on the produce from their land but also on anything which they acquired by purchase (Matt. 23:23; par. Luke 11:42).

The Pharisees believed that when the people were prepared in purity and holiness their Messiah would appear as the Son of David and would gather the scattered tribes of Israel and reestablish the kingdom. The more the pious rejected the increasingly worldly Hasmonean rule, the greater was their expectation that the Anointed One from David's lineage would soon appear to cleanse Jerusalem of the heathen, overthrow the ungodly, and take over political rule. This belief in a warrior-Messiah was based on the Psalms of Solomon, a Pharisaic work of the first century B.C. Although the Pharisees themselves were not particularly militant in this hope, the founder of the Zealot party was a Pharisee, as was the renowned Rabbi Akiba, who was involved in the revolt of Bar Kochba (A.D. 132).

Let us look briefly now at the relation of the Pharisees to the New Testament. For our purposes, only a few points will be mentioned. For a more detailed study, see Everett F. Harrison, *A Short Life of Christ*, where he discusses at length the conflict between the Pharisees and Jesus.

It is interesting to note that the famous Pharisee Rabbi ben Zakkai lived in Galilee as a contemporary of Jesus for eighteen years, only a few miles away. The "silent years," the public ministry, the crucifixion, resurrection, and ascension of Jesus all took place during this period. Could it be that Ben Zakkai met or heard Jesus? The encounter of Jesus with a Galilean schoolteacher named Zacchaeus is preserved in the *Gospel of Thomas*, and Neusner suggests that "Zacchaeus" could represent the Greek translation of "Ben Zakkai."

Neusner also suggests that the story of Jesus disputing with the scholars at the age of twelve arose after A.D. 70 in order to liberate the Christian community from the authority of Ben Zakkai's Academy of Yavneh. "Those who held that the destruction of Jerusalem represented divine retribution for the rejection and crucifixion of Jesus could hardly acknowledge the continuity of Jewish religious authority and the legitimacy of Yohanan's institution at Yavneh" (Neusner, 55).

In terms of beliefs and practices Jesus stood near the Pharisaic position on several points—for instance, the resurrection of the dead and the call to repentance and conversion. Jesus actually expressed some Pharisaic principles such as the Sabbath being made for man rather than man for the Sabbath (Mark 2:27) and that only a deliberate oath was binding (Matt. 23:16).

Jesus broke with the Pharisees, however, by eating with tax collectors and sinners (Mark 2:15), thus violating the Pharisees' law of purity. Jesus was above the Sabbath rules (Mark 2:23-3:6) and was not bothered by intricate rules of Pharisaic purity (Mark 7:1-5). Jesus in fact called Pharisees hypocrites for being so intent on observing the Law outwardly yet oblivious to purity of heart (Luke 11:39-43). This was not the only point on which Jesus opposed the Pharisees. He criticized the power of the Pharisaic scribes

(Matt. 23:2-31) and considered his own revelation as superior (Matt. 7:29; 12:23f.). He also criticized their interpretation of law as nullifying or neutralizing the force of a given commandment.

Even so, Jesus was on friendly terms with some Pharisees; for example, Simon (Luke 7:37), and some who warned him about Herod (Luke 13:31).

Most of the time, however, we see them plotting against his life (Mark 3:6; John 11:47-57). Jesus had criticized them because "The Pharisees, led by Yohanan ben Zakkai, were attempting not merely to rule the sanctuary but to *exclude* from the Temple all who did not accept their rulings....Whatever had not been done in the Pharisaic manner was thereby to be declared profane" (Neusner, 80). We see these practices in John, Chapter 9, where the blind man and the followers of Jesus are excommunicated from the Synagogue.

Other New Testament references to the Pharisees could be cited. We know that Paul studied with the famous Pharisee Gamaliel (also Ben Zakkai's predecessor). Thus, it is not surprising to see some likeness in writing style of Paul and Gamaliel. (For a comparison of Paul's epistles with Gamaliel's letter, see Neusner, p. 67.)

Josephus names the Sadducees as one of the three major sects of the Jews. Most of our information comes from his *Antiquities* and his *Wars,* and though he gives a somewhat biased viewpoint, he describes them quite at length. As for other sources, the New Testament gives us some idea of the beliefs and practices of the Sadducees, but obviously it shows no sympathy for them; it shows them mainly in opposition to Jesus. In Talmudic literature (the Mishna and the Tosephta) we see them in conflict with other scholars on questions of religion and law. We have at the present time no source that is acknowledged to have been written by a Sadducee since the sect disappeared after the destruction of Jerusalem in A.D. 70. Thus, no actual sources were preserved.

Most scholars attribute the origin of the Sadducees to the priesthood of Zadok, established by David. Lohse agrees on this as the inspiration of the sect, but traces its actual origin more precisely to the time of Ezekiel.

> The label 'Sadducees' certainly is to be connected with the name Zadok who, long ago under King Solomon, was installed as high priest (I Kings 2:35) and from whom, as their ancestor, the priests traced their lineage. In the sketch of the future of Israel, of the land, and of the sanctuary which is presented in Ezekiel 40-48, the priestly ministry is committed to the sons of Zadok (Ezek. 40:46; 43:19; 44-15; 48:11). Then in the construction of the postexilic community the Zadokites played a crucial role and as legitimate priests in Jerusalem, took care of the temple service. (Lohse, 74)

Rhoads points out that during the Maccabean revolt several groups claimed to be "sons of Zadok"; for example, the Qumran group: a group that retained control of Jerusalem; and a group that cooperated with the Hasmoneans and eventually came to be called "Sadducees" (Rhoads, 39-40).

Another theory regarding the origin of the name *Sadducee* is that rather than being connected with the high priest Zadok it came from an association with the word *Saddikim*, "righteous ones" (*cf. Assumption of Moses*, 7:3). Russell, however, sees such a connection as etymologically impossible (Russell, 157).

T. W. Manson puts forth another theory. He says that the origin derives from the Greek *Syndics*, meaning "legal counsel."

> It is that the meaning of the name is to be found, not in the priestly connexions of the party, but rather in the realm of international politics. He finds its derivation in the Greek word *sundikoi* (Syndics) which can be traced back in Athenian history as far as the fourth century B. C. and is also mentioned in documents from Roman and Byzantine times. (Russell, 157)

Bo Reicke counters that this derivation does not adequately explain the vowels of the words as found in the New Testament and Josephus, or the consonants found in rabbinic literature, although "Manson has, however, emphasized some historically important facts" (Reicke, 153-54).

Still another theory is that the origin is a *scholar* named Zadok, active in the second century B.C.(Abot, R. Nath. 5). But Bo Reicke also criticizes this theory on the ground that since it is so similar to another passage about a certain Böethus who is an ancestor of the Böethus priests, the rivals of the Annas priests, "the passage is merely an etiological legend" (Reicke, 153).

Bruce combines Manson's theory with another theory. Like Manson, he says that it is "probable" that *Sadducee* is a Hebraization (*Sadduqim*) of the Greek word *syndikoi* (Syndics), members of the Council; but unlike

Manson he goes on to say "that it marks them out as the councilors of the Hasmoneans; although they themselves come to associate the word with the Hebrew *saddiq*, 'righteous'" (Bruce, 74).

In view of these many theories, it is next to impossible to conclude with any certainty just where the Sadducees originated. It is possible, though, that they began not as a religious sect but as a civil party with close ties to the Temple and the priesthood; and because politics and religion could not easily be separated from one another they eventually took on a religious character.

We can be certain of a few facts, however. Unlike the Pharisees, they were members of the aristocracy, and their membership included both laymen and priests, traders and high-ranking government officials (Jos., *Ant.* xviii. 1,2-3).

In later Talmudic literature, the Sadducees appear as men without religion or morality. Enoch presents them as pagans. If these sources are reliable, then the Sadducees were extreme Hellenists. In regard to their behavior Josephus remarks, "But the behavior of the Sadducees one toward another is in some degrees wild; and their conversation with those that are of their own party is as barbarous as if they were strangers to them" (Jos., *Wars* ii. 8,14).

It is possible to trace briefly the history of the Sadducees from the time of the Seleucids (third and second centuries B.C.) to the time of their disappearance in A.D. 70. They were influenced by the Hellenization of the Jews during the time of the Seleucids. As their political authority grew, their religious devotion apparently decreased. The writer of I Maccabees regards such leaders as renegades and traitors to the heritage of the fathers (I Macc. 1:15). During the time of the Romans and the Herods, the Sadducees were so politically prudent and skillful that they occupied high offices in Jerusalem. The high priests were always chosen from the Sadducees.

Rhoads comments,

> From the time of Herod (37-4 B.C.E.) the high priests were appointed and deposed at will by the Roman representative in Palestine, either the Herodian king or the procurator. They quite naturally appointed people, usually from several leading families, who were sympathetic to the Roman presence in Palestine. This close association between high priests and

Romans has led to the traditional characterization of the Sadducees as 'collaborators' with the Romans. (Rhoads, 41)

By the time of the first century A.D. it is difficult to trace the Sadducees except through the high priesthood and, to some measure, the aristocracy.

The Sadducees opposed the revolt against Rome. But as Rhoads explains, "Although the evidence for resistance to Rome is scant in the case of Joazar [a Sadducee]...the Sadducees played an important role in the national resistance against the Romans in subsequent years." The Sadducees opposed the Zealots' active resistance and the Pharisees' rejection of Gentile authorities, but the Sadducees' power and influence were limited. Therefore, as Josephus says, "For whenever they gained office, they held firm—even though under compulsion and unwillingly—to what the Pharisees say, because otherwise the people would not tolerate them."

During Jesus' time the Sadducees were a small group with widespread influence in Politics and religion. But the war of A.D. 70 spelled doom for the group. With the fall of Jerusalem and the Temple, the Sadducees disappeared. The Pharisees of course did not preserve the Saducean documents or writings, so even their views no longer exist. We can get glimpses of their beliefs, however, from Josephus.

The Sadducees were conservative in regard to the Law. They rejected the oral tradition of the Pharisees and did not admit legal or doctrinal deductions from the Prophets (Jos., *Ant.* xiii. 10,6; xviii. 1,4). To them, the Torah alone was authoritative. Russell, however, feels that it is not likely that they denied the sacredness of the Prophets and Writings as some Church Fathers suggest. They merely rejected any doctrines which could not be justified by the Torah (Russell, 159). In practice also the Sadducees were more strict than the Pharisees; for instance, they saw no way to avoid or "get around" the Sabbath commands. Also, they always prescribed penalties exactly according to the Law; for example, the death penalty was always stoning.

The Sadducees denied the belief in angels and demons (Acts 23:8). They rejected the idea of the immortality of the soul. Josephus says, "They also take away the belief of the immortal duration of the soul, and the punishments and rewards in Hades" (Jos., *Wars* ii. 8,14). Hence it follows that in the view of the Sadducees there was no resurrection of the dead.

The Sadducees believed in man's free will, that man is responsible for his actions (Jos., *Bell.* ii. 164; *Ant.* xiii. 5,9). They held that man must make good his transgressions on earth since there is no life after death (Acts 23:8; Jos., *Bell.* ii. 165; *Ant.* xviii. 1,4). In their doctrine of free will, they "do away with Fate altogether" and "remove God beyond the sight of will" (Jos., *Wars* ii. 8,14).

The Sadducees, since they had no belief in apocalyptic intervention or Fate, embraced, a "this-worldly eschatology" in which they hoped to see the nation of Israel free, as it was under David's rule. Rhoads states that "In practice, however, the Sadducees sought to bring about their eschatological vision of an independent temple-state by trying to achieve as much autonomy as possible within the Roman Empire by use of the realistic political and diplomatic means at their disposal" (Rhoads, 41).

The lack of a doctrine of retribution or recompense in the world to come was possibly one of the reasons that the Sadducees could not cope with the disaster of A.D. 70. After their central sacrificial system was gone, they were left without anything to compensate for it.

In regard to political views, the Sadducees are usually seen as sympathizers with the Hellenists of the Maccabean times, who subverted the pure Jewish faith. Russell points out that the Sadducees lent support to the Hellenizers but that, after the Maccabees, sympathy for Hellenistic culture is not a feature that distinguishes the Sadducees from the other sects (Russell, 158).

They did hold political offices and positions which committed them to practical action and a realistic view of their situation. They adjusted to the existing politics. Lohse comments, "As the Sadducees had always been concerned with linking their beliefs with an attitude of receptiveness to the world at large, they recognized the existing government and strove to moderate the hostility toward the Romans which was increasing among the people" (Lohse, 76). Rhoads suggests that the Sadducees had more freedom in their way of life than the Pharisees because decisions about matters not in the written law were left up to the individual. Thus the Sadducees had greater flexibility than the Pharisees to adapt to the Roman and Hellenistic cultures, but "most...maintained a basic commitment to the Jewish institutions of the Law, the Temple, and the state" (Rhoads, 40).

Russell points out that "As conservatives in politics they [the Sadducees] stood for the Israelite ideal of a theocratic state under the leadership of the High Priest" (Russell, 159). Thus, any suspicion of a popular Messianic faith and hope for the future would be seen as a direct threat to the existing social and political order. Jesus' teaching was a direct threat to their wealth and their social and political positions.

According to Mark 12:18-27, the Sadducees argued against the resurrection of the dead on the grounds given in Deuteronomy 25:5-6. By their example of the woman with seven husbands, the Sadducees hoped to show Jesus that belief in the resurrection was absurd. Instead, Jesus showed their position to be absurd – he merely said that after the resurrection there would be no marriage; relationships would be different from those on earth.

The High Priest Annas and his colleagues were closely associated with the Sadducees, so Luke equates supporters of the high priest with the Sadducees (Acts 5:17). As mentioned, the Sadducees opposed popular movements which threatened the power of imperial officials and high priests. Accordingly they attacked Jesus in conjunction with the Pharisees (Matt. 16:1, etc.).

Tcherikover expresses the conflict between Pharisees and Sadducees very well.

> The sources describe the conflict between them in various ways. Josephus on one occasion speaks of them as philosophical schools preoccupied with questions struggling for power. In Talmudic literature (the Mishnah and Tosephta) the conflict assumes the character of differences of opinion between scholars on various questions of religion and law.
>
> These accounts do not in fact contradict one another: for this sectarian strife lasted more than two hundred years and quite naturally took various forms at various periods. Under the Hasmoneans the quarrel between the Pharisees and Sadducees was mainly political, and two strong parties, each supported by certain social strata, fought for power in the state. Herod put an end to the independent political life of the Jewish community, and henceforward anyone desiring to engage in politics was forced to tread the path of revolution. This road

was taken by the 'left' wing of the Pharisees, the Zealots, who under Herod split off from the former and founded an independent sect, while the Pharisees themselves gave up interfering in affairs of state and restricted themselves to activity within the walls of the schools. The Sadducees also, whose political power had been broken under the last Hamoneans by Rome and Herod, now turned their attention to questions of religion and law. The parties appeared again as political forces for the last time during the Jewish war with Rome (66-70 C.E.). (Tcherikover, 253)

On key theological issues we can summarize by saying that the Pharisees and Sadducees held diametrically opposed views. Pharisees believed in foreordination, the Sadducees in free will. Pharisees taught the soul's immortality, the resurrection, rewards in a future life, and a belief in angels and demons, all of which the Sadducees rejected, as they recognized only the explicit prescriptions of the Torah. The Pharisees recognized both the Torah and a subsequent oral tradition of expansion and interpretation. Both groups were opposing religious factors in Jesus' ministry and played key roles in the scene of the New Testament.

THE BIBLICAL INSTRUMENTS *are divided into three categories: strings, winds and percussion. The family of stringed instruments were most important in the musical practice of the ancient Hebrews. The winds were the next important, and the percussion instruments were the last integral part of the music.*

The Bible mentions sixteen musical instruments as having been used in ancient Israel. Daniel refers to six more that were played in King Nebuchadnezzar's court; their names characterize them as non-Jewish instruments. In the third chapter of the Book of Daniel we have probably the sole specimen of Babylonian or Chaldean music.

There was to be no playing of instruments on the Sabbath except for accompaniment for singing at worship. Stringed and wind instruments, when not in use, were wrapped in napkins or kept in special receptacles. Different kinds of receptacles were made for kinnorot *and* nebalim. *Wind instruments were kept in either "cases for pipes" or "bags for pipes." There was a distinction made in the regulations for cleanliness as to whether an instrument could be laid in the case from above or from the side.*

Stringed Instruments

Kinnor – *The invention was ascribed to Jubal. It was "David's harp," the preferred instrument in Israeli music. The work has two plural forms, one masculine,* kinnorim, *one feminine,* kinnorot, *which is an unexplainable peculiarity not found with any other name of instrument.*

The Bible mentions kinnor *in 42 places. Biblical scribes do not reveal anything about the shape of the* kinnor *and there are no authentic pictures found in Hebrew antiquities. Opinions about its nature are controversial.*

Modern research says that kinnor *was not a harp-like instrument or type of lute with long-necked fingerboard, but an instrument similar to the Greek* kithara, *similar to the* lyra. Kithara *was the larger of the two, had lower tones and more voluminous sound, had large side-arms, mostly hollow, and produced an increased resonance. The players hung* kithara *with a strap around shoulders while marching.* Lyra *was smaller and more delicate in type. Side-arms were mostly of one piece, fixed directly upon the sounding box.*

Nebel – *This stringed instrument was used for accompaniment of singing, and is mentioned 27 times in the Bible. Plural of the word is* nabalim. *The original meaning of the word is "to inflate," "to bulge." In Hebrew,* nebel *(or* nevel) *is also the term for leather bottles and other bulky vessels, also pots of clay.*

This instrument had twelve strings and was plucked with fingers; the sounding box was on the upper part. It was lower pitched than the kinnor, *also larger and had a stronger sound. The strings were made from entrails* (meyav) *of sheep. It was an upright, portable harp which might have been in various sizes. The basic form has not been modified much at all through the centuries.*

The inventors of these instrument were the Phoenicians, inhabitants of Sidon.

'Asor – *This instrument is found only three times in the Old Testament – Psalms 33:2; 92:3; 144:9 – and the word is derived form a root meaning "ten." In all three passages* 'asor *is connected with another instrument. Some people think that since* 'asor *means "ten" it was connected with other instruments and meant they had ten strings. It is still undecided whether or not it is a separate instrument or connected in some way to instruments with which it is mentioned.*

Gittit – *This instrument is found in headings of Psalms 8, 81, and 84. Literal meaning is "that from Geth." It might refer to an instrument that could have originated in Geth (Gath) where David stayed for some time.*

The Gittit *was a sort of lute; the Targum translates it "on the zither."*

Sabbeka – *References to this instrument are Daniel 3:5, 7, 10, 15. It is mentioned as one of the instruments played at Nebuchadnezzar's court. It is generally agreed that this is identical with the Greek* sambykē *and the Roman* sambuca.

It was a horizontal angular harp, similar to the triangular, four-stringed, high-pitched sambykē *of the Hellenes.*

Pesanterin – *References to this instrument are Daniel 3:5, 7, 10, 15. This instrument was also played at Nebuchadnezzar's court. Not much is known about its characteristics except that it must have been a stringed instrument with probably eight strings stretched above a slightly arched sound-box. The box had ten small round openings – sound holes – and the player struck the strings with a rather large stick.*

Kathros – References: Daniel 3:5, 7, 10, 15. *This instrument was also played at Nebuchadnezzar's court.* Kathros (or kithros) – *the name of this instrument does not give any clue to what it was like – its form or its character. The name indicates an instrument of the most varied type. The Greek* kithara *and Roman* cithara *were lyres.*

The origin of the word points to the Far East. Kithros *could have come from another part of the Mediterranean Sea and been exchanged in trade. The instruments Daniel mentions are not of the family of instruments used by the Israelites in Palestine, but are exotic types used for pagan worship.*

Neginot – *General meaning of the term* bineginot *or* 'al-neginot *is to sing to the accompaniment of stringed instruments, but also simply "song." However,* neginot *is frequently interpreted as a musical instrument.*

References are Psalms 4, 6, 54, 55, 61, 67, 76; Lamentations 3:14; 5:14; Isaiah 38:20; Psalms 77:7; Job 30:9.

Early Bible translators already show discrepancies with regard to the meaning of this word. Nevertheless, the root of the word refers to its meaning. Neginot *derives from the verb* naggen *"to touch," "to strike" – indicating clearly the manner of playing stringed instruments. This probably refers to stringed instruments for the accompaniment of singing.*

Shushan – References: *Psalms 45, 60, 69, 80 contain the word* shushan. *From* Rashi *some expounders think the word has a double meaning – an instrument of six strings in the shape of a lily. It is most likely not an instrument at all, but a popular song whose melody has been utilized for these psalms.*

Chapter 5

ESSENES

THOUGH THEY ARE not mentioned in the New Testament, the Essenes were another religious sect of Judaism at the time of Jesus.

There are four major ancient sources for our knowledge of the Essenes. The most extensive is Flavius Josephus who describes them at some length after having actually spent some time with them. His fullest description is in his *Jewish Wars* (written a few years after A.D. 70); they are also mentioned more briefly in the *Antiquities*, book xiii., written about twenty-thirty years after *Wars*. F. F. Bruce cautions that Josephus must be read with some reserve and "as his 'close familiarity' with the Essenes was wedged in along with his other experiences between his sixteenth and nineteenth years (c. A.D. 53-56) it does not appear to have been extended." Also, it must be remembered that Josephus was writing for a Gentile audience, and so it appears that he describes the sects as Greek philosophical schools. For the most part, though, Josephus' account is "factual and reliable" (F. F. Bruce, 85).

Another quite lengthy account of the Essenes is found in Philo's *Every Good Man is Free*, and a shorter account in his *Hypothetica*, an apology for the Jews. Since both accounts were written between 20 B.C.-A.D. 50 these are some of the earliest records existing.

Pliny has left us a valuable paragraph about the Essenes in his *Natural History* (v. 73) written between A.D. 73 (the year that Masada fell) and A.D. 79 (Pliny's death in the eruption of Vesuvius). Pliny's account is especially significant because it gives us some indication of where the Essenes lived and is important for the debate about whether the Essenes were the sect which lived at Khirbet Qumran. Although Pliny tends to exaggerate (he writes for instance, that the Essenes have existed for "thousands of generations"), his information concerning locations of cities and other basic questions seem to be quite accurate.

The fourth source is Hippolytus, *Refutation of All Heresies*, book 9, written in the early years of the third century. Although he presents the Essenes as an heretical sect and his account follows Josephus quite closely, he does make fresh contributions to our knowledge.

Until recently, scholars have depended for their knowledge of the Essenes only on these ancient writers from outside the sect itself. Now, a body of probable Essene literature has been found so that the Essenes can possibly be seen from within. These are the Dead Sea Scrolls.

The Essenes were an ascetic sect whose origins can be traced to the early decades of the second century, B.C. They existed until the Jewish war of A.D. 66-70. Their history is uncertain. Philo says that Moses started the order and Josephus states that they existed "ever since the ancient time of the fathers." As mentioned, Pliny says that their history covers "thousands of generations." Although this must be an exaggeration, it agrees with other indications that the Essenes had existed for a long time. We are certain that they existed since the second century, B.C. and lived among Jewish communities. They later settled at Qumran and at scattered communities in Palestine and Syria. The Scrolls indicate that the Essenes have their historical basis in Judaism. Bo Reicke points out that there are some analogies to Persian and Greek dualism, but since these analogies do not extend to terminology or organization, they "should therefore be considered more as formal convergences" (Reicke, 169-70).

The first documentary evidence for the name "Essene" refers to a time about 144 B.C. Josephus mentions the Sadducees, Pharisees and Essenes in connection with negotiations carried out by the High Council with Rome and Sparta. Bruce suggests that there is a thorny case for the derivation of "Essene" from the Aramaic 'āsyā (healer). This in interesting in view of the fact that it is similar to the "Therapeutai," a pious community of Jews in

Egypt mentioned by Philo (*De unita contemplatiua*, 2ff.). Russell suggests that the word could be derived from the Greek form of the Aramaic equivalent of the Hebrew *Hasidhim*. Thus, the origin of the name "Essene" is uncertain.

It is generally agreed, however, that the ancestry of Essenes is found in "pious ones" of the Maccabean and pre-Maccabean era who resisted Hellenism and showed zeal for the Torah. The Scrolls further indicate that the sect was associated with the Hasidim of the period around 167 B.C., and may in fact have participated in the Maccabean struggle.

However they began, by the first century B.C. the Essenes had become a monastic order of priests and laymen, dedicated to the ritual and fulfillment of the Torah and to an interpretation different from that of the Sadducees and Pharisees.

The best description of the Essenes comes from Josephus.

> For there are three philosophical sects among the Jews. The followers of the first...are the Pharisees; of the second the Sadducees; and the third sect, who pretends to a severer discipline, are called Essens. These last are Jews by birth, and seem to have a greater affection for one another than the other sects have. These Essens reject pleasures as an evil, but esteem continence, and the conquest over our passions, to be virtue. They neglect wedlock, but choose out other person's children, while they are kindred, and form them according to their own manners. They do not absolutely deny the fitness of marriage, and the succession of mankind thereby continued; but they guard against the lascivious behaviour of women, and are persuaded that none of them preserve their fidelity to one man.
>
> These men are despisers of riches, and so very communicative as raises our admiration. Nor is there anyone to be found among them who had more than another; for it is a law among them, that those who come to them must let what they have be common to the whole order – insomuch, that among them all there is no appearance of poverty or excess of riches, but every one's possessions are intermingled with every other's possessions; and so there is, as it were, one patrimony among all the brethren. They think that oil is a defilement; and if one of them be anointed without his own approbation, it is wiped off his body; for they think to be sweaty is a good thing, as they do also to be clothed in white garments. They also have stewards appointed to take care of their common affairs, who every one of them have no separate business for any, but what is for the use of them all.

They have no certain city, but many of them dwell in every city; and if any of their sect come from other places, what they have lies open for them, just as if it were their own; and they go into such as they never knew before, as if they had been ever so long acquainted with them. For which reason they carry nothing with them when they travel into remote parts, though still they take their weapons with them, for fear of thieves. Accordingly there is, in every city where they live, one appointed particularly to take care of strangers, and provide garments and other necessaries for them. But the habit and management of their bodies are such as children use who are in fear of their masters. Nor do they allow of the change of garments, or of shoes, till they be first entirely torn to pieces, or worn out by time. Nor do they either buy or sell anything to one another; but every one of them gives what he hath to him that wanteth it, and receives from him again in lieu of it what may be convenient for himself; and although there be no requital made, they are fully allowed to take what they want of whomsoever they please.

And as for their piety towards God, it is very extraordinary; for before sunrising they speak not a word about profane matters, but put up certain prayers which they have received from their forefathers, as if they made a supplication for its rising. After this every one of them are sent away by their curators, to exercise some of those arts wherein they are skilled, in which they labour with great diligence till the fifth hour. After which they assemble themselves together again into one place; and when they have clothed themselves in white veils, they then bathe their bodies in cold water. And after this purification is over, they every one meet together in an apartment of their own, into which it is not permitted to any of another sect to enter; while they go, after a pure manner, into a dining-room, as into a certain holy temple, and quietly set themselves down; upon which the baker lays them loaves in order; the cook also brings a single plate of one sort of food, and sets it before every one for them; but a priest says grace before meat; and it is unlawful for any to taste of the food before grace be said. The same priest when hath dined, says grace again after meat; and when they begin and when they end, they praise God, as he that bestows their food upon them; after which they lay aside their [white] garments, and betake themselves to their labours again till the evening; then they return home to supper, after the same manner; and if there be any strangers there, they sit down with them. Nor is there every any clamour or disturbance to pollute their house, but they give every one leave to speak in their turn; which silence thus kept in their house appears to foreigners like some tremendous mystery; the cause of which is that perpetual sobriety they exercise, and some settled measure of meat and drink that is allotted to them, and that such as is abundantly sufficient for them.

And truly, as for other things, they do nothing but according to the injunctions of their curators; only these two things are done among them at every one's own free will, which are, to assist those that want it, and to shew mercy; for they are permitted of their own accord to afford succour to such as deserve it, when they stand in need of it, and to bestow food on those that are in distress; but they cannot give anything to their kindred without the curators. They dispense their anger after a just manner, and restrain their passion. They are eminent for fidelity, and are the ministers of peace; whatsoever they say also is firmer than an oath; but swearing is avoided by them, and they esteem it worse than perjury; for they say that he who cannot be believed without [swearing by] God, is already condemned. They also take great pains in studying the writings of the ancients, and choose out of them what is most for the advantage of their soul and body; and they inquire after such roots and medicinal stone as may cure their distempers.

But now, if any hath a mind to come over to their sect, he is not immediately admitted, but he is prescribed the same method of living which they use, for a year, while he continues excluded; and they give him a small hatchet, and the formentioned girdle, and the white garment. And when he hath given evidence, during that time, that he can observe their continence, he approaches nearer to their way of living, and is made a partaker of the waters of purification, yet is he not even now admitted to live with them; for after this demonstration of his fortitude, his temper is tried two more years, and if he appear to be worthy, they then admit him into their society. And before he is allowed to touch their common food, he is obliged to take tremendous oaths; that, in the first place, he will exercise piety towards God; and then, that he will observe justice towards all men; and that he will do no harm to any one, either of his own accord, or by the command of others; that he will always hate the wicked, and be assistant to the righteous; that he will ever shew fidelity to all men, and especially to those in authority, he will at no time whatever abuse his authority, nor endeavour to outshine his subjects, either in his garments, or any other finery; that he will be perpetually a lover of truth, and propose to himself to reprove those that tell lies; that he will keep his hands clear from thefts, and his soul from unlawful gains; and that he will neither conceal anything from those of his own sect, nor discover any of their doctrines to others, no, not though any one should compel him so to do at the hazard of his life. Moreover, he swears to communicate their doctrines to no one any otherwise than as he received them himself; that he will abstain from robbery, and will equally preserve the books belonging to their sect, and the names of the angels [or messengers]. These are the oaths by which they secure their proselytes to themselves.

But for those that are caught in any heinous sins, they cast them out of their society; and he who is thus separated from them does often die after a miserable manner; for as he is bound by the oath he has taken, and by the customs he hath been engaged in, he is not at liberty to partake of that food that he meets with elsewhere, but is forced to eat grass, and to famish his body with hunger till he perish; for which reason they receive many of them again when they are at their last gasp, out of compassion to them as thinking the miseries they have endured till they come to the very brink of death to be a sufficient punishment for the sins they have been guilty of.

But in the judgments they exercise they are most accurate and just; nor do they pass sentence by the votes of a court that is fewer than a hundred. And as to what is once determined by that number, it is unalterable. What they most of all honour, after God himself, is the name of their legislator [Moses]; whom, if any one blaspheme, his is punished capitally. They also think it a good thing to obey their elders, and the major part. Accordingly, if ten of them be sitting together, no one of them will speak while the other nine are against it. They also avoid spitting in the midst of them, or on the right side. Moreover, they are stricter than any other of the Jews in resting from their labours on the seventh day; for they not only get their food ready the day before, they may not be obliged to kindle a fire on that day, but they will not remove any vessel out of its place, nor go to stool thereon. Nay, on the other days they dig a small pit, a foot deep, with a paddle (which kind of hatchet is given them when they are first admitted among them); and covering themselves round with their garment, that they may not affront the divine rays of light, they ease themselves into that pit, and after they put the earth that was dug out again into the pit; and even this they do only in the more lonely places, which they choose out for this purpose; and although this easement of the body be natural, yet it is a rule with them to wash themselves after it, as if it were a defilement to them.

Now after the time of their preparatory trial is over, they are parted into four classes; and so far are the juniors inferior to the seniors, that if the seniors should be touched by the juniors, they must wash themselves, as if they had intermixed themselves with the company of a foreigner. They are long-lived also; insomuch that many of them live about a hundred years, by means of the simplicity of their diet; nay, as I think, by means of the regular course of life they observe also. They contemn the miseries of life, and are above pain, by the generosity of their mind. And as for death, if it will be for the glory, they esteem it better than living always; and indeed our war with the Romans gave abundant evidences what great souls they had in their trials, wherein, although they were tortured and distorted, burnt and torn to pieces, and went through all kinds of instruments of torment, that they might be forced either to blaspheme their legislator or to eat what was forbidden them, yet could they not be made to do either of them, no, nor once to flatter their tormentors, nor to shed a tear; but they smiled in their very pains, and laughed those to scorn who inflicted the torments upon them, and resigned up their souls with great alacrity, as expecting to receive them again.

For their doctrine is this: – That bodies are corruptible, and that the matter they are made of is not permanent; but that the souls are immortal, and continue for ever; and that they come out of the most subtile air, and are united to their bodies as in prisons, into which they are drawn by a certain natural enticement; but when they are set free from the bonds of the flesh, they then, as released form a long bondage, rejoice and mount upward. And this is like the opinion of the Greeks, that good souls have their habitations beyond the ocean, in a region that is neither oppressed with storms of rain or snow, nor with intense heat, but that this place is such as is refreshed by the gentle breathing of the west wind, that is perpetually blowing from the ocean; while they allot to bad souls a dark and tempestuous den, full of never-ceasing punishments. And indeed the Greeks seem to me to have followed the same notion, when they allot the islands of the blessed to their brave men, whom they call heroes and demi-gods; and to the souls of the wicked, the region of the ungodly, in Hades, where their fables relate that certain persons, such as Sisyphus, and Tantalus, and Ixion, and Tityus, are punished; which is built first on this supposition, that souls are immortal; and thence are those exhortations to virtue, and dehortations from wickedness collected; whereby good men are bettered in the conduct of their life, by the hope they have of reward after death, and whereby the vehement inclinations of bad men to vice are restrained, by the fear and expectation they are in, that although they should lie concealed in this life, they should suffer immortal punishment after death. These are the divine doctrines of the Essens about the soul, which lay an unavoidable bait for such as have once had a taste for their philosophy.

There are also among them who undertake to foretell things to come, by reading the holy books, and using several sorts of purifications, and being perpetually conversant in the discourses of the prophets; and it is but seldom that they miss in their predictions.

Moreover, there is another order of Essens, who agree with the rest as to their way of living, and customs, and laws,

> but differ from them in the point of marriage, as thinking that by not marrying they cut off the principal part of human life, which is the prospect of succession; nay rather, that if all men should be of the same opinion, the whole race of mankind would fail. However, they try their spouses for three years; and if they find they have their natural purgations thrice, as trials that they are likely to be fruitful, then they actually marry them. But they do not use to accompany with their wives when they are with child, as a demonstration that they do not marry out of regard to pleasure, but for the sake of posterity. Now the women go into the baths with some of their garments on, as the men do with somewhat girded about them. And these are the customs of this order of Essens. (Jos., *Wars* ii. 8)

Hippolytus mentions the Essenes' intolerance toward Gentiles, especially toward those who spoke of God but were not circumcised. In fact, Hippolytus claims that if a group of Essenes came upon a Gentile speaking of God, they would surround him and force him to be circumcised or be killed. This attitude toward Gentiles caused the Essenes to be sometimes confused with Zealots or *sicarii*. The Essenes were definitely not pacifists. Bruce observes that this is "further indicated by the appearance of an Essene named John as an energetic commander of the insurgent Jewish forces in the war against Rome" (Bruce, 90).

Most practices of the Essenes are clearly described in the passage from Josephus, but a few clarifications are needed. In reference from Josephus, which could be taken to imply that the Essenes were sun-worshipers, the Essenes did not actually worship the sun, as is clear from Philo and Hippolytus. Their worship began at sunrise so that it only appeared that they made supplication to the sun as it rose.

Hippolytus gives several examples which illustrate the Essenes' strictness in regard to the Sabbath and the Law. Some Essenes would not handle coins with the Emperor's image because this was against the second commandment (idolatry) (Hipp., *Ref*. ix. 21). The Essenes abstained from *all* work on the Sabbath; some were so strict that they did not even get out of bed on the Sabbath (*Ref*. ix. 25). The *Damascus Document* of the Dead Sea Scrolls says that it is unlawful to lift an animal out of a pit on the Sabbath. This was considered extreme even by the Pharisees (*cf*. Matt. 12:11).

From our sources, it is clear that the Essenes were competent in farming, herding and other occupations. They took no role in politics.

Evidently there were varieties of Essenes; for instance, there were some which forbade marriage and others who allowed it for the sake of childbearing. All the groups seem to be characterized by an "ascetic ideal which sought separation from the ritual impurities of the world around them" (Russell, 165). That there was more than one settlement is clear for we are told that members of the sect were welcome in any of the Essene colonies. In fact, they went out of their way to help the traveling Essene even to providing clothes as well as provisions.

The Essenes considered only the Scriptures of Judaism as authoritative, and studied them diligently and often. They were devoted more esoterically to apocalypticism and to a future spiritual deliverance than were the Pharisees or Sadducees. Several apocalyptic books such as Daniel and I Enoch were found in their library at Qumran. Josephus also regards apocalyptic teaching as typical of the Essenes.

There is some contradiction between Josephus and Hippolytus on the Essenes' doctrine of resurrection. Josephus states "that bodies are corruptible and that the matter they are made of is not permanent; but that the souls are important and continue forever" (Jos., *Wars* ii. 8,11). Hippolytus, on the other hand, states, "For they confess that the flesh rises again and will be immortal, which soul, when it departs from the body, abides in an airy and well lighted place until judgment" (Hipp., *Ref.* ix. 27). Bruce suggests that the contradiction may be resolved in the following way. Both Josephus and Hippolytus attest to the Essenes' belief in the immortality of the soul (which is not characteristic of Judaism), but Josephus makes a further concession to Greek thought by implying that the Essenes did not expect a bodily resurrection (which Greeks did not accept) (Bruce, 90-91).

In regard to angels, the Essenes (in the Scrolls) believed that "the 'prince of light' battles against the 'angel of darkness' for control of the universe, and the 'spirit of truth' struggles with the 'spirit of error' for control of the heart of man." It is debatable what the Essenes believed in regard to the Messianic hope. Different versions appear in the Scrolls (*cf.* Russell, 173). "But the sect of the Essenes affirm that fate governs all things, and that nothing befalls men but what is according to its determination" (Jos., *Ant.* xiii. 5,9).

The Essenes rejected the temple cultus so revered by the Pharisees and Sadducees. They claimed to represent spiritually the priesthood of Zadok, spoken of by Ezekiel and the Chronicles (Ezek. 40:46; I Chron. 24:6). They saw themselves as an exiled community (174 B.C.) led by the true Zadokite priests. To become comrades of the true sons of Zadok, the members had to pledge themselves to asceticism, that is, strict obedience to the Law and self-control. These vows and tests were clearly more difficult than those of the Pharisees.

The Essenes were organized like the Pharisees with Scribes in authority; they also lived in previously determined associations. They differed from the Pharisees in that they remained apart from society and sought to realize socially the cultic holiness of the priesthood. Thus, they wore white robes and had their own priesthood. Members formed communities under the supervision of these priests and all goods and property were in common.

Josephus describes several individual Essenes significant in history for one reason or another. The first he mentions is Jonathan (160-143 B.C.) who lived during the reign of Aristobulus I; he was renowned for his ability to predict the future. It is said that he correctly predicted the day and place of the death of Antigonus, one of the King's brothers.

Simon was another Essene prophet. He was remembered with others before Archelaus (in A.D. 6) to interpret a dream. He interpreted it to predict Archelaus' downfall. Five days later, Archelaus was summoned before Augustus in Rome and banished to Gaul. Here is Josephus' account of another Essene's early encounter with Herod:

> Now there was one of these Essens, whose name was Manahem, who had this testimony, that he not only conducted his life after an excellent manner, but had the foreknowledge of future events given him by God also. This man once saw Herod when he was a child, and going to school, and saluted him as king of the Jews; but he, thinking that either he did not know him, or that he was in jest, put him in mind that he was but a private man; but Manahem smiled to himself, and clapped him on his backside with his hand, and said, 'However that be, thou wilt be king, and wilt begin thy reign happily, for God finds thee worthy of it; and do thou remember the blows that Manahem hath given thee, as being a signal of the change of thy fortune; and truly this will be the best reasoning for thee,

that thou love justice [toward men], and piety towards God, and clemency towards thy citizens; yet do I know how thy whole conduct will be, that thou wilt not be such a one, for thou wilt excell all men in happiness, and obtain an everlasting reputation, but wilt forget piety and righteousness; and these crimes will not be concealed from God at the conclusion of thy life, when thou wilt find that he will be mindful of them and punish thee for them.' Now at that time Herod did not at all attend to what Manahem said, as having no hopes of such advancement; but a little afterward, when he was so fortunate as to be advanced to the dignity of king, and was in the height of his dominion, he sent for Manahem, and asked him how long he should reign. Manahem did not tell him the full length of his reign; wherefore, upon that silence of his he asked him further, whether he should reign ten years or not? He replied, 'Yes, twenty, nay, thirty years;' but did not assign the just determinate limit of his reign. Herod was satisfied with these replies, and gave Manahem his hand, and dismissed him, and from that time he continued to honour all the Essens. We have thought it proper to relate these facts to our readers, how strange soever they may be, and to declare what hath happened among us, because many of these Essenes have, by their excellent virtue, been thought worthy of his knowledge of divine revelations. (Jos., *Ant.* xv. 10,5)

Now let us ask: What relation does this sect have to the group which lived at the recently discovered Khirbet Qumran?

To answer this question, we must look at Pliny's paragraph which raises the question whether their headquarters may be identified with Khirbet Qumran – the more so since Pre de Vaux and other archaeologists assure us that there is no other installation west of the Dead Sea which could satisfy Pliny's description.

The Scrolls themselves (especially the Qumran Manual, found at the Qumran Library) show, according to Bo Reicke, "clear points of agreement with the statements of Philo and Josephus about the Essenes, and there is no doubt that Qumran and Essenism represent the same movement in different stages of development" (Reicke, 172).

In order to see the relation between the Essenes and the Qumran sect, we here set out a summary of Yigael Yadin's description of the sect of the Scrolls. Since we have already looked at Josephus' description of the Essenes, we can easily compare.

> The sect is opposed to the unification of the priesthood and the kingship in one person. It believes that the lay leader

should be a descendant of the House of David, and the religious head a descendant of the Sons of Zakok of the House of Aaron.

The sect, following its particular interpretation of the first chapter of Genesis, kept a three hundred and sixty-four day calendar, based on the solar months of thirty days, with an additional four intercalary days, one after every three months. They could thus obviously not follow the calendar in use in Jerusalem, which was a lunar calendar. As a result their festivals occurred on different days. They could therefore not partake in the holy service in the Temple, where the official calendar was observed.

The deeds and thoughts of the sect were guided by the law of Moses. They are the most orthodox in adhering to the rules of the Torah, and their interpretation of its laws is far more strict than was customary in Jerusalem at the time. Part of their daily life is devoted to studying the Pentateuch. The sect does not oppose the marriage of its members, but it is quite clear from its writings that their rules of personal status were extremely rigid and the Manual of Discipline even indicates that within the sect itself there were groups of members who refrained from marrying.

Members of the sect attached particular importance to cleanliness of soul and body. This is evidenced in all their writing. They believe that everything has been preordained, and that all creatures are divided into the Lot of Light and the Lot of Darkness...The sect, accordingly, had considerably developed belief about angels and their part in battle, which may account for the fact that the names of the angels were inscribed on their battle shields.

They place great emphasis on knowledge and wisdom, with whose help they study the phenomena of the world and learn the secrets of creation. The words 'truth,' 'justice' and 'judgment,' which appear often on their standards, represent their principal beliefs.

The sect rejects city life and its members live out of bounds. As far as concerns the members of the Dead Sea area, we know from their writings that they were organized in military fashion, and led a communal life devoid of individual possessions; newcomers swore to give the *Yahad*, or community, their 'wealth, wisdom and strength.' They are divided into groups in order of seniority, and the younger must obey the older. Severe punishments are inflicted on transgressors of all kinds whether against religious belief or against daily behaviour.

They have special rules for promotion and demotion in seniority. They eat together and follow a ceremonial pattern reminiscent of the ceremonies of sacrifices and offerings, with the priest officiating and uttering a special blessing. They have special functionaries such as supervisors and judges, whose duties are clearly laid down and who must be obeyed...They lead a life of modesty and fanatical orthodoxy, and spend their days studying the Bible and interpreting it. They prepare code and rules for their way of life in the future, and wait patiently for the day of vengeance against all enemies of the Sons of Light. (Yadin, *The Message of the Scrolls*, 173-76)

This description shows clearly the similarity between the Essenes and the sect of the Scrolls. With regard to discrepancies between the Qumran sect and Philo's account of the Essenes, these differences do not discount the identification since these are also the discrepancies between Josephus' and Philo's accounts of the Essenes.

Pliny gives us a most significant passage which directly links the Essenes with the Scroll sect:

> On the west side of the Dead Sea but out of range of the noxious exhalations of the coast, is the solitary tribe of the Essenes, which is remarkable beyond all the other tribes in the whole world, as it has no women and has renounced all sexual desire, has no money, and has only palm-trees for company. Day by day the throng of refugees is recruited to an equal number by numerous accessions of persons tired of life and driven thither by the waves of fortune to adopt their manners. Thus through thousands of ages (incredible to relate) a race in which no one is born lives on forever; so prolific for their advantage is other men's weariness of life.
>
> Lying below the Essenes was formerly the town of Engedi, second only to Jerusalem in the fertility of its land and in its groves of palm-trees, but now like Jerusalem a heap of ashes. Next comes Masada, a fortress on a rock, itself also not far from the Dead Sea. This it the limit of Judaea. (From Yadin, 185)

This passage is significant because Pliny specifies that the Essenes lived on the western shore of the Dead Sea, and his description of Engedi probably refers to the town lying south of the Essene settlement, and then Masada. So Pliny is mentioning the places from north to south, consistent with the location of Qumran.

Yadin concluded that there are two alternatives: "Either the sect of the Scrolls is none other than the Essenes themselves; or it was a sect which resembled the Essenes in almost every respect, its dwelling place, its organization, its customs" (Yadin, 185-86).

Because the Essenes are not actually mentioned in the New Testament, some have said that Jesus himself was an Essene in sympathy if not in origin. Renan called Christianity "an Essenism which succeeded on a broad scale" (quoted by Pfeiffer, p. 118). E. Schure went so far as to say that Jesus had been initiated into the secret doctrines of the Essenes (*cf.* Pfeiffer, 118).

These theories do not hold up in light of Jesus' own teaching and practice. In fact, Jesus was diametrically opposed to the legalism and asceticism of the Essenes. For example, the Essenes considered contact with even their own members defiling; Jesus ate and drank with publicans and sinners (Matt. 11:19; Luke 7:34). The Essenes kept the Sabbath rigorously while Jesus continued to heal and to do good on the Sabbath, declaring that the Sabbath was made for man, not man for the Sabbath (Matt. 12:1-2; Mark 2:23-28; Luke 6:6-11; 14:1-6). The Essenes considered that matter was evil; Jesus said that evil emerges from within a man. The Essenes repudiated Temple worship and sacrifice; Jesus came to the feasts; his disciples, Peter and John, did likewise (Acts 3:1). The Essenes were a monastic, ascetic order which departed from society; Jesus came to the "common people" who "heard him gladly" (Mark 12:37). He was called "wine-bibber," "friend of publicans and sinners" (Luke 7:34).

John the Baptist is closer to the Essenes than is Jesus. He grew up in the desert of Judah and baptized near Qumran. His eschatological preaching was similar to the Essenes in that he emphasized spiritual purity. Both John and the Essenes used the passage from Isaiah, "Prepare ye the way of the Lord." Baptism was a central feature of Essenism as well as John's ministry. There are several notable differences between John the Baptist and the Essenes, as well. First, the Essenes were more isolated than John. John spoke to the crowds (see Mark 1:5: "And all the country of Judaea was going out to him, and all the people of Jerusalem..." (NAS); also Matt. 3:5). Second, John's baptism was not merely a ritual cleansing as that of the Essenes appears to have been. John's baptism was clearly for the forgiveness of sins and for repentance (Mark 1:4; Matt. 3:6; Luke 3:3; John 1:23).

The Scrolls

In 1947, seven antique rolls of leather were found by two Bedouin shepherds in the Judean wilderness near the northwest shore of the Dead Sea. Several years went by and the scrolls came in contact with many people before their full significance was realized. Their discovery set off further discoveries of manuscripts, most of which occurred in the caves of Wadi Qumran, a gorge through the cliffs bordering the Dead Sea, seven or eight miles south of Jericho. The caves of Wadi Murabba't, twelve miles southwest of Qumran, have also produced a number of manuscripts and manuscript fragments. Besides these caves, a place south along the Dead Sea known only to the Bedouin, and the ruins of Khirbet Mird (Ancient Hyrcanus), lying inland from Qumran in the west side of Judean Buq, have yielded manuscripts and information concerning ancient generations. In the eleven caves of Qumran more than 500 manuscripts have been found and placed in the museums of Israel. Some are well preserved while others are only mutilated fragments. The largest single cache of manuscripts was found in Cave IV (1952), which yielded tens of thousands of fragments belonging to over 380 manuscripts. Many years lie ahead before the knowledge from these finds will have been assimilated and related to relevant biblical and auxiliary disciplines.

The discovery of these scrolls captured the attention of the public and many books have been written trying to shed light on the circumstances surrounding the first discovery. The story has been so obscured by time and legend that perhaps the complete truth will never be known. But certain facts have been established through interviews with the Bedouin and the middlemen in the discoveries and the events that followed.

We include the conflicting accounts of these events since so much controversy has arisen concerning them, although the points of conflict will probably never be resolved.

An ancient discovery of scrolls near the Dead Sea was recorded by Origen (c. A.D. 185-254), who mentions that Greek and Hebrew manuscripts were found stored in jars near Jericho. Eusebius quotes him: "The sixth edition, which was found together with other Hebrew and Greek books in a jar near Jericho in the reign of Antonius the son of Severus..." (A.D. 198-217). Also, in abut A.D. 800, Timotheus I (the Nestorian Patriarch) wrote to Sergius (the

Metropolitan of Elam) describing a discovery of Hebrew manuscripts in a cave near Jericho. It is interesting to note the similarity in the account of this early discovery to the 1947 discovery in Cave I of Qumran; when a Bedouin was searching for his lost dog he entered a cave and found a library containing biblical and secular books. Possibly these books influenced the theology of the Karaites, a medieval Jewish group who rejected the rabbinical interpretation of the Scriptures. The Jewish writer Kirkisani in a history written in A.D. 937 speaks of a sect of Jews, the al-Maghariya–the "Cave people"–so called because their books had been found in a cave. The Moslem writer Shahrastani dates these people around the middle of the first century B.C. Thus, it is possible that "Dead Sea Scrolls" were available to those people.

The following is a description of the Qumran area by J. T. Milik:

A cliff 1,100 feet high towers above the northwestern corner of the Dead Sea; its upper edge is level with the Mediterranean and marks off the eastern limit of the plateau called the Wilderness of Judea. Its impressive reddish limestone face is honeycombed with countless natural caves, and, at its foot, a terrace of marl spreads out and falls away toward the Dead Sea, 1,292 feet below sea level. Long ages ago, the entire bed of the Jordan valley was covered with water, and the salt deposited at that time makes the soil barren even now. In the spring, however, a little vegetation appears and then the semi-nomad Ta'mireh tribe brings its sheep and goats down into the valley. They can water the flocks at 'Ain Feshka, a strongly flowing but brackish spring lying to the south of the area. Towards its centre, this area is divided by the course of a seasonal torrent, the Wadi Qumran: a group of ruins on the terrace or marl to its left is called analogously Hirbet Qumran (the word 'hirbeh' means 'ruin'). (Milik, 11)

Dupont-Sommer describes Cave I as follows: "The cave opens onto a narrow gully; there are two openings; the one, fairly high, acts as a window; the other, almost level with the ground, can only be entered on hands and knees" (Dupont-Sommer, 9).

It was in this cave, in the spring or summer of 1947, that two Bedouin shepherds of the Ta'mireh tribe found the first scrolls of the Qumran area. They had been grazing their sheep and goats along the cliffs of the Dead Sea near Qumran when one of the animals strayed. While trying to find it, one shepherd threw a stone into one of the small openings in the cliff face. A shattering sound came from the cave. The boys ran away but later returned, hoping to find buried treasure. In the cave they found eight large jars intact, five on one side and three on the other side of the cave. Some were covered with bowl-like dishes.

G. Lankester Harding in The Times *(August 9, 1949)* describes this find: "Instead, however, of the expected golden treasure they drew forth a number of leather rolls covered in, to them, an unknown writing – had they but known it, a treasure far greater than any gold. Seven of the eight jars were empty, and there are varying accounts as to how many scrolls were found on the first visit. Barthelemy and Milik say that only one jar contained scrolls – one large scroll and two small ones.

A variant account of the discovery was given by one of the Bedouin in Arabic to R. S. Khoury of Bethlehem, and it appeared in the Journal of Near Eastern Studies *in October of 1957.* In 1945, this Bedouin entered the cave alone and found the jars. He broke nine of them but they contained only reddish seeds. The tenth jar was sealed with a substance like red clay and contained an inscribed roll of leather. This roll he took with hopes of making sandal straps. He even gave some pieces of the scroll to his two companions for this purpose. When he arrived home, he put the scroll in a bag and it hung in his room for two years, after which time his uncle took it to an antiquities dealer in Bethlehem to find out its value. This version of the discovery, though agreeing in some points with the other account, is most likely an exaggeration, since Bedouin are noted for their stretched stories. The precise details will probably never be known.

The fact has been established, though, that the Bedouin realized the Scrolls' value as curios and took them to Bethlehem, where they tried to sell them to a Muslim antiquities dealer for twenty pounds. When the dealer said the price was too high, the shepherds went to another dealer. This dealer, a member of the Syrian Orthodox Church, thought the documents might be Syriac manuscripts, so he contacted the Syrian Metropolitan of Jerusalem, Mar. Athanasius Yeshue Samuel. The Metropolitan recognized the writing as Hebrew and the material as leather or parchment, but he did not know the significance of the Scrolls. He decided to buy them, but he was away when the dealer and the Bedouin came to his house. The monk who answered the door saw the men with the "dirty rolls" written in Hebrew and, not realizing the situation, sent them away. The Metropolitan eventually contacted the dealer again and, after *negotiations, bought four scrolls. He also dispatched monks to explore the cave but they returned empty-handed.*

The Metropolitan then began to search for expert opinion on the antiquity and value of the Scrolls with the result that an official of the Mandatory Government Antiquities Department, a member of the cole Biblique, the Syrian Patriarch of Antioch, and two officials of the Hebrew University and the Jewish National Library – all failed to recognize the significance of the Scrolls. A Dutch professor, Father J. P. M. van der Ploeg, visited the monastery and examined the Scrolls, but when he returned to the cole Biblique, others convinced him it was unreasonable that such ancient manuscripts would still be in existence. Thus, he was persuaded that they were spurious and abandoned any further consideration of them. The Metropolitan also tried to arrange an interview with G. L. Harding, but with no success. He did not give up, however; he continued searching for expert opinion and, with his limited knowledge of the subject, investigated the Scrolls for himself. With the help of a Jewish journalist, the Metropolitan identified the large scroll as an Isaiah text with slight divergences from the Masoretic version.

In the meanwhile, Professor E. L. Sukenik, senior archaeologist of the Hebrew University, had returned from the United States (1947). On November 23rd a friend of his, an Armenian antiquities dealer, telephoned Sukenik and told him about an exciting "find" he had to show him. They met at the gateway to Military Zone B in Jerusalem and discussed the matter through the barbed wire separating the two divided parts of Jerusalem. The antiquities dealer told Sukenik about some scrolls that the Bedouin was trying to sell to an Arab dealer in Bethlehem. He said they were found in a cave near Jericho, and the Arab wanted to know if they were genuine. If they were genuine the Armenian friend wanted Sukenik to buy them for the Museum of Jewish Antiquities of the Hebrew University. To Sukenik, the letters of the script resembled those of the period before the Roman destruction in A.d. 70 and he felt that they were not a forgery, but actually genuine. He almost immediately decided to buy the scrolls, but he asked first to be able to see and examine them more thoroughly.

On November 29th, the Armenian dealer took Sukenik to Bethlehem to see the scrolls and negotiate with the Arab dealer. At this time Israel was in the midst of war between the Jews and Arabs; there was great risk involved for a Jew to go to Arab Bethlehem, but Sukenik did not wait. The Arab dealer told his version of the scrolls' discovery, which coincided with the story previously related—that the scrolls were found by a Bedouin looking for his goat. This account stated, however, that only a few weeks had elapsed between the discovery and the sale in Bethlehem. As Sukenik examined the scrolls, his excitement mounted; he thought that perhaps the cave had been a "genizah," or book morgue. He later wrote, "It is written in beautiful Hebrew...suddenly I had the feeling that I was privileged by destiny to gaze upon a Hebrew scroll which had not been read for more than 2000 years." Sukenik took the scrolls for further investigation, and two days later was convinced of the originality of the text and of the scrolls' importance for biblical study. He sent word that he would buy them. On December 1, 1947, he wrote in his diary: "I'm afraid of going too far in thinking about them. It may be that this is one of the greatest finds ever made in Palestine" (Harrison, 4).

A few days later Sukenik told a friend, an official at the Hebrew University, about the scrolls he had purchased. The friend was astonished and told Sukenik that Dr. Magnes had written to the University Library and asked for two officials to come and look at some manuscripts in the Syrian Monastery of St. Mark, in the Old City, that were owned by the Metropolitan Samuel. The officials went and were told by the Metropolitan that the Scrolls had been in one of the monastery libraries near the Dead Sea, and he wanted an opinion on their age and content. He also wanted to know if the University Library was interested in buying them. The official thought the Scrolls were not very old and that the texts were in Samaritan. They recommended that a specialist be called in. They called the Monastery later to find out what the Metropolitan had decided, but he was away and could not be reached. Thus, nothing came of the visit.

Until this time, Sukenik had been aware of the five scrolls that the Metropolitan had purchased for the Syrian Monastery. Now he realized that the Scrolls his friend was telling him about must be from the same group as the ones he himself had purchased, and that they must have been found in the caves, as his had been. Sukenik then went to Dr. Magnes and received authority to visit the Syrian Monastery. In the meantime, he urged the Armenian dealer to get more scrolls from the Bedouin.

At the end of January, 1948, Sukenik received a letter from Jerusalem, saying that someone had the Hebrew scrolls for Sukenik to see. Upon seeing the scrolls, Sukenik thought one of the manuscripts looked very much like the Book of Isaiah, and he was told that the Metropolitan had bought them from the same Bethlehem dealer from whom his scrolls had been purchased. The dealer had bought them from a Bedouin of the same Ta'âmireh tribe. Sukenik then told the Metropolitan he was willing to buy the five scrolls for the Hebrew University, and he took them home for further investigation. He read the scrolls, showed them to Dr. Magnes and his other colleagues and made copies of some of the texts. He could not decide on the price to offer; he wanted to offer 2000 pounds cash but there was no place to secure a loan because of the tension of the war.

On February 6th, 1948, Sukenik returned the scrolls to the Monastery, planning to meet the following week to decide the price. In the meanwhile, Sukenik had talked to the Bialik Foundation, and Ben-Gurion and the Jewish Agency leaders were so impressed by the fragments from the scroll that they put at Sukenik's disposal any sum that would be necessary. Sukenik anxiously waited for the Syrian letter naming the meeting place and time, but it never came.

Later, a letter came saying they had changed their minds – they wanted to wait for peace to find out the market value of the scrolls before they would sell. Sukenik found out later that one of the Syrians, Father Sowmy, had gone to the American School of Oriental Research and had let the Americans photograph the scrolls. They had assured the priest of far higher prices for the scrolls after their publication in the United States. Sukenik wrote in his diary: "Thus the Jewish people have lost a precious heritage." He died believing this, in 1953.

Yigael Yadin says in his book: "He (Sukenik) was not to know that the Scrolls were to be restored to the Jewish people and permanently housed in Jerusalem, and that I, his son (Yadin), in the strangest possible way, would have something to do with their acquisition." However, Sukenik did see the first three scrolls that he had acquired published in Jerusalem. They were a compilation of thanksgiving psalms or hymns, an imperfect copy of Isaiah, and "The War of the Sons of Light Against the Sons of Darkness" (Dupont-Sommer, 13; cf. Harrison, 5).

At the time the Metropolitan was searching for an expert opinion on his scrolls, Dr. Burrows, the Director of the American School in Jerusalem, had gone to Baghdad and left Drs. Trever and Brownlee in charge. On February 18, 1948, Father Sowmy telephoned the American School and told Dr. Trever that "while working in the library of the Convent, cataloging the books, he had come upon five scrolls in ancient Hebrew about which their catalogue contained no information." Father Sowmy asked if Dr. Trever would look at the Scrolls. Since the Orthodox Christian garb of the Syrian priests made it safe for them to move around Jerusalem, Father Sowmy and his brother, Ibrahim, brought the Scrolls to the American School. When they arrived, they told Dr. Trever that the former Metropolitan had purchased these documents for the Monastery forty years earlier from the Bedouin who had found them in a cave near 'Ain Feshka, on the northwest shore of the Dead Sea.

Trever describes his first impression of the Scrolls: The first scroll "a very brittle, tightly rolled scroll of cream-colored leather, less than two inches in diameter...written in a clear, square Hebrew script, not at all like Archaic Hebrew." The second scroll was 10-1/2" long and 6" in diameter, a thinner, softer leather, more pliable, the same color as the first except with a darkened center. Of the three other scrolls, one was the same size, texture and color as the first; one was narrower, on dark brown leather and inscribed with large clear characters with its lower edge disintegrated; and the third was too brittle to open and in an advanced state of decay. But the script of all of them was extremely puzzling.

As Dr. Trever looked at the scrolls the words of Dr. Burrows came to his mind: "Let your evidence lead you where it will." Dr. Trever was sure it would take time to decipher the evidence before he could pass judgment on the antiquity and value of the scrolls, so he copied a few lines to compare with other ancient manuscripts. That night Dr. Trever found that the copy's words matched Isaiah 65:1 word for word, almost letter for letter: "I am sought of them that asked not for me; I am found of them that sought me not..." (Isa. 65:9). Brownlee, in his account, remarks: "But to me, in retrospect, the scroll has said something different: 'I was ready to be sought by those who did not ask for me; I was ready to be found by those who did not seek me.' The Scroll had been seeking me, but I had successfully escaped it" (Trever, 23, 27).

That night Dr. Trever also found that the script was very similar to that of Nash Papyrus, the oldest known existing Hebrew manuscript. The Nash was from the second half of the second century B.C., so Dr. Trever and Dr. Brownlee estimated the Isaiah Scroll to be around the same age or older.

Dr. Trever was now convinced that the Scrolls should be published so they could be studied and debated by scholars. The Metropolitan agreed to let Trever photograph them, and gradually Trever won the confidence of the Syrians so that they left the Scrolls to be photographed at the American School. Trever examined the Isaiah Scroll again and found the evidence of authenticity that he had been looking for—corrections in the margins with a different script and ink. There had also been rips repaired with pieces of leather. He now realized that this scroll was the entire Book of Isaiah.

After photographing the Scrolls, Trever sent negatives to Professor W. F. Albright, one of the leading authorities on the subject, and wrote: "...it has some indications to show it may be earlier than the Nash Papyrus...." And to a friend-colleague, Edgar J. Goodspeed, he wrote: "If Dr. Albright is correct in dating the Nash Papyrus in the second century B.C., then this is as old or older!..." At the same time, Trever sent a set of photographs to the Metropolitan (Trever, 22-27).

Here there is an unresolved conflict as to what really happened. The Metropolitan says that after he received the photographs, the Armenian dealer Kiraz asked permission to show the Scrolls to Sukenik. The Metropolitan suggested that Kiraz take the photographs instead of the Scrolls themselves, but Kiraz said they were not large enough. This disagrees with Sukenik's account that "after copying some of the Isaiah manuscript, he returned the Scrolls to Kiraz on the sixth of February, three weeks before Trever's photographs were finished." This conflict seemingly cannot be resolved (cf. Burrows, 12).

Dr. Trever also took the photographs and showed them to R. W. Hamilton, Director of the Department of Antiquities, and asked him for help in securing more adequate film for more photographs of the manuscripts, but besides giving a few suggestions, Mr. Hamilton was of little help.

Dr. Burrows returned and Dr. Trever told him about the Scrolls, but being a cautious scholar he would not be convinced of their authenticity until he could see more evidence. Dr. Burrows then visited the Monastery and after seeing the fourth scroll, he exclaimed, "This is Aramaic!" The full significance of this *realization did not show up until later.* Now that Dr. Burrows was becoming convinced of the Scrolls' value, he joined Dr. Trever in trying to persuade the Syrians to let them photograph the Scrolls again. Eventually the Syrians agreed and told Dr. Trever the true story of the discovery. "We have been keeping something from you, Dr. John [Trever], until we were certain we could trust you. The scrolls have not been in our Monastery for forty years, as I told you. They were purchased last August from some Bedouin who lived near Bethlehem." Naturally, Drs. Burrow and Trever were shocked to hear this.

Now the subject of an expedition arose, and with it came many problems: To make the expedition, the friendship of the Syrians was necessary, but the Syrians did not want to work in cooperation with the Department of Antiquities. Moreover, the permission of this Department was needed to excavate. Dr. Trever therefore went to Mr. Hamilton and received permission to go to the cave with the Syrians and photograph everything in sight without disturbing anything; to take any potsherds or other objects on the surface back to the school; and to report back to the Department of Antiquities. But when Trever approached the Metropolitan about the expedition, he was told that the situation in the area was much too dangerous at that time.

Thus the Department of Antiquities was not uninformed about the Scrolls. Actually, Stephan H. Stephan (of the Department) was one of the first to examine the Scrolls, and he appeared skeptical, so he did not report the matter to the Director of the Department. Mr. Wechsler, who was with him, also saw the Scrolls, but was misled by the marginal corrections in one of the manuscripts – the ink was so black that he felt it could not be very ancient. He said, "If that table were a box and you filled it full of pound notes, you couldn't even then measure the value of these scrolls if they are two thousand years old as you say!" He did not realize that he was speaking the truth. Thus, the Department of Antiquities knew about the Scrolls, but just did not realize their significance. This denies the charge made later by Mr. Harding that the Metropolitan, Dr. Trever and others involved simply ignored the Department of Antiquities when they knew that the Scrolls rightfully came under the Department's jurisdiction.

On March 15, Dr. Trever received a letter from Dr. Albright:

> *My heartiest congratulations on the greatest manuscript discovery of modern times! There is no doubt in my mind that the script is more archaic than that of the Nash Papyrus....I should prefer a date around 100 B.C....What an absolutely incredible find! And there can happily not be the slightest doubt in the world about the genuineness of the manuscript....*

Dr. Trever felt that the Syrians should now be told about the antiquity and value of the Scrolls and should be urged to let them be taken to a safer place than Jerusalem. At this time, the Metropolitan told Dr. Trever that Dr. Magnes, President of the Hebrew University, wanted to see the Scrolls, and that Dr. Sukenik wanted to buy them. Trever, who did not know the whole background, urged the Metropolitan to tell Dr. Magnes that the Scrolls were already being handled by the American School. This was the reason that Sukenik received the letter saying the Scrolls were no longer for sale. Dr. Trever was able to impress the Metropolitan with the urgency of the Scrolls' need to be taken to a safer place, and soon afterward Father Sowmy left Palestine with them.

On April 11, 1948, the news of the discovery of the Scrolls was released to the American press. Dr. Burrows had written, "The Scrolls, were acquired by the Syrian Orthodox Monastery of St. Mark." The press, however, said the Scrolls had been "preserved for many centuries in the library of the Syrian Orthodox Monastery of St. Mark in Jerusalem." No one know who was responsible for the error (Burrows, 17).

The announcement of the discovery set off many reactions besides those of joy. Until the article in Biblical Archaeologists *about the Scrolls came out in May, G. L. Harding had known nothing about the discovery. He had been placed in charge of explorations in Arab Palestine and Transjordan and was responsible for everything found there. Under Jordanian Law, the Scrolls belonged to the government. Thus, when Sowmy and the Metropolitan exported the Scrolls they broke the law and put Harding in a very bad situation. Harding describes the Metropolitan's decision to take the Scrolls to the United States: "Later he smuggled out of the country the Isaiah Scroll, the* Manual of Discipline, *the* Habakkuk Commentary, *the* Lamech Apocalypse, *some large fragments of Daniel, and eventually took them to the USA with him" (Yadin, 36).

Harding's attitude is understandable, since now the original site could not be located and examined without proper supervision. Yadin smooths over the situation by saying that it was hard for scholars to keep in touch because of tensions arising from the Palestinian war. But it was not that simple: the government of Jordan threatened to punish the Metropolitan unless he returned the Scrolls. In response the Metropolitan answered that when the Scrolls were exported the British Mandate had expired, and therefore there was no established legal body to regulate and enforce procedures. The Metropolitan also told the Jordanian government that the money from the sales of the Scrolls would go for "the expansion of religious and educational facilities in the Syrian Orthodox Church."

In January, 1949, three of the four Scrolls were edited by Burrows and published by the American School. The fourth Scroll could not be unrolled. The Scrolls' publication did not increase their monetary value as Trever had thought. On the contrary, their value decreased and none of the Americans institutions would buy the Scrolls because of the legal problems involved. Finally, in desperation, the Metropolitan advertised the Scrolls in the Wall Street Journal under "Miscellaneous Items." Dr. Yigael Yadin in the United States on a lecture tour, saw the ad and after complicated negotiations with the Metropolitan bought the four Scrolls for Israel for $250,000. On February 13, 1955, Premier Sharett announced that the Dead Sea Scrolls were now owned by the State of Israel and the Government planned to erect a special museum for these and the other manuscripts that Professor Sukenik had given to the Hebrew University in 1947. This special house, called the Shrine of the Book, is in the shape of a huge scroll and can be lowered into the ground to preserve the manuscripts in time of war. Eight years had passed, and finally, the Dead Sea Scrolls were under one roof.

Yigael Yadin says,

> Thus ended the adventures of the seven Dead Sea Scrolls, from the moment of their chance discovery by the Bedouin on the shores of the Dead Sea until their return to their home in Jerusalem. There, in the Shrine of the Book which is about to be built, they will be the most prized exhibits in what is intended as a center for Biblical and scroll research for scholars all over the world. (Yadin, 52)

Discoveries did not end with these Scrolls. Already, Captain Lippens of the Belgian Army had taken a great interest in the cave in which the Scrolls were supposedly found, and with an Arab legion of soldiers had searched for three days in the Qumran area for it. This set off a series of systematic excavations in the area: On February 15, 1949, Harding and Pre de Vaux led an expedition, but several non-professional excavators also began "some barbaric and illegal digging." When Harding and Pre de Vaux began investigating Cave I, they found what these illegal excavations had left behind—shards, cloth and leather. The cave was filled with fine powdery grey dust and stones for a depth of about fifty centimeters, and the work had to be done with tools such as penknives, brushes, tweezers and fingers because of the "delicacy of the fragments." Harding relates that each day the excavators would put the newfound fragments under glass for observation. Harding also found linen wrappings and broken jars corresponding to those that had housed the original Scrolls, but the tribesmen had already removed many of the manuscripts or fragments.

Dupont-Sommer says that altogether there were fifty jars found in Cave I, and four to five scrolls could have been in each jar, so there must have been 200-250 scrolls in this library at one time. Harding says, however, that this idea is "no longer tenable" because similar pottery not housing scrolls had been found in the settlement at Qumram. The number of different books represented by the fragments is the only evidence for the possible quantity of scrolls. About 75 books are represented. The cause of the scrolls' removal from the jars or the reason for their damage, is unknown.

The location and contents of Cave I linked it to the ruins of Khirbet Qumran, the ancient community center of a monastic order whose identity is still controversial. These ruins, located nine miles southeast of Jericho, were identified in the nineteenth century as the site of biblical Gomorrah, but this idea was corrected in the twentieth century by Dalman, who identified them as indications of Roman habitation. E. deSaulcy says that the name Qumran, as pronounced by the Bedouin, sounds something like Gomorrah, and thus some European explorers identified it with Gomorrah. In any event, Gomorrah was not located in this vicinity.

From 1951-1956, these monastic ruins were systematically investigated by a team of archaeologists. In Byzantine writings, this monastery was called

Castellion or *Marda*, both of which are Aramaic terms for "fortress"; it was built over the site of the ancient Hasmonean fortress, Hyrcanian. In its underground chamber, archaeologists found a library of manuscripts – Arabic, Greek, Christian, and Palestinian-Aramaic, reflecting the late Byzantine and early Arab periods. They also found there a jar similar to the ones at the Qumran cave that definitely links the people who inhabited the Qumran settlement to those who owned the scrolls found in the Qumran caves. Evidence was also found establishing the fact that the material must have been put in the caves in the first century A.D.

Although many of the archaeologists digging in the Qumram area held the view that Cave I was the only one of its kind, the tribesmen continued searching. In November, 1951, some documents turned up for sale at cole Biblique – the Bedouin had been successful. The new cave was eleven miles south of Cave I, in Wadi Murabba't. Closer investigation revealed three more caves near the summit. Three months later an official party visited these caves and found 34 Bedouin engaged in clandestine excavation.

Some of the tribesmen were hired by the archaeologists, and excavation continued. There were hazards involved in these caves: erosion had caused great crevices in the floors, the dust created added inconvenience, and the roofs were quite insecure because of a partial rock fall. Investigation yielded several important discoveries of pottery, coins, and papyrus, including one of the earliest papyri in Hebrew (from the seventh century B.C.), Greek, Aramaic and Hebrew documents from a cache belonging to Bar Kochba (late first and early second centuries A.D.), and a scroll of the minor prophets (second century A.D.). Evidence of five distinct periods of human occupation was revealed: Chalcolithic period (c. 4500-3000 B.C.), Middle Bronze Age (c.1700-1550 B.C.), Iron Age (eighth-seventh century B.C.), Roman period, and the Arab occupation.

In the meantime, while scientists explored the caves of Wadi Murabba't, the Bedouin began searching in the area of the original discovery, and they were not disappointed. In a cave near Cave I they found some fragments (1952). The archaeologists came running, and very soon many archaeological schools mounted expeditions to explore all of the caves north and south of Khirbet, an area of five miles. Dr. W. L. Reed and Pre de Vaux led an expedition in the vicinity of Wadi Qumran and located Cave II south of Cave I, and Cave III, north of Cave I. These finds were not made without difficulties – the team had some 200 unsuccessful soundings amongst the crevices and areas from Hajar el-'Asba' to Ras Feshka, a distance of six miles. In forty locations, they found pottery, fragments, lamps, utensils, jars, and two tiny fragments. The manuscript fragments from Cave II had already been sold by the Bedouin, and Cave III was in a bad state since its roof had collapsed. However, Cave III housed the two copper scrolls, which contained directions for finding the buried treasure of the Essene Monastery.

By the end of March (they had begun in February), the heat, malaria and fatigue brought the expedition to a halt. The archaeologists had explored the caves of the limestone cliffs, but had ignored the artificial caves and clefts in marl terrace at the foot of the cliffs. When the expedition ended, the Bedouin carried on in the marl terrace around Khirbet Qumran. One evening in September, 1952, the Bedouin were discussing their recent finds. One of the older men told a story of chasing a partridge into a hole near the ruins of Khirbet Qumran. He found the partridge in a cave, and while he was there he collected a terracotta lamp and some potsherds. The young Bedouin took careful note of the topographical details of the old man's tale, took a bag of flour, ropes, and primitive lamps, and went to Qumran. They found the cave, investigated, and found thousands of manuscript fragments. Later they took them to various archaeological schools, giving false clues as to where they were found. Eventually, the archaeologists found the cave – Cave IV, the "main lode," which was almost as important as Cave I. Harding and de Vaux explored carefully and found fragments of more than 100 manuscripts, some matted and decayed beneath the floor. During the excavation, Cave V was found by scientists in the marl north of Cave IV, and Cave VI was found near the waterfall of Wadi Qumran by the Bedouin. Both caves held significant finds.

In the summer of 1952 a series of manuscript discoveries in the wilderness remote from Qumran took place. The most significant of these were found by the Bedouin in an unknown site south of Murabba't in one of the wadis emptying into the Dead Sea. These documents appeared in Jerusalem in 1952. Most of them are from the era of the Jewish revolts against Rome; the most important item is the Greek minor prophets representing a lost version of the Septuagint, from the third to the second century B.C. This find was most helpful to the textual critics.

Quiet settled on the Qumran area for about three years, except for the excavations at Khirbet Qumran. Then in 1955, during a "campaign" at Qumran, four more caves were discovered, Caves VII, VIII, IX, and X, in the marl. However, they had collapsed from erosion and produced only a handful of fragments. The others must have been washed away by torrents that had rushed down the gorge. A little later, Cave XI, located near Cave III, north of Cave I, was found and excavated by the Bedouin. It contained several scrolls, excellently preserved: the Psalter, two copies of Daniel, and part of Leviticus. Cross mentions that not since the discovery of Cave I had the Bedouin broken pieces off the manuscripts; rather, they realized and appreciated the value of this material and worked patiently, skillfully and gently with the documents.

These scrolls of Caves I-XI have had a most suspenseful and exciting discovery, and are of priceless value to biblical and archaeological scholars. One of the main questions remaining is, who were the people who put these scrolls into these caves, and why did they put them there? It is doubtful that we will ever know the answers with certainty, but there are several theories based on existing evidence found in the caves. After excavating Khirbet Qumran, Professor Pfeiffer says it is evident that the people who lived in these caves were active in the community center and hid the scrolls when they saw their community about to be destroyed by the Roman legion. (There is evidence in Khirbet Qumran of Roman occupation after A.D. 68.) Harding agrees and adds that the charred ruins of Khirbet Qumran prove its destruction by violent means, after which it was never rebuilt.

So discoveries continue, and translations and publications are increasingly produced, casting more light on the ancient past. There is no way of knowing what information may still be buried in the remote wilderness of Judea.

DEAD SEA SCROLLS

SCROLL'S NAME	WHERE FOUND	CONTENTS (WHEN NECESSARY)
4Q158-186 – *Pesharim*	Cave IV	Interpretations of Biblical Writings
4QEnoch	"	Fragments of the Book of Enoch
6QD(6Q15) – "Damascus Document"	Caves IV and VI	Fragments related to CD (see below)
11QPs^a – Psalms Scroll	Cave XI	Psalms
11QEzek	"	Exekiel fragments
11QapPs	"	Apocryphal Psalms fragments
11QMelch	"	Melchizedek Scroll
11QtgJob	"	Targum of Job
11QTemple	"	Temple Scroll
5MurXII	5th Wadi Murabba 'ât Cave	Hebrew Scroll of Minor Prophets
8HerXII gr	Nahal Hever Cave VII	Greek Scroll of Minor Prophets
XQPhyl	Unidentifeied Qumran Cave	Phylactery fragments
MasSirSabb – "Songs of the Sabath Sacrifices	Masada	Angelic Liturgy, "sectarian liturgical scroll"
CD – "Damascus Document"	Cairo Genizah	"Zadokite Fragments"
Copper Scroll (in two pieces)	Cave III	A list of treasures stored in remote and vaguely identified places.

DEAD SEA SCROLLS

SCROLL'S NAME	WHERE FOUND	CONTENTS (WHEN NECESSARY)
1QIs^a – Isaiah "A"	Cave 1	The Great Isaiah Scroll
1QIs^b – Isaiah "B" Scroll	"	—
1QDan^a – Daniel "A"	"	Fragments from "matted mass of leather" (layers 8 and 9)
1QDan^b – Daniel "B"	"	Fragments from "matted mass of leather" (layers 6 and 7)
1QpHab – *Pesher* to Habakkuk	"	Habakkuk Commentary
1QapGen – 1Q20	"	Genesis Apocryphon, Book of Lamech, Apocalypse of Lamech, Fourth Scroll
1QS – Manual of Discipline	"	Rule of Community
1QSa – Rule of the Congregation	"	Probably part of 1QS Scroll
1QSb – Collection of Benedictions	"	Probably part of 1QS Scroll
1QPrayers – 1Q34^{bis} 1Q34, Litergical Prayer Scroll	"	From "mattes mass of leather," (layers 1-5)
pap1Q70^{bis}	"	Unidentified papyrus fragment
1Q19^{bis} – The Book of Noah	"	Fragment of 1Q19
1QH – *Hodayot*	"	Thanksgiving Hymns, Songs of Thanksgiving
1QM – War Scroll	"	"Battle between the Sons of Light and the Sons of Darkness

Wind Instruments

'UGAB – 'UGAB *is one of two instruments mentioned in the earliest musical reference in the Bible (Gen. 4:21), their initial use having been attributed to Jubal who was the "father" of the musical profession. This word is also used in Job 21:12; 30-31 and Psalms 150:4.*

Not enough is known about it to make an absolute statement, but most likely the word "'ugab" did not refer to a specific instrument but rather to a whole family of some type. This seems to be indicated in Psalms 150:4. "Praise Him with stringed instruments (minnim) *and the pipe* ('ugab)." *"Stringed instruments" is used here as a collective term, and because of the construction of biblical poetry it is almost certain that* 'ugab *refers here to the family of wind instruments.*

Halil – *plural is* halilim – *This instrument occurs six times in the Old Testament – I Samuel 10:5; I Kings 1:40; Isaiah 5:12; 30:29; Jeremiah 48:36, twice in last-mentioned passage. It is of Asiatic origin. Babylonians had used it mainly for lamentations. (It was some type of flute, maybe even a double-reed mouthpiece.)*

Use of halilim *in every ritual is confirmed in several biblical passages – I Samuel 10:5 in which* halil *is mentioned as one of the instruments played by "a band of prophets." Use in religious ceremonies is directly referred to in Isaiah 30:29: "Ye shall have a song...and gladness of heart, as when one goeth with the pipe* (halil)...."

Halil, 'ugab *and* 'abub *are the three words found in the Bible which indicate wind instruments, individually as well as collectively. The timbre of the halil is shrill and penetrating, similar to oboe-type, blown with a mouthpiece of reed.*

This instrument is one of joy and gaiety and was played at all merry occasions, such as festivals, banquets, popular entertainments, coronations, etc. At the Feast of Tabernacles wealthy people frequently hired halil-players *for domestic entertainment. In contrast, the tone could also be mournful and wailing and was appropriate for funeral ceremonies, too. Its shrill tone could also simulate a state of ecstasy.*

Nehilot – *The expression 'el ha-nehilot is used only once in the Bible, in the heading of Psalm 5. This expression is probably an instrument for accompanying Psalm 5 with woodwinds (pipes), whereas with most psalms, stringed instruments were used, or especially called for.*

Mahol – *This instrument is thought to be used in the Bible as a musical instrument at certain times. In the superscriptions of Psalms 53 and 88 'al mahalot refers to musical renditions of these Psalms, indicating the accompaniment with woodwinds.*

Mashrokita – *The* mashrokita *was among the instruments of Nebuchadnezzar's court (Dan. 3:5, 7, 10, 15). The word could be derived from Hebrew* sharak *"to hiss," "to whistle," but it is generally assumed that it refers to a foreign instrument, one of the instruments that were considered "exotic."*

There are some insurmountable difficulties in trying to find out exactly what this instrument was like, so for want of a better, more definite solution we will identify it with the syrinx *which had a row of pipes of different length, which produced a hissing sound. This peculiarity seemed to justify the derivation of the word from the Hebrew* sharak.

Sumponyah – *This instrument is not mentioned in the Hebrew text of the Bible. It appears in the Book of Daniel among the instruments played in Nebuchadnezzar's orchestra (3:5, 10, 15). It is not certain if this was a wind or stringed instrument or if it was an instrument at all. Some musicologists still think it was a type of bagpipe.*

Hazozerah – *plural* hazozerot – *This instrument was a long straight trumpet built by the Israelites after Egyptian models. It was in Egypt during the reign of Tut-Ankh-Amen. Two of these, a silver and a bronze, were found in his tomb. Trumpets were also used by the Assyrians, as bas-reliefs show us.*

The hazozerah *was one ell long, its straight tube somewhat wider than* halil *and widened at the lower end into a bell. The mouthpiece was rather broad. The form was identical with today's signal trumpets, called "herald's trumpets." The* hazozerah *was made of metal, either bronze or, for sacred trumpets, beaten silver.*

God commanded Moses to make two trumpets (Num. 10:2). The sounding of the hazozerah was the exclusive privilege of Aaron's descendants (Num. 10:8). Players were called hazozerim and they played the sacred trumpets. Unlike pagan worship (with instruments) Israelites blew trumpets not to awaken their god-like pagans, but "for a memorial before your God" (Num. 10:10).

Trumpets (secular) were used to gather the congregation, to cause camps to set forward, to invite princes for a gathering, to sound alarms in danger, to give signals when going to war; (religious) for religious feasts, the New Moon, daily burnt and peace offerings and all important ritual ceremonies. The Old Testament mentions hazozerah 29 times.

Shofar – plural shofarot – The shofar is still used in the Jewish liturgy and is the only instrument of Ancient Israel that survived the millennia in its original form. The Hebrews took over the shofar from the Assyrians. The word is derived from shapparu Assyrian meaning "wild goat" and the instrument is made of a ram's horn. The original form of the shofar was curved, like that of the natural ram's horn.

The Year of the Jubilee is like the New Year in the blowing of the shofar and in the Benedictions. The shofar blown in the Temple was made from the horn of a wild goat, straight, with its mouthpiece overlaid with gold. Later when the shofar was blown on New Year's Day, this was to remind God symbolically of His promise given to Abraham, Isaac and Jacob. The blowing on other days was also symbolic in that the faithful should remember the ram Abraham sacrificed in the place of his son.

The shofar was the only instrument permitted to be blown after the burning of the sanctuary in Jerusalem, all music being prohibited as a sign of mourning.

The primitive shofarot were made by cutting off the tip of the natural horn or boring a hole into it; therefore there was no mouthpiece and only crude sustained tones could be produced. The shofar with a mouthpiece represents a more developed form of the instrument, but even then the tones were limited to two or perhaps three in number.

If shofarot *were damaged, they could be used again only if they were expertly repaired. They were not to be painted over with colors, but ornaments and inscriptions could be carved on them.*

The shofar *was blown only by priests and Levites on special occasions, in secular events by laymen, by children and by women in cases of emergency, and was frequently blown on other than ritual occasions.*

The shofar *is mentioned most frequently in the Bible – 72 times. By this we know its great importance in the religious and secular life of the Jewish people.*

Examples of religious use included: transfer of the ark of the covenant by David (II Sam. 6:15); renewal of the covenant by King Asa (II Chron. 15:14); announcement of the New Moon (Ps. 81:3); and thanksgiving to God for His miraculous deeds (Ps. 98:6; 150:3). Examples of secular festivities included: Absalom's accession to the throne (II Sam. 15:30); Solomon's anointment as king (I Kings 1:34); and Jehu's accession to the crown (II Kings 9:13).

The shofar *was the regular signal instrument in times of war for assembling the warriors, attacking the enemy, pursuing the vanquished or announcing the victory. The* shofar *played a decisive role in the siege of Jericho.*

Keren – *The literal meaning of the word* keren *is "firm," "solid." It refers to the hard horn of the neat in contrast to the soft flesh of the bovine cattle.*

It is implied that the keren *was made from animal horn and was powerful, that is, loud. It also served as a signal instrument; it was made entirely of neat horn and had no metal parts. It is not connected in biblical text with the sacred service and, therefore, it is assumed it was used exclusively as a secular instrument.*

Yobel – *This term appears for the first time in the Bible in Leviticus 25:9-54. It was used especially for announcing the Year of Jubilee. The* yobel *was much louder than the* shofar *or* keren; *therefore, it was bound to have a larger shape. It had a wide resounding bell of metal that could be put on and taken off and functioned like a megaphone. The description of Moses' ascension of Mt. Sinai (Exod. 19:13, 16, 19) indicated that such a larger horn type with a resounding bell was used.*

The characteristic feature of the yobel *was the metal sound bell that, no doubt, was put together of several parts. The adequate translation of* yobel *would be "horn of the Jubilee," or "high-sounding horn."*

Chapter 6

THE SAMARITANS

"...FOR JEWS HAVE no dealing with Samaritans" (John 4:9).

Why? Who were these mysterious people looked down upon as idolaters by the Pharisees, but made an object of Christ's ministry of reconciliation and healing, and evangelized by the early Jewish Christians? What were the origins, beliefs, religious practices and Messianic expectations that distinguished them from other Jews of Jesus' day? Samaritans were regarded by Jesus as part of the "lost sheep of the House of Israel" and as closer adherents to the Law, in some ways, than the Jews themselves.

The Jewish people identify the Samaritans as a schismatic sect claiming to be a remnant of the House of Israel, and still surviving as a small community in Nablus, site of ancient Shechem, in Samaria, Palestine. Members of this "schismatic sect" are thought to be descendants of colonists that King Shalmaneser of Assyria brought back from Cutha, Babylon, Hammath and other places after he had conquered Samaria and deported the native population in 722 B.C.

The widely believed story begins when the first imported "settlers" bring their own gods into Samaria and worship them according to their own customs. Josephus says:

> ...they provoked Almighty God to be angry and displeased at them, for a plague seized upon them, by which they were destroyed; and when they found no cure for their miseries, they learned by the oracle that they ought to worship Almighty God as the method for their deliverance. So they sent ambassadors to the king of Assyria, and desired him to send them some of

> those priests of the Israelites whom he had taken captive. And when he thereupon sent them, and the people were by them taught the laws and the holy worship of God, they worshipped Him in a respectful manner, and the plague ceased immediately; and indeed they continue to make use of the very same customs to this very time....
>
> And when they [the Samaritans] see the Jews in prosperity, they pretend that they are changed, and allied to them, and call them kinsmen, as though they were derived from Joseph, and had by that means an original alliance with them; but when they see them falling into a low condition, they say they are in no way related to them, and that Jews have no right to expect any kindness or marks of kindred from them, but they declare that they are sojourners that came from other countries. (Gaster, 337)

The Samaritans, therefore, were regarded by the Jews as a "mixed stock." They were even dubbed *Kuthim*, or men of *Cuthah*, in order to stigmatize them as non-Israelite. John Bright, a leading Old Testament scholar, supports this view as he says, "These foreigners brought their native customs and religion with them and, together with others brought in still later, mingled with the surviving Israelite population. We shall meet their descendants later as the Samaritans" (Gaster, 337).

Samaritans of today dismiss this view as Jewish folklore. They say that the deportation in 722 B.C. of the native population was neither total nor final, and that the exiles returned to Samaria after 55 years. It is the descendants of these native Israelis that they claim to be.

> The origin of this people is of the tribe of our lord Joseph...,who are the descendants of Ephraim and Manasseh. Their priests are of the house of Levi, the descendants of Aaron....Once there followed this people some of the other tribes, though now there is none among them who is not from the tribe of our lord Joseph...,excepting the family of the priesthood, which is of the tribe of Levi, as we have already stated. (Priest Amram Ishak, *The History and Religion of the Samaritans*, A Modern Samaritan Document, p. 5)

According to the Samaritan version the breach with the Judeans goes back to the time of Eli, who took it upon himself to set up an apostate sanctuary to Yahweh at Shiloh, instead of the true "chosen place" prescribed in the law of Moses, Mount Gerizim.

> *Gerizim the Original Holy Place* – Now the causes of their separation from the remnant of the tribes of Israel and the causes of their attachment to the faith which they now have

and which differs in many points from the faith of the Jews are many. The principal cause happened during the life of Eli, the priest, who lived in the year 280 of the entrance of the children of Israel into the land of Canaan. For when the children of Israel...entered the holy land, their high priest was the wise Eliazar the son of Aaron....His place of dwelling was in Gerizim, where he served in the tabernacle, which was built in the wilderness, according to the commandments of the Truth...,and according to the plan of our lord Moses...,as it was given from Him....Those who made its vessels were the wise men Bezaleel and Eliab, and other skilled men who joined in with them, as it is narrated in the Holy Torah. (*Hist. and Rel. of Samaritans*, 5-6)

Misinformation regarding the place of worship was allegedly later reinforced by the "accursed Ezra," who falsified the sacred text and thereby seduced the people on their return from the Babylonian exile to erect the second temple beside the Judean capital.

The Inventions of Ezra – When Ezra and his people became settled in that land, and had found the people of Joseph were in the best conditions so far as fulfilling their religious duties is concerned, many of his people were convinced to turn from their foolish way and to return to their true religion. The Jews had no book in their possession, and they could not read the Torah and they only had the name Israelite, but the majority of them were in ignorance and negligence like illiterate people, for the Torah was lost from among them during the reign of Sorday the king.

And Ezra, seeing these things, began to gather books from the legends and from some chronicles and narratives. He invented things which never occurred, and he wrote them in the Assyria writing, which is still found in the books of the Jews. He began to gather into books as he thought best, and he gathered narratives of the Israelites, and began to alter according to his judgment. Then he mentioned the people of Samaria whose origin is from the tribe of Joseph and descendants of the tribe of Phinehas, and he called them Samaritans. He said that they were Gotin (Gentiles?). It is recorded in the book of Kings, the seventeenth chapter, and he filled it with many phrases which are refuted by us and which have no truth in them. All of this was because of his hatred of the aforesaid people, whom he called Samaritans. (*Hist. and Rel. of Samaritans*, 34)

According to Landman, Samaritans do agree that pagan colonists were brought in by Assyrian monarchs but feel that they, the true natives, Israelites, should not be confused with them. In keeping with this view the

Samaritans prefer to call themselves *Shamerim*, which means the "observant," rather than *Shomeronim*, "inhabitants of Samaria" (Gaster, 336).

One of the most recent views is propounded by Coggins, who rejects both the assumption that Samaritan origins date back to the eight century B.C. and the idea that the later Samaritans were descendants of foreigners settled in the land by the Assyrian conquerors. He also maintains that "there is nothing in the references to those who remained in the land which would connect them with the Samaritans by way of religious practice or even geography." Coggins argues furthermore against the idea of any sudden event that divided Jews and Samaritans. "All the evidence," he concludes, "suggests that the decisive formative period for Samaritanism was the epoch from the third century B.C. to the beginning of the Christian era; and that it emerged from the matrix of Judaism during this time, with some measure of communication continuing well into the Christian era between Samaritans and various Jewish groups" (Gaster, 336).

If the solution to finding the correct view were a simple matter the Samaritans and Jews would not have continued arguing over their identity throughout the epochs, and books would not have been written pro and con. There is truth within each view, as well as folklore and plain untruth, and thus it seems that the ultimate truth lies between the extremes.

Following the fall of Samaria in 722 B.C. the Biblical story is confirmed by Assyrian records. These show that it was Sargon, Shalmaneser's successor, who completed the siege that effected the exchange of the races in question. These documents also show that the colonization (mentioned in II Kings 17:24) took place over several years and under different rulers. Hamathithes were probably brought to Samaria after Sargon had stopped a revolt in their city in 721 B.C. An introduction of Babylonians and Cutheans evidently should be assigned to Ashurbanipal rather than to Sahlmaneser; it could have been an act of retribution by Ashurbanipal for their share in a civil war.

But the fact that the biblical account is generally confirmed by the archaeological documents does not prove that Jews are right in regarding Samaritans as merely the offspring of colonists. The Samaritans have much to support their claim to be true descendants of Israel.

To begin with, Sargon himself evidently records that he deported 27,290 persons, and a count based on a contemporary record in II Kings 15:19 shows that wealthy land owners alone numbered 60,000 at that time. In II Chronicles 34:9 we read of a "remnant of Israel" still residing in Ephraim and Manasseh in the days of Josiah, about one century later. II Kings 24:24 reads: "And he carried away all Jerusalem, and all the princes, and all the mighty men of valour, even 10,000 captives, and all the craftsmen and smiths: none remained, save the poorest sort of the people of the land." Through this we can infer that the influential citizens were driven into exile while the lowliest of the lot were left. We must realize that there is nothing in Samaritan doctrine that shows any indebtedness to Assyrian ideas, and that the attitude of Samaritans toward Jews is likely a continuation of the immense hostility between Israel and Judah.

The conclusion seems to be that after the fall of Samaria in 722 B.C., the local population consisted of two distinct peoples living side by side: the remnants of the native Israelites, and the foreign colonists. The Jewish version ignores the former and the Samaritan version, the latter.

The Creed of the Samaritans states, "We believe only in God and in Moses, the son of Amram, His servant, and in His sacred laws, and in the Mount Gerizim and in the day of punishment and reward."

The main tenets of the Samaritans can be seen in six concepts: Belief in God, Moses as the supreme apostle of God, the Torah as the only authentic law of God, Mount Gerizim as the chosen place of god, the day of Punishments and Rewards, and the Taheb.

God exists beyond time and space and transcends a physical body. He is in all things and yet cannot be localized. He cannot be described; His being is epitomized by the phrase: "I am who I am" (Exod. 3:14). He created all things and sustains all things. The esteem and respect of the Samaritans is so intense that they avoid using the name of God (Tetragrammaton) and substitute it with *Shëma*, which means "the Name." The Samaritans express their belief of God in this way:

> God did not bear, and was not born; He has no second, no companion, and is incomparable. He is alone, separate, pristine, eternal, by Himself. God dwells in an isolated state, has no form; there is none like Him; He is matchless,

incomparable. He has no place, no bound. Apart in Oneness, having none second to Him in His divine state..... (Macdonald, 67)

Moses is considered as "the exalted prophet," "the seal of the prophets," "the apostle," and "the choicest of creatures." He is "the light of the world" and existed before creation, which in fact was created for him (Marqeh, 67b). He intercedes for the people and is the prophet foretold in Deuteronomy 18:18. Apparently the Samaritans revere Moses as Christians do Jesus Christ (*cf.* Macdonald, 67).

The Samaritans recognize the Torah as sacred Scripture but reject the Prophets and the Writings. The Samaritans' Torah, moreover, is different than the Jewish Torah (since they hold that Ezra "invented" parts of the Text). They consider that the Torah was given by God to Moses on Sinai, along with the Ten Commandments. Samaritans cling faithfully to the Ten Commandments mentioned in the Torah in Exodus (20th chapter, 1) (Deuteronomy 5th), expressed as follows: recognition of the monotheism of God; making no false oaths by God; taking into consideration the importance of the days of the Sabbath in its blessing and holiness; the necessity of avoiding stealing; respect and homage to the parents; the necessity of avoiding murder; the necessity of avoiding committing adultery; the necessity of avoiding the giving of false testimony; the necessity of avoiding having a lust for another's woman; and faith in Gerizim mountain. They observe circumcision as well (Hasanein Wasef Kahen, *The Samaritans: Their History, Religion, Customs*).

Every Samaritan prepares for the approaching Sabbath by executing three essential duties: performance of bathing; performance of wearing new and clean clothes; performance of required prayers. Prayers are done seven times during Friday night and Saturday morning and noon; they are made up largely of phrases of gratifying, exalting, naming, extolling and thanking. Sabbath restrictions include bans against talking about business and outdoor work, against voyaging by sea, and against strolling or going out in the streets.

The Samaritan child is circumcised on the eight day following his birth or sentenced to death, even if the eight day is a Saturday or the child is in need of a cure from illness (Gen. 17:12). In regard to such aspects of the

Law, Rabbi Simon Gamaliel comments, "Every command the Samaritans keep, they are more scrupulous in observing than Israel."

Instead of the Jewish Jerusalem, Mount Gerizim is the special place where God abides on earth; it is the Mount of Blessing. The Patriarchs are said to be buried upon it, and regular pilgrimages are made to their graves. It was also the scene of Jacob's dream, Noah's altar, and is believed to be the navel of the earth. An addition to the Ten Commandments in Deuteronomy, as mentioned, ordains its sanctity.

The "day of punishments and rewards" is taken from the Samaritan text of Deuteronomy 32:34,35 which reads: "Is it not stored and sealed up in my treasures, against the day of vengeance and reward?" At that time the deeds of men will be weighed on the scales and angels will prosecute and defend. The text (v. 39) continues, saying that God will cry out, "See now that it is I, even I?" The earth will split open, graves will open and the dead will rise. The righteous will be dressed in clean robes while the wicked are seen in tatters. Following judgment, the former will enter Eden while the wicked will be sent to the fire (Marqeh, 189b-191a).

The Samaritans believe in the Messiah, who is called the Taheb or "Restorer." He will appear on earth to initiate the new dispensation and to restore the Temple on Gerizim, where he will reinstate the sacrifices. He is expected to live 110 years. Although the exact date of his coming is uncertain, they hold the idea that the earth will dissolve after 6,000 years. The Taheb will announce this event. (See chapter on Messianic expectations for Jewish beliefs.)

Another point of interest is the Samaritan interpretation of historical figures which differs from that of the Jews; for example, Samuel (a Jewish prophet of God) is called by the Samaritans "a sorcerer."

The Samaritans are seen in the New Testament in contact with Jesus and also in illustrations of his teachings. In the parable of the Good Samaritan (Luke 10:25-37) Jesus cites the Samaritan, in contrast to the Jews in the story, as the one who reflected the true attitude of the Law of love for one's neighbor regardless of circumstances. The story indicates the manner in which Jesus regarded the Samaritans, those hated by his own people.

The account of the healing of the ten lepers, in which the Samaritan alone returned to give thanks to Jesus, shows that they were included in his ministry and treated him with reverence and respect even to a greater degree than did the Jews.

The account of Jesus and the Samaritan woman (John 4:7-26) is the most detailed story of Jesus' interaction with the Samaritans. The conflict between the Jews and Samaritans is reflected in verse 9, where John comments, "for Jews have no dealings with Samaritans." Certain beliefs are also seen in the woman's words; for example, "our father Jacob" and "the place of worship," and in her belief that the Messiah was coming. The story concludes with the Samaritans' reception of Jesus as Saviour.

In the early church the Samaritans again appear. Jesus includes them in the plan for evangelization: "Ye shall be my witnesses both in Jerusalem, and in all Judea and Samaria, even to the remotest part of the earth." Acts, chapter 8, tells of the ministry of Philip, Peter and John in Samaria and later Luke, in Acts (9:31) speaks of the churches there enjoying peace.

Percussion – Shaking and Rattling Instruments

TOF – PLURAL – TUPPIM – *This is a collective term for all kinds of hand-drums of the ancient Hebrews. The form of this instrument is not given in the Scriptures so we have to rely on analogies with similar instruments of other ancient Oriental people and on pictorial reproductions provided by the antiquities of Egypt and Assyria.*

The tof consisted of a wooden or metal hoop covered with an animal skin and played with either the fingers or the clenched fist. There is no indication it was played with sticks. It was the most primitive, common instrument of ancient Israel and could be played easily by anybody.

In Israel the tuppim were played by the girls and women and occasionally by the men, and were used much for dancing. They were the symbol of joy.

The tof was used in religious ceremonies in the early history of the Jews. Dancing, singing and playing are the three elements with which they glorified God.

Meẓiltayim, Ẓelzelim – *The only percussion instruments admitted unreservedly in the sacred service were the bronze cymbals which were named in the plural form* – meẓiltayim.

The Egyptian cymbals had a broad, flat rim and large bulge in the center. They were held upright and played sideways. The Jewish ẓelzelim *were no doubt similar. According to Josephus they were large bronze plates played with both hands. The cymbals of the Temple were made of brass "to sound aloud" (I Chron. 15:19).*

These instruments are found for the first time in the Bible at the transfer of the ark of the covenant to Jerusalem (II Sam. 6:5). At the institution of the regular music the meẓiltayim *acquired an important ritual function, being played by three precentors heading a group of singers and leading their groups by beating the cymbal. They were often played by the Temple Levites.*

Jewish song was not metrical like our Western music; therefore marking of the beats with cymbals, as we know it, could not be applied in the music of the Temple. The sounding of the cymbals was the signal for starting the choir-

singing in later Jewish ceremonies. Cymbal-playing Levites are mentioned at the rededication of the Temple by Hezekiah (II Chron. 29:25).

Shalishim – *This word appears only once in the Bible (I Sam. 18:6) and it is not certain whether it is even an instrument – it is very vague. By analogy with Ugaritic (+⌊+⌋) – metal (meaning three) they could be cymbals or metal bowls.*

Mena'an'im – *This word appears in biblical text only in II Samuel 6:5. It originates from the very nu'a which means "to shake," "to move about." They are a shaking instrument, like the Egyptian sistrum, though not quite so richly adorned. They consisted of a metal frame, inserted with rods and carrying loose rings. The frame, had a handle which the player held to shake the instrument, thereby creating a tinkling sound.*

Pa'amonim *(derived from very* pa'am *meaning "to strike") – In Exodus 28:33, 34 and 39:25, 26, it signifies the little bells attached to the lower seam of the high priest's purple garment. These bells were made of gold and had a bright sound which was just loud enough to indicate the whereabouts of the high priest. Since bells proper were used only in the seventh century B.C. E., these must have been metal platelets. Later, they were substituted by actual bells.*

Mezillot – *This is mentioned in Zechariah 14:20 and is rendered generally as "bells" which were hung upon horses. The Jewish* mezillot *must have been larger and more compact than the dainty* pa'amonium *on the high priest's garment, because they were supposed to carry an inscription on them – "Holy Unto The Lord."*

The pa'amonim *and* mezillot *were not musical instruments as we consider such. They did not serve musical or artistic aims; their purpose was to exert an extra-musical effect by their sound.*

Chapter 7
MESSIANIC EXPECTATIONS[*]

THE GREEK WORD χριστός (from χρίω , to anoint), is a translation of the Hebrew *Mashiah*, in Aramaic, *Meshiha*, from which the Greek form *Messias* is derived. In the Talmud, it appears sometimes without the article as a proper name (Aramaic משיח), sometimes with the article (Aramaic משיחא). Besides its use in rabbinic literature, this word is used in Baruch 29:3, 30:1, II Esdras 12:32 (lat. Syr. Armen. Text); Enoch 7:28; Ar. 2: Slavonic Josephus, *B.J.* 1 364. "Messiah" means "anointed" (with oil). Anointing with oil had a special significance – it was thought to symbolize the transition of the person or object to a sanctified status. In the Old Testament, kings (foreign and Israelite) and high priests are described by this word. "The Anointed" denoted a special relationship with God. Saul, the King of Israel, is called "the Lord's anointed" (I Sam. 24:7; Heb. 24:6-Eng.).

As a king of the final age, the founder of a glorious kingdom, "Messiah" does not occur in the Old Testament; it first appears in the literature of later Judaism. It does occur, however, in the Old Testament as a religious title for the reigning king in Israel. Thus when "messiah" acquired the connotations of an eschatological figure, it also still carried, through the historical association of ideas, a political significance: The Messiah will restore Israel, conquer other nations, rule over Israel as king.

---

[*] For a more elaborate text on this topic see R. Patten "The Thaumaturgical Element in the Gospel of Mark," Dissertation for Drew Univ., 1976.

The Political Messiah

"The political part of the belief in the Messiah," according to Joseph Klausner, "took place in ancient times during periods of trouble and distress precisely because it proclaimed...comfort and hope that political freedom would return to the Jewish people....The people of Israel did not have a *glorious past*, hence it was forced to direct its gaze toward a *glorious future*. It longed for a...redeemer and savior" (Klausner, 15-16).

Klausner traces the idea as beginning with Moses, who not only redeemed Israel from her material troubles and political servitude, but also from her ignorance and spiritual bondage. He became the symbol of the redeemer (Klausner, 17-20). A quote from the authors of the Talmud and Midrash show how closely the future Messiah is to compare with Moses:

> ...just as Moses brought redemption to his people, so also will Messiah bring redemption; just as Moses was brought up in the house of Pharaoh among the enemies of his people, so also will Messiah dwell in the city of Rome, among the destroyers of his land; just as Moses, after revealing himself to his brethren in Egypt and announcing to them that deliverance was near, was forced to go into hiding for a time, so also will Messiah be forced to hide himself after the first revelations; just as Moses crossed from Midian to Egypt riding on an ass (Exod. 4:20), so also will Messiah come riding on an ass; just as Moses caused manna to rain from the sky, so will Messiah bring forth different kinds of food in a miraculous way; and just as Moses gave to the children of Israel wells and springs of water in the wilderness, so also will Messiah make streams of water flow in the desert. (Klausner, 17-18)

The Mosaic concept of the Messiah was just one aspect of the expected redeemer. Israel also developed a King-Messiah ideal. The official Israelite conception of the king was that he was a superhuman, divine being; an "elohim," a powerful, superior being: a god.

It was believed that when the king was anointed he was endowed with the divine Spirit and filled with superhuman power and wisdom. The anointing signified Yahweh's "choice" of him to be king over the people. This sacramental act, which more than anything else linked the king with Yahweh, was probably practiced by the Canaanites, and also among the Egyptians and Babylonians. According to Sigmund Mowinckel:

> When, in Ps. 2:7 Yahweh says to the king on the day of his anointing and installation, 'You are My Son; I have begotten

you today,' He is using the ordinary formula of adoption, indicating that the sonship rests on Yahweh's adoption of the king. The act of adoption is identical with the anointing and installation.

The true king judges Yahweh's people with justice, relieves the oppressed, the helpless, and the unprotected, gives justice to the widow and the fatherless, protects them from the oppression of the wicked, and avenges them when their rights have been violated and their blood shed....The righteous king also conveys good fortune. (Mowinckel, 78, 68)

David was thought to have been such a king. It is emphasized that he was a "warrior chosen from among the people" that Yahweh exalted when he made David king (Ps. 89:20). He was considered the true "prototype" of the Messiah. His political prowess in unifying all the tribes of Israel, his courage in battle, his defeat of Israel's enemies, made him the "greatest political savior" in the eyes of Israel. Also, in spite of accounts of his human weakness, he was considered spiritually ideal. The Messiah came to be known as "Son of David," and was expected to set up an earthly kingdom which would even exceed that of David. Thus the two great "saviors" of Israel, Moses and David, influenced the people's concept of a future deliverer.

The Messiah in the Qumran Literature

The Qumran sect expected two types of Messiah. One was the Priestly Messiah, the Teacher of Righteousness, Interpreter of the Law. These names were also used to refer to their own priestly founder, thus the idea originated that they were one and the same. The Qumran sect also expected an Anointed One, a prince of the line of David. In the *Manual of Discipline* both the Messiah of Israel and the High Priest are mentioned. This Davidic Messiah is a war leader, and a judge. In the *Manual of Discipline*, he is described:

He will renew for Him the Covenant of the Community (charging him) to establish the kingdom of His people for[ever, to judge the poor justly, and] to reprove with e[quality the hum]ble of the land, to walk before him in perfection, and in the way of [...] and to restore his [hol]y alliance [in] the time of distress with all those who seek his [hol]y alliance [in] the time of distress with all those who seek [Him. May] the Lord li[ft th]ee up to an everlasting height like a fortified tower on a high wall, that thou [mightest smite the peoples] with the might of thy [mouth], with thy sceptre devastate the land, and with the breath of thy lips kill the wick[ed, armed with the spirit of coun]sel and everlasting might, the spirit of knowledge, and the fear of God. And the righteousness shall be the girdle o[f thy loins, and fai]th the belt of thy reins. [And] may he make thy horns of iron and thy hooves of brass to gore like a young bu[ll...and tread down the peop]les like the mire of the streets. For God has established thee as a sceptre over rulers. Bef[ore thee shall they come and do obeisance, and all the na]tions will serve thee, and by His holy name He will strengthen thee. And thou shalt be like a l[ion...] prey with none to resto[re], and thy [mess]engers will spread over the face of the earth.... (Allegro, 167)

The study of the Messianic expectation in Qumran is not without problems. There is a great debate over whether there was one, two or three messiahs. Some scholars see references to three types: messianic king, messianic priest, and messianic prophet. There is also the question of whether the Messiah is eschatological or whether the word *messiah* is simply a common noun for "anointed one."

Although opinions are varied regarding the Qumran sect's messianic expectations, it is clear, however, that it was thought that the messiah either included two aspects – priest and king – or that two separate persons would come, priest and king. Both would have significance for the restoration of Israel as a nation.

Concept at the Time of Jesus

There were two concepts of the Messiah which were not consciously distinguished. "One," Mowinckel explains, "was the national, political, this-worldly [concept], with the particularistic tendencies, though universalistic at its best. The other was a super-terrestrial, other-worldly [concept] rich in religious content and mythological concepts, universalistic, numinous, at home in the sphere of 'Holy' and the 'wholly other'" (Mowinckel, 281).

The expectation of an earthly kingship developed more fully during the Babylonian exile when the throne of David no longer existed, and the Jews were forced to postpone the promise to a distant future. It became more active under the rule of Greece as Jewish nationalism developed, and the expectation of a political warrior emerged. This concept of Messiah (political, national warrior) prevailed at the time of Jesus.

This older, nationalistic future hope prevailed among the masses because it addressed economic, social and political pressures, whereas the other-worldly concept was current in certain literary circles, among the learned, religious sects. That the Messiah was regarded as an earthly figure is evident by the accounts of several people being proclaimed as such. For example, Zerubbabel was proclaimed king of the restoration by Zechariah and Haggai; Simon, during the Hasmonean rule, was considered the Messiah (I Macc. 14:4ff.); the false messiahs, mentioned by Josephus, were called brigands, rioters, and saboteurs. Hezekiah, the "robber-chief," so called by Josephus, was called "Messiah" by R. Hillel. Other messiahs mentioned by Josephus are Hezekiah's son Judas the Galilean form Gamala, and his brother Menahem ben Hezekiah, the unnamed Jew who appeared during the rule of Festus and took his followers into the wilderness where they were massacred by the Romans (Jos., *Ant* xvii. 271; *B. J.* ii. 118, 433ff.; *Ant.* xx. 97f.; Acts 5:36; *Ant.* xxi. 38; xx. 169ff., 188; *B. J.* ii. 266ff.), and Simon bar Kochba, "Son of a Star," who claimed to be the "star out of Jacob." Rabbi Akiba called him Messiah (Buhl, 437ff.; Mowinckel, 285). This king or Messiah also appeared among the Samaritans (Jos., *Ant.* xviii. 85f.). It is evident that the people generally expected an earthly, political man.

At the time of Jesus, the mission of the Messiah was the salvation of Israel, i. e., to restore Israel as a people to her former glory, to a leading position among all nations; to free her from enemies and destroy the world powers. This concept was influenced by the growing intolerance of everything foreign as a result of the Maccabean revolt and Roman rule. The future hope concentrated more and more on deliverance. The Messiah would be primarily a royal deliverer, enemy of Rome, a zealot. His qualities and deeds would surpass ordinary standards, but had also been done by others, as in the miracles of Elijah. "Only as a mighty ruler and an exalted and unequaled moral personality," Klausner says, "would the Messiah be superior to all the rest of the saints and prophets of Israel. His kingdom was still *of this world"* (Klausner, 465-66).

There was still no conception of a "suffering Messiah." Mowinckel says the idea existed of a mortal messiah who would suffer or die in battle, but this had nothing to do with atonement; "Judaism knows nothing of a suffering, dying and rising messiah" (Mowinckel, 326-29). (See Mark 8:31; 9:31.)

The concept of a messiah being an eternal Being is due to its association with the Son of Man concept. As he became unique and eternal, significant for salvation, he also became pre-existent.

As for the Messiah's appearances, Mowinckel notes:

> The day when the Messiah appears and accomplishes his Messianic work of salvation is the day when he 'is revealed' as what he is destined to be, as the Messiah. These expressions imply that it is this Messianic work which makes him the Messiah. He cannot be known and acknowledged as such until these actions have revealed his identity. By performing Messianic works he 'reveals his glory' (his dignity as Messiah).... (Mowinckel, 337)

If it is the Messiah's work which makes him and reveals him as the Messiah, there may be a time in his human life when he is "hidden"–even without his own consciousness. It was thought he would have to be announced by Elijah who would make the human one of David's line renowned in performing Messianic deeds (Mowinckel, 304-06).

Thus at Jesus' time the people of Israel were expecting a political, national type of messiah who would deliver them from the oppression of Rome. Political messiahs were expected to authenticate their claims and leadership by miracles. There were many such claimants at the time of Jesus who are mentioned by Josephus. These figures appealed to nationalistic sentiments of liberation associated with Moses and the exodus, and attempted to organize the people into a revolutionary movement. They authenticated their claims by attempting to repeat the miracles which were thought to have been done by the first wilderness generation.

A Samaritan, during the procuratorship of Pilate (c. A.D. 26-36) led an armed group towards Mt. Gerizim. Josephus writes:

> Neither was the Samaritan nation exempt from disturbance. For a man, who had little concern about lying and manipulated everything according to the whim of the crowds, rallied them with the command to accompany him to Mount Gerizim, which is regarded by them to be the most sacred mountains. He vigorously insisted that when they arrived he would show them the sacred vessels which were buried there where Moses had deposited them. Since they regarded the story as credible, they armed themselves and established themselves in a certain

> village called Tirathana, taking in others who could be collected since they planned to make the ascent to the mountain as a great multitude. Pilate appeared and blocked their ascent with a detachment of cavalry and armed infantry, who killed those whom they engaged in a battle as they were gathered in the village and took prisoner many of those who fled, of whom Pilate killed the leaders and those who were most influential. (Jos., *Ant.* xviii. 85-87)

Festus, who succeeded Felix, also had to cope with claimants who promised salvation if the people would follow them. These figures hoped to document their claims by signs in the desert.

> Festus also sent a force of cavalry and infantry against those who had been misled by a certain fraud who promised salvation and rest from troubles, if they would follow him into the desert. Those who were sent killed both the deceiver himself and the followers. (Jos., *Ant.* xx. 188; *cf.* Tiede, 201)

Such revolutionary activity did not cease with the fall of Jerusalem; neither was it limited to Palestine. Josephus reports about Jonathan of Cyrene (c. 73 A.D.), a wilderness miracle-worker from North Africa.

> The madness of the Sicarii even touched the cities around Cyrene like a disease. Jonathan, a most evil man and a weaver by trade who had taken refuge there, convinced many of those without resources to listen to him and he led them into the desert, promising to show them signs and apparitions. His knavish activity was not noticed by others, but the Jews who were in high positions in Cyrene reported his exodus and preparations to Catullus, the governor of the Libyan Pentapolis. He sent his cavalry and infantry which quickly overcame the unarmed, most of whom were killed in the encounter, and some of whom were taken prisoner and brought to Catullus. At that time, Jonathan the leader of the plot escaped, but was caught after a long and weary meticulous search of the country. (Jos., *B.J.* vii. 437-41; Tiede, 201-02)

In observing these figures mentioned by Josephus, several points seem clear. Josephus links miracle workers (mostly imposters) with Messianic movements to secure Israel's freedom. "It would accordingly appear," S. G. F. Brandon notes, "that Zealotism was closely linked with Messianic expectation, and that the accepted evidence of Messianic leadership was the ability to work miracles or the claim to be able to work them at some crucial moment" (Brandon, 112-13; *cf.* also 100, 108-09).

Thus, the connection between revolutionary activity and miracles as authentication of claims to leadership is apparent. The people followed these claimants into the desert usually under the assumption that signs and wonders would authenticate their claims that God would aid in deliverance. The motif of the wilderness also stands out as a significant feature of these revolutionary activities; references to the wilderness probably have symbolic associations with the first wilderness generation (Moses, Joshua, etc.) where the nation gathered for the conquest of the land. Thus, Messianic figures attempted to demonstrate, by working signs and wonders in the desert, that God was with them in their attempt to conquer the enemies of Israel.

The Prophet Figure

Another type of Messianic expectation was that of the prophet figure, based on the belief that one of the great prophets of the Old Testament would return. These were eschatological prophets. The most popular were Elijah and Moses, although any of the prophets could fill this role.

Elijah is generally viewed as an eschatological prophet. In both the Old Testament and Intertestamental periods the belief existed that a prophet would return at the endtime. This general expectation of a returning prophet took several forms. Some expected a prophet to appear at the endtime, one who would fulfill all earlier prophecy. The idea also existed that since all prophets proclaimed basically the same truth, the same prophet had been successfully incarnated in different prophets, and would appear again at the endtime. This idea is found in the Pseudo-Clementine writings and in the Gospel of the Hebrews. Pseudo-Clement writes that the "true prophet" has appeared repeatedly in different forms and names since Adam, and in the endtime will come as Son of Man.

That the expectation of a returning prophet was widespread is attested to by religious groups outside of Judaism, such as the Samaritans and the Qumran sect. The Samaritans, on the basis of Deuteronomy 18:15ff., expect *Ta'eb* whom they identify as Moses *redivisus*: he works miracles, restores the law and true worship, and brings knowledge to other nations. The concept of a returning prophet was important for the Jewish sect, which is known through the *Damascus Document* (discovered in Cairo in 1896) as the "Community of the New Covenant." In the *Manual of Discipline* a prophet as well as two messiahs are expected. The precedent for this expectation is found in Deuteronomy 18:18 where a prophet like Moses is promised; apparently the sectarians still expected him, accompanied by an anointed priest and an anointed king. This is the clearest reference to the expected prophet by the Qumran literature. The *Commentary of Habakkuk* also gives valuable information about the founder of this sect – the Teacher of Righteousness. This title is one of honor and was bestowed on Elijah in later Jewish literature. Philo also believed in the coming of a prophet on the basis of Deuteronomy 18. He saw the function of this prophet as bearing salvation and beginning the new era. According to Gaster (*Samaritan Esch.*, 247), the Sadducees expected a liberator or prophet from the house of Levi. Josephus speaks of a leader of the people, a prophet who will bring salvation. Thus, there existed the expectation of the return of prophecy in the form of a prophet who would arise to bring salvation and to announce the new era, the Kingdom of God. There were several variations of this hope as far as who the prophet(s) would be. The most popular opinions were Moses, Elijah, Enoch, or one of the more famous ancient prophets.

The belief that Elijah would return to earth in the endtime has its origin in the biblical text (II Kings 2:11) which relates how Elijah did not die but ascended to heaven in a chariot. This unique honor not only caused him to appear superior in the minds of the Jews, but the fact that he was still alive would make a return to earth possible. The vividness of the historical account caught the popular imagination: Who was more fitting to announce the Kingdom of God than the great miracle-worker and anointed of prophets and kings – Elijah? Another reason for the prominence of the belief in Elijah's return was the passage in Malachi 4:5, 6:

> Behold, I will send you Elijah the prophet before the coming of the great and dreadful day of the Lord.
>
> And he shall turn the heart of the fathers to the children, and the heart of the children to their fathers, lest I come and smite the earth with a curse.

This prediction of the return of an individual is unique in the Old Testament. In order to find a parallel one must go to II Esdras 2:18: "For thy help I will send my servants Isaiah and Jeremiah."

The Elijah tradition developed by various interpretations and legends, most of which originated from the interpretation of the Malachi passage.

The interpretation based on the Massoretic text in Malachi 4:5,6 is simply that "To turn the heart of the fathers to the children" refers to repentance: Elijah will bring about reconciliation between families. Throughout the development of the tradition this continued to be considered one of the main reasons for Elijah's return (Scott, 490; Temple, 3; Teeple, 4).

The first step of development appears in the LXX: "The heart of the children to their fathers" has become "the heart of a man to his neighbor," the plural of "father" has been replaced by the singular, and most important, the translation has changed from "repent" to "restore." Thus, Elijah is now expected to bring restoration as well as repentance (*cf.* Sirach 48:10; Ecclus. 18:10).

Ben-Sirach marks the next step of development. In the section 48:1-12 (on Elijah), verse 10 reads as follows: "Who art ready for the time as it is written, to still wrath before the fierce anger of God, to turn the heart of the fathers unto the children, and to restore the tribes of Israel." Here, the idea of restoration is firmly established.

The third step in the development of the Elijah traditions revealed in the rabbinic writings where "Elijah redivisus" has become connected with the idea of the resurrection of the dead. This translation was probably due to the account of the raising of the widow's son by Elijah at Zarephath, as well as the record of his own translation. Scott points out the difficulty involved in attempting to date with any amount of certainty the Talmudic materials. He notes, however, that "The New Testament period with which we are concerned, fortunately, comes at the beginning of the growth of the Talmud, so that if the material can be arranged in sequence, that which seems to be primary will approximate to the thought of the first century" (Scott, 492-93).

Primary material of this tradition includes the Mishna, some Talmudic an some Midrashic material. Scott calls the Mishna "practically contemporary (with the New Testament) material" (Scott, 493; *cf.* also Christie, *JTS* [July 1925]; Thackery, 25-27).

"The Mishnah is the Oral Law of the rabbinic schools as it had become stereotyped about the end of the second century A.D." (Scott, 493). It was descended from the first century Mishnahs through the collection of Rabbi Akiba (c. A.D. 120) to Patriarch Rabbi Judah ha-Nasi. Thus, it is almost contemporary with the Gospels. Tractate 'Eduyot 8:7, an exposition of Malachi 4:5, 6 says,

> R. Joshua says, 'I have it by tradition from R. Johanan ben Zakkai, as he from Hillel, as he from his teacher, as a Halokka of Moses at Sinai, that Elijah will come not to declare (families) clean or unclean, to remove or to bring near, except to remove those who were brought near by force, and to bring near those who were removed by force.' R. Judah says, 'To bring near only, not to remove.' R. Simeon says, 'To settle disputes,' but the Wise say, 'Not to remove and not to bring near, but to make peace forever, as it is said...(quoting Mal. 4:5, 6).'

Thus Elijah's activity includes: the decision of questions about Israelite descent; settlement of religious controversies; and establishment of peace. These are all derived from the Malachi passage about turning the fathers' heart to the children. Also in the tractates Baba Metsia 1.8; 2.8; c:4, 5; Shekalim 2.5 (and Yebamot 102a), Elijah is expected to establish the pure doctrine and to settle disputes over the Law (also see I Macc. 2:58); personal disputes are left undecided "until Elijah comes" (Baba Metsia 1.8; 2:8, etc.). For example, someone found a document under his papers and, not knowing what significance it had, he left it alone "until Elijah comes."

These materials further define the functions of Elijah. He is to raise the dead.

> Sota ix. 15 (an addition which appears in some editions of the Mishnah and Talmud): "The Holy Spirit leads to the resurrection of the dead, and the resurrection of the dead comes by the prophet Elijah."
>
> Yalkut Shim'oni on Psalm 60:9: "If a heretic denies the resurrection, take the prophet Elijah as witness."
>
> j. Shabbat i.3 (Jitomir ed., tractate "Shabbat," p. 9 bot.): "Party leads to the resurrection of the dead, and the resurrection of the dead leads to Elijah."
>
> j. Shekalim iii. 3 (Jitomir ed., tractate "Shekalim," p. 25): "The resurrection of the dead leads to Elijah as it is said, 'Behold I will you Elijah the prophet before the great and terrible day of the Lord come.'"

He is to purify the Israelite descent.

> Midrash Shir ha-Shirim Rabba 27:3: "Elijah will come to pronounce clean and unclean."

> Kiddushin 72b. The Amora Judah in the name of the Amora Samuel speaks of Elijah as purifying Israel from illegitimate admixture.

And he is to settle religious controversies.

> Menachot 45a. R. Johanan and R. Judah (pupil of Akiba) says: "This section (i.e., of Scripture) Elijah will interpret one day."
>
> Pesachim 13a (ch. j. Pesachim iii.6). In a dispute about doubtful meat, R. Eliezer ben Judah says: "Perhaps Elijah will come and declare it clean."
>
> j. Yebamot xii. 1: "If Elijah should come and say what is permitted, he would be listened to."

Other Talmudic and Midrashic material, according to Scott, cannot with absolute certainty be dated back to New Testament times, but "beneath the accretion of legend, may be traced the old times which connected the return of the Tishbite with repentance and reconciliation, restoration and resurrection" (Scott, 497). Examples refer to Elijah as helping someone in trouble or distress, appearing as witness in someone's defense, disclosing celestial mysteries, instructing about Scripture passages, etc.

Also included in these materials are legends and tales of wonder which have embellished the Messianic hope after the period of the Tannaim. Some of these deal with the time and manner of Elijah's coming. Another group of these stories includes tasks which will be performed by Elijah in the Messianic age. In Shir ha-Shirim Zuta 38, Elijah will appear with the Messiah and will be asked by the Jews to raise their loved ones from the dead. Mekilta, tractate Wajissa 5 (Midrash on Exodus 16:33) says that Elijah will bring back three things – a cup of manna, a cup of the lustration water, and a cup of the anointing oil. Deborim Rabbah 3 refers to the coming of Elijah "to console you." Similar to this is the theory of Ruth Rabbah 2:14 and Kohelet Rabbah 11:2 that Elijah acts as an intercessor in heaven for the people.

In apocalyptic circles Elijah is mentioned as the forerunner of the Messiah (I Enoch 90:31; IV Ezra 6:26: also Justin's *Dialogue with Trypho*, c. 8:49). The *Apocalypse of Elijah* also predicts the return of Elijah and Enoch. Their function is to announce the beginning of God's reign. In some sources, Elijah is considered to be the forerunner of God himself, to prepare the way for the reign of God.

In Hellenistic Judaism, Elijah is also considered a miracle-worker, an intercessor for the elect, a healer of the sick, and a helper for those in trouble (Dieter, 148, 216; Jeremias, *TDNT* 2, 930; Weeden, 58).

From this brief survey, four aspects of Elijah's expected activity emerge: repentance, reconciliation, restoration, resurrection. These activities are to prepare Israel for the imminent coming of the Kingdom of God. In all of these traditions – Old Testament, Qumran, and apocalyptic circles – the prophet is seen against an eschatological background as the servant of redemptive history and eschatological expectation: The prophet is expected to announce and to prepare for the imminent coming of the Kingdom of God.

Moses was another of the ancient prophets whom the Jews expected to arise again at the endtime. This belief, although not so prevalent as that in the return of Elijah, arose through the general opinion that Mosaic times would return to Israel. Moses is known as the great prophet of Israel, the Savior of Egypt, the prophet mediator, the author of the Torah. His miracles were seen in connection with God's redemptive plan for Israel.

Later Judaism held Moses in high regard: The more the authority of the Torah increased, the more the respect for its author arose. The *Assumption of Moses* (A.D. 7-30) considers Moses as its central figure: He is the man of the world, his tomb is the whole world (11:8), he is a great angel, the universal Lord of word, the godly prophet of the world, the accomplished scholar of time, the intercessor for the people. According to II Baruch 59:3ff. (A.D. 50-100) the secret things of the heavenly realm will be revealed to Moses; in the *Life of Moses*, Moses is declared to be the partner of God; all the elements belong to him; as the friend of God he has joint possession of God's power. Philo (*Sacrifice of Abel*, 8f.; *Life of Moses* I, 158), *The Pesikta* k. 32 (200b) and *Testament of Levi* 8 (109-107 B.C.) speaks highly of Moses. The Samaritans also respect him: He is the prophet of god, prophet of the whole world, perfect priest, the first king (Deut. 33:5), intercessor for those in need. The task of the returning Moses was to establish the new age in a national sense. Moses was also to be a witness of the nations of the world, to serve the shekinah (Zohar), and to be companion of the Messiah. Thus, Moses appears in an eschatological setting as the servant of God.

In Exodus 4:16; 7:1 Moses is assigned a role as "God" before Pharoah and Aaron–the presence of the divine is verified by miraculous acts. In Deuteronomy, after Moses' death is recounted, the qualifications of prophet are mentioned: knowing God face to face, signs and wonders, mighty powers and great and terrible deeds.

In Josephus, the figure of Moses is varied according to the audience which Josephus is addressing: Moses appears as sage, lawgiver, miracle-worker, prophet and military genius (Jos., *Ant.* iii. 180). In the *Contra Apionem*, Josephus' apologetic interests are quite clear: He presents Moses as the virtuous Lawgiver of the Jews, who excels the Greek heroes. Nowhere in this work does Josephus refer to Moses as miracle-worker. The image of Moses in Josephus' *Antiquities* is more varied. "Josephus' frequent use of a rationalistic disclaimer in his conclusion of miracle stories," according to David Tiede, "must also be regarded as an apologetic nod to the cultured tastes of his audience" (Tiede, 215). This does not mean that Josephus doubted the reliability of miraculous accounts.

Josephus, however, subordinates Moses to God in miracle-working. "While Josephus does not recount the miracles as Moses' miracles," Tiede explains, "he does treat Moses as the lawgiver of the Jews who possesses and displays ἀρετή and he documents Moses' unique status before God in his roles as lawgiver, prophet, and general by pointing to his ἀρετή " (Tiede, 230; *cf.* also 227f.)

There were traditions, however, which presented Moses almost totally as a miracle-worker. Moses is treated by Greek and Roman literary authors as the Lawgiver of the Jews but John Gager has recently discovered that:

> On the whole, however, the Moses of the magical documents is a figure unto himself. Here he emerges as an inspired prophet, endowed with divine wisdom and power, whose very name guaranteed the efficacy of magical charms and provided protection against the hostile forces of the cosmos. (Gager, 312)

Also, in such a tradition as Artapanus represents, Moses is presented as "...the leader of an oppressed people who controls the animal cults, strikes terror in the heart of the king, commands the great goddess, Isis, and surpasses the accomplishments of the heroes of romantic Egyptian legends at every turn" (Tiede, 177).

Thus, the nature of miracles as authentication of a prophet's status is viewed differently by different traditions. In literary circles, such as Josephus and Philo represent, Moses is presented as sage, lawgiver, possessor of virtue. In other spheres, miracles play a greater role and Moses is presented as the great miracle-worker, prophet and magician. The writers emphasized the elements which would be most appealing to their audiences. In whatever context Moses appears, it is noteworthy that he appears in the connection with the Exodus, the redemption of Israel. Even in the magical traditions, his magic is performed in order to redeem Israel. Thus, even when Moses appears as a magician, the Exodus can be perceived in the background; the miracles are set in an eschatological setting; they have a broader purpose than the exaltation of the performer, rather they are seen in the context of God's redemptive history: The prophet appears as God's agent on earth.

The prophet figure as Messiah can be seen further in Josephus' accounts of the "prophets" in Judea in the first century who organized masses of people while authenticating their claims by promising to work miracles (*cf.* Tiede, 197; Brandon). Of these figures mentioned by Josephus, only two are actually referred to as "prophets," Theudas and the Egyptian.

Theudas arose during the procuratorship of Cuspius Fadus (c. A.D. 44-88).

> While Fadus was procurator, a certain fraud named Theudas persuaded the majority of the masses to gather their possessions and follow him to the Jordan river. He claimed to be prophet and that at his command the river would divide and provide easy passage for them. He misled many by saying these things. But Fadus did not allow them to thrive on such folly. He sent a squadron of cavalry against them which fell on them unexpectedly and killed many and took many prisoners. Having captured Theudas himself, they beheaded him and took the head to Jerusalem. (Jos., *Ant.* xx. 97-98)

The Egyptian arose during the time of Felix (c. A.D. 52 to 55 or 60).

> And a certain Egyptian came to Jerusalem at this time claiming to be a prophet. He advised the masses to accompany him to a mountain called the Mount of Olives, which lies opposite the city at a distance of five furlongs. For he claimed that he wanted to show them from there that the walls of

Jerusalem would fall at his command, promising to provide entrance to the city through them. When Felix was advised of this, he commanded his soldiers to take up their arms, and accompanied by a large cavalry and infantry, he rushed from Jerusalem and fell on those with the Egyptian, slaying four hundred and taking two hundred prisoners. The Egyptian himself was not to be found since he had run from the battle. (Jos., *Ant.* xx. 167-72)

Both of these prophet figures attempted to authenticate their claim of charismatic leadership by miracles, but it is significant to note that their miracles were not merely in order to exalt their own person, rather they were to validate their claims of political redemption. Whether political or spiritual, the prophet's miracles were performed in order to indicate redemption for Israel. Thus the miracles of the prophets had a broader scope than the mere glorification of the miracle-worker; they had redemptive significance.

All these Messianic expectations were in the minds of the people at the time of Jesus. The disciples voiced these influences when Jesus asked: "Who do men say that I am?" (Mark 8:27). The disciples' answers reflected these views – Elijah, or one of the other prophets. Even Peter's confession of Jesus as Messiah may have had political overtones. Jesus modified this expectation by saying that the Messiah must be killed and then rise again (Mark 8:33).

FROM THE COMPOSITION of the orchestra of the first Temple it can be seen that Israel accepted and adapted the same type of arrangement of religious orchestra as was used in Egypt at its cultural height. There is a legend that when Solomon married Pharoah's daughter she brought with her 1,000 varieties of instruments. This seems to have some validity in historical fact, for the instruments used in the first Temple and the orchestra arrangement were similar to those in Egypt.

Instruments used in the first Temple included:

I. *Strings*
   Nebel
   Kinnor

II. *Non-Musical Wind Instruments*
   Shofar
   Chatzotzerah

III. *Musical Wind Instruments*
   'Ugab
   Ḥalil
   'Alamoth

IV. *Percussion*
   Tof
   Meẓiltayim
   Pa'amonim

The instruments used in the Second Temple were perhaps not quite so elaborate, but there is no reason to expect that the order and method of worship through music had drastically changed. Thus, these instruments were probably heard by Jesus and the disciples since they attended the Temple on several occasions, especially at the time of the Feasts. Music was undoubtedly important to Jesus himself, since he led the disciples in a hymn on the way to his betrayal at the Garden of Gethsemane (Mark 14:26).

> *And there will be a son of Mars; his mother*
> *Is Ilia, and his name is Rumulus,*
> *Assarcus' descendant. On his helmet*
> *See, even now, twin plumes; his father's honor*
> *Confers distinction on him for the world. Under his auspices*
> *Rome, that glorious city, Will bound her power by earth, her pride by heaven*
> *....One promise you have heard*
> *Over and over: her is its fulfillment,*
> *The son of a god, Augustus Caesar, founder*
> *Of a new age of gold, in lands where Saturn Ruled long ago; he will extend his empire Beyond the Indies, beyond the normal measure*
> *Of years and constellation, where high Atlas*
> *Turns on his shoulders the star-studded world.*

SO VIRGIL CELEBRATES *Rome and the Augustan Age in* The Aeneid. *Augustus as a title means "majestic," a term that quite accurately describes the reign of the emperor Augustus (27 B.C. - A.D. 14), who also set the scene for the coming of Jesus and the early church.*

Juluis Caesar's assassination had been followed by the political warfare among Antony, Brutus, Cassius and Octavian. Rule of the empire rocked between Mark Antony and Lepidus and Octavian. Augustus, Julius Caesar's grand-nephew, came to rule for twelve years with Antony, then finally ruled on his own for 44 years.

Augustus began to deal with the political chaos in a moderate yet effective way. He returned discipline to the army, began an ambitious building program, reorganized the provinces, expanded borders, stabilized the empire's finances and introduced a moderate administration of justice.

In the early part of his rule, Augustus was horrified at being addressed as "Lord" and later brushed aside the title "Father of his Country" given by the commons. Suetonius describes that episode and Augustus' response:

> In a universal movement to confer on Augustus the title 'Father of his Country,' the first approach was made by the commons, who sent a deputation to him at Antium; when he declined this honour a huge crowd met him outside the Theatre with laurel wreaths, and repeated the request. Finally, the Senate followed suit but, instead of issuing a decree or acclaiming him with shouts, chose Valerius Messala to speak for them all when Augustus entered the House. Messala's words were:

> 'Caesar Augustus, I am instructed to wish you and your family good fortune and divine blessings; which amounts to wishing that our entire City will be fortunate and our country prosperous. The Senate agree with the People of Rome in saluting you as Father of your Country.'

With tears in his eyes, Augustus answered – again I quote his exact words: 'Fathers of the Senate, I have at last achieved my highest ambition. What more can I ask of the immortal gods than that they may permit me to enjoy your approval until my dying day?'

M. C. Tenney describes clearly and succinctly the effect of Ausustus' rule:

> He was, in effect, dictator of Rome, though he seemed to be singularly discreet in his exercise of these tremendous powers. He desired 'to make life secure and tolerable for every class in the empire.' To the limit of his ability he endeavored to do so, for during his reign he visited almost every province and evinced keen interest in the welfare of his subjects. He succeeded in establishing a system that survived the shocks of external attack and the blight of internal decay for more than four centuries after his death – an achievement that has probably been equaled by no other political administrator. (Tenney, Times, 132)

In Judea, the representative of Rome and Augustus was Herod the Great, who attempted to secularize Jewish culture and give it a more Roman and Hellenic cast.

It was into this Roman world that Jesus was born.

PART II
BIRTH, SURVIVAL, IDENTITY

Chapter 1

THE IDENTITY OF THE CHURCH

THE CHURCH WAS not born alone and it did not develop alone. It flourished in a rich, turbulent environment of politics, religion and philosophy, an environment that reflected the great cultures of Judaism, Hellenism and Rome. This environment confronted the church's beliefs, teachings, and values. The result was often severe conflict between "the church" and "the world." The church had to survive within a political government while teaching a kingdom not of this world; had to preserve and develop its doctrine within a polyreligious, often pagan culture while teaching worship of a god not made with hands; and had to confront the rational world while teaching faith in a Saviour who was both human and divine. The church struggled not only against physical annihilation but also against the threat of absorption as just another syncretistic cult.

Of course, the church today is a vast institution reaching throughout the world and into almost every culture. Though it now appears in various physical structures and propounds divergent doctrines, the church as a whole traces its roots back to the first-century life of Jesus. And yet if one searches the Four Gospels, one may be amazed at the absence of Jesus' words concerning the church. Besides the one reference in Matthew 16:18 – "And I say also unto thee, That thou art Peter, and upon this rock I will build my church; and the gates of hell shall not prevail against it" – Jesus never referred to any kind of plan for the formation of such an institution as the church; He never discussed with the disciples a constitution or structure.

Could the church, then, have been a creation of the disciples after Pentecost? If so, they apparently did not adopt the idea from an existing movement within Judaism, Hellenism or the Roman religions. For though some have related the church to Socrates and his school, or to the Essenes' Teacher of Righteousness and his followers, or even John the Baptist and his converts, the general conclusion seems to be that Jesus and his church is without analogy.

If we define the term "church" ἐκκλησία as "called out ones," we can suggest that the church actually did begin with Jesus' calling of the twelve disciples. He taught them principles of conduct (e.g., in Mat. 5-7), gave authority to heal the sick and cast out demons (Matt. 10:1ff, and finally declared the great commission, "Go therefore and make disciples of all the nations, baptizing them in the name of the Father, and the Son and the Holy Spirit, teaching them to observe all that I commanded you; and lo I am with you always, even to the end of the age" (Matt. 28:19, 20).

These were the elements that Jesus gave to the disciples. The organizational structure was begun by Peter and developed by Paul in order to meet physical and social needs of the people.

The church, then, was created as a vehicle to promote a belief. To Jesus the important factors of its continued existence were apparently not inherent in a particular type of organizational structure, but in the faith and teachings which He imparted to His followers and in their commitment to spreading that faith to others. Therefore, the final words of Jesus to Peter in His post-resurrection appearance at Galilee were addressed to Peter's own love of Jesus and his subsequent commitment to "feeding the sheep." Jesus did not tell Peter exactly *how* he was to carry this out.

It appears that on the Day of Pentecost the disciples did not consciously "begin the church" but merely witnessed to the faith which they had received from Jesus. As many listened and were converted, the need arose for some way to promote the continued existence of the movement through such activities as instruction, fellowship and prayer. Thus the church began.

The disciples did not conceive of themselves as founders of a new religion, but as members of the Jewish faith, to whom had been revealed the final step in God's plan of salvation for Israel and then the world. They continued the observance of temple ordinances and followed many Jewish practices. It was not until much later that the church was given the name "Christians" (Acts 11:26) and a separation process began – a process which took some years to complete.

The church was based on faith in Jesus Christ, His death and resurrection. Anyone who came to such a belief became a member. Therefore, the charge of Jesus, "Go ye therefore into all the world and preach the Gospel..." (Mark 16:15), was also the goal of the apostles. The church was merely a visible means of carrying out and promoting an invisible faith.

Constituency

The church was made up of different groups of people. On the Day of Pentecost, 120 disciples gathered together, primarily Jews, all of whom had been associated with Jesus during His ministry and were committed to His cause. This number included the eleven disciples, Jesus' mother and brothers, and other men and women who were united in prayer (Acts 1:13-14) in anticipation of the promise of power that Jesus had told them was coming (Luke 24:49).

To these were added more than 3,000 people soon after the event of Pentecost (Acts 2:41). These were Hellenist Jews and proselytes from all over the Roman Empire who represented various cultures and languages but who were united in the bond of Jewish belief. It is likely that these people later helped to form the link between the Jewish church and the Gentile world. The church grew steadily in Jerusalem, soon increasing to 5,000 (Acts 4:4), including men and women (5:14) and even Jewish priests (6:7).

Then, because of persecution that sprang up, the church evangelized beyond Jerusalem, converting Samaritans (Acts 8:5), Ethiopians (Acts 8:27ff.), Jews as far as Phoenicia, Cyprus and Antioch (Acts 11:19), and finally large numbers of the Gentile world broadly. The outreach to the Gentiles was a slow, painful process begun by Peter's witness to Cornelius (Acts 10, 11), continued by men of Cyprus and Cyrene to the Greeks at

Antioch (Acts 11:20) and finally expanded to Asia, Greece and Rome by Paul.

Thus, though the church began with a few men and women united by a common cause and belief, it soon spread to thousands, reaching people of all races. The reasons for this growth were several: a constant preaching by the disciples, the manifestation of miracles, and finally persecution, which helped to drive the evangelists into other geographical areas.

Requirements for entry into this constituency were simple: repentance of sins through faith in Jesus and baptism, which was a visible confession signifying a commitment to the cause of the church (Acts 2:38, Rom. 6:3f.). Those who met these requirements were given the promise of the Holy Spirit.

Organization

The church began more as an organism than an organization, and in the beginning its government was simple and informal. Leadership rested with the original disciples, who assumed responsibility for preaching (Acts 2:14), teaching (2:42), administration of funds (4:35), discipline (5:1-11), business (1:21; 6:2) and laying on of hands for service (Gal. 2:9). They witnessed individually, and as a following developed they met in houses (Acts 2:46).

As the assembly grew, however, a more complex assignment of tasks became necessary. For example, deacons were chosen to supervise the distribution of food, leaving the apostles free to continue their preaching ministry (Acts 6:2, 4). Decisions such as the choosing of these deacons were carried out by a democratic process in which the entire congregation took part.

Later emerged the more formal government represented by James and a council of elders. These participated in theological decisions (Acts 15), supervised the founding of new churches (11:22), and reviewed reports from the traveling ministers (21:18). The Council, which operated out of Jerusalem, became the seat of government for the church.

As the outreach of Gentile territory expanded, Antioch of Syria became another center for the church, second only to Jerusalem. Here there were both prophets and teachers who had authority to teach, preach and to ordain men for the ministry (11:26,27; 13:1-3). Evangelists such as Paul and Barnabas, who conducted missions to Asia and Greece, reported to this center periodically.

As we have seen, the activities of the early church were few but very important: teaching, breaking of bread, fellowship and prayer (Acts 2:42). Instructions were most likely based on Jesus' teachings and included the Old Testament-Jewish Scriptures, which were interpreted in the light of His mission. They included both ethical instruction and doctrinal explanations. Teaching probably took place at the sacramental meal, as in Jewish customs, and in homiletical discourses.

Breaking of bread may have been related to Jewish feasts like the Passover and would therefore have had the character of a worship service. After giving thanks, the leader began the meal by breaking of bread. Then followed a regular meal, teaching, and prayer, ending with the sacramental eating and drinking which Jesus had instituted in the Upper Room.

The fellowship function of the church was a bond of togetherness in which everyone shared words of encouragement, prayer and even material possessions (Acts 2:44, 46). It appears that certain members gave their possessions to the leaders, who then distributed them to the needy. This was done mostly in the Jerusalem church because many had left their homes and means of income. It seems to have been a personal, voluntary act of love in order to meet the needs of the community.

These basic activities were passed on to the new churches as they were established through Asia, Greece and Rome. Because of the many different cultures, however, problems often arose which made it necessary to define the order of services, such as the Lord's Supper and prophecy, and to answer such questions as attire in church, some of which are addressed in I Corinthians. Paul took responsibility for outlining the order of conduct in the church services and soon set up a system of deacons, elders, pastors and overseers who met his prescribed qualifications. These he left in charge of the new churches (I, II Tim., Titus). Nevertheless, he continued to address himself to problems of doctrine and conduct through frequent visits and correspondence.

Therefore, the organization of the church was not pre-planned by Jesus, but grew up to meet the physical and social needs of the people. Responsibility, which at first rested with a few men, soon had to be shared by many to meet the needs of growth and expansion. The basic activities, which at first reflected the Jewish environment, soon had to be carefully defined as they were carried out and adapted to Gentile cultures.

It was this simple church based on faith which faced the divergent Judaic, Hellenistic and Roman worlds.

IN THE YEARS *before he became emperor, Tiberius established an illustrious career, securing the Roman frontiers and becoming in turn quaestor, praetor and consul at a very young age. He fought several successful campaigns in the Alps, Pannonia, Germany and elsewhere.*

Suddenly, at the height of his career, while in excellent health and the prime of life, Tiberius decided to retire from state affairs. Suetonius speculates that perhaps it was his dislike of his wife Julia, or his desire not to bore his countrymen by remaining in sight too long, or his wish to increase his reputation by a prolonged absence from Rome. At any rate, he left Rome for about seven years and returned only after learning that he was in danger. He still believed in a glorious future that had become fixed in his mind from early childhood by presages and prophecies. He ascended to the throne and showed that he was emperor in practice as well as in principle. At first his policy was not always consistent, he nevertheless took considerable pains to further the national interest. At first, too, he intervened in matters of state only when abuses had to be checked; revoking certain orders published by the Senate, and sometimes offering to sit on the tribunal beside the magistrates, or at one end of the curved dais, in an advisory capacity. And if it came to his ears that influence was being used to acquit a criminal in some court or other, he would suddenly appear and address the jury either from the floor or from the tribunal; asking them to remember the sanctity of the Law and their oath to uphold it, and the serious nature of the crime on which their verdict was required. He also undertook to arrest any decline in public morality due to negligence or license (see Suetonius, chapter on Tiberius).

But eventually Tiberius returned to Capri, where he found seclusion from public scrutiny and practiced all kinds of perversions. He began to become suspicious and to take property and wealth from his heirs and other leading provincials on the charge that they were keeping it for revolutionary purposes. He became so cruel that many satires were written against the evils of his rule.

Tiberius was thus embittered and suspicious, living in degeneration and perversion on his island of retreat. As a result, the Roman senate was tense and jittery, and the entire empire began to feel the unrest. Little wonder that the leaders of Palestine were also fearful, even though the provinces generally were well governed.

If Augustus' reign was one of peace and prosperity, Tiberius' was one in which peace and prosperity were taken for granted. This complacency allowed a measure of degeneration to set in. Tiberius did, however, leave behind a strong commonwealth.

It was during Tiberius' reign that the ministries of John the Baptist and Jesus took place. Judea was governed by Herod Antipas, who did not see their ministries as a political threat, even though he later executed John to please his wife.

Jesus referred to Tiberius when the Herodians approached him with the question concerning paying taxes to Caesar. The coin that Jesus asked to see was the one bearing Tiberius' image, and of which He said, "Render to Caesar the things that are Caesar's and to God the things that are God's" (Matt. 22:21).

We further see Tiberius' reign reflected in the tension present in Jesus' trial before Pilate. The unrest and tension caused by Tiberius' suspicious nature help account for Pilate's fear and his ultimate decision to surrender Jesus to the Jewish religious leaders who threw out the taunt, "If you release this Man, you are not a friend of Caesar; Everyone who makes himself out to be a king opposes Caesar" (John 19:21). Since Tiberius removed anyone suspected of the least treasonous action, to be "not a friend of Caesar's" was an extremely dangerous thing.

Soon after Jesus' resurrection, on the day of Pentecost, the church was born. For the duration of Tiberius' reign, it did not come into contact with Rome, but rather grew under the aegis of Judaism.

Chapter 2

PERSECUTION OF THE CHURCH

JESUS CHRIST CAME into a world filled with its share of both intelligence and ignorance, superstition and barbarism. Despite currents of enlightened rationality in learned culture, and of intelligent civilization in everyday pursuits, people were generally ignorant in their knowledge of Divinity; they were often superstitious regarding the movements of nature, and barbarous to those who opposed their superstitions. They loved their gods and feared lest by Christ's influence they would lose them. This fear produced enmity in their hearts and led to efforts on the part of the Romans, for example, to crush Christianity by a series of slow persecutions, by confiscation and pillage, by fire, murder, crucifixion and other atrocities. Some yielded under this pressure and renounced their faith, but others stood faithful and unmoved. Through these persecutions came visions of reward, the triumph of truth and the establishment of the Church, founded on Christ, the Rock of Salvation.

"The hand of God," according to F. Norwood, "purified the Church by affliction and distress; the enemies were but the instruments used by God to establish a permanent religion." Persecutions of the early church came from both Jewish and pagan sources.

While Jesus was on earth He discussed the future several times with the Twelve Disciples, telling them what they would have to endure.

> Behold, I send you out as sheep in the midst of wolves; therefore, be shrewd as serpents and innocent as doves. But beware of men; for they will deliver you up to the courts and

scourge you in their synagogues; and you shall even be brought before governors and kings for my sake, as a testimony to them and to the Gentiles. (NAS)

You will be hated by all on account of My name, but it is the one who has endured to the end who will be saved.

But whenever they persecute you in this city flee into the next....

And do not fear those who kill the body, but are unable to kill the soul;... (Matt. 10:16-18, 22-23, 28)

These and other instructions and warnings by Christ give glimpses of the disciples' future persecutions: trials in courts, scourgings in the synagogues, appearances before kings and governors, and finally martyrdom. The warnings showed that the agents of persecution would be both political and religious.

Jesus told His disciples to flee when persecuted (Matt. 10:23), and often they did just that. It may seem strange that Jesus would advocate apparent "cowardice." But as Clement of Alexandria explains, "Given a choice, we ought to avoid persecution lest we become accessories to the crime of evil...'God may test His servants. But He also bids us to take care of ourselves'" (Norwood, 85). Origen says that we are not to expose ourselves to danger rashly or unreasonably or without good grounds.

At first the Christian Church was looked on with favor by the Jewish community because of the piety of the believers and the Divine power among them. But from time to time difficulties arose with the authorities that resulted in the arrest of Church leaders. The grounds of arrest were usually revolutionary and seditious utterance.

Chapters three and four of Acts illustrate these difficulties. As Peter and John were going up to the Temple to pray, they happened to pass a lame man who was begging. Peter healed him. A large crowd gathered immediately and Peter, taking the opportunity, preached the gospel to the people. The commotion aroused the suspicion of Saducean priests who performed the services in the Temple and preserved order there. They imprisoned the apostles because it was too late in the day to take judicial action.

Henry Milman says that the Sanhedrin had stood aloof until they were assailed in the heart of their own territory – by the healing of the lame man—when they found it necessary to interfere. It is noteworthy that even then the Pharisees, the religious leaders, were not the ones to take offense; it was the Sadducees, the most political of the Jewish factions. Thus, the apostles were arrested for disturbing the peace, not necessarily for teaching another religion or being enemies of the Law. The Sadducees may have feared that any type of rioting might lead to trouble with their Roman patrons.

The Sadducees may also have felt that the great enthusiasm of the people would result in a shrinkage in the funds available for the ritual and sacrifice of the Temple.

Peter and John were brought before the court the next day. The question put to them concerned the power or name by which they had performed the miracle. Speaking in their own defense, they astonished the Sanhedrin court. They were not educated in the Jewish schools, yet they spoke confidently. One fact could not be denied: the lame man was walking. The trial resulted in their release, with a warning not to speak again in the name of Jesus. They were released so soon because the purpose of their arrest was only to restrict their freedom of speech and stop the tumults and disturbances that their public preaching was causing. After hearing the apostles' report, the Church was filled with joy and praise to God (Acts 4:23-31).

The Sadducees' reprimand was not enough to hinder the apostles' ministry. The Church grew and many were healed and freed from unclean spirits (Acts 5:14-16). The high priest and the Sadducees, who were frantically jealous, again imprisoned them, perhaps charging them with casting out demons in the name of Jesus rather than Jehovah, which in their eyes was on a level with the exorcism of Gentiles. The council decreed that the apostles not preach in the name of Jesus (Acts 4:18). But the angel of the Lord released them during the night and they continued their preaching. This caused great confusion among the religious leaders, who once again arrested Peter and stood him before the council.

Gamaliel, a Pharisee, spoke in his behalf, saying:

And so in the present case, I say to you, stay away from these men and let them alone, for if this plan or action should be of

> men, it will be overthrown; but if it is of God, you will not be able to overthrow them; or else you may even be found fighting against God. (Acts 5:38, 39)

This man was most likely the one who is distinguished in Jewish tradition as president of the Sanhedrin, although the high priest, if present at the council, would have taken the chief place.

Gamaliel's speech has been doubted by some, but there is no reason why he should not have counseled moderation. His attitude did not imply a secret belief in Christianity. It was simply an attitude of a wise, cool-headed man who believed that control would accomplish the desired purpose better than repression. That there was nothing unusual in this is evident in the long period of peace that followed after this incident. Gamaliel was also a freethinking Jewish theologian who could easily have been moved by an impression of the Divine. And the apostles' observance of the Law and Gamaliel's hostile attitude toward the Sadducees may have favorably disposed him toward them, as well.

The council's consent to Gamaliel's advice may have been conditioned by any or all of several factors, including the belief that the "sect" would die anyway, the thought that it would run to wild excess and provoke the Roman government to deal with it, the fact that it contradicted the Sadducees, its human principles, or simply awe, piety or perplexity on the part of the council regarding what the church was doing.

The apostles were released after a flogging. The result of this persecution was numerical increase as well as joy in the church, and a short period of peace. There is no certain date that marks this period except the death of Herod in A.D. 44 (although scholars disagree even on this date). Peace must have existed for at least three or four years, time enough for the infant church community to mature.

This persecution was a fulfillment of Christ's words that they would be delivered up to courts and scourged in the synagogues (Matt. 10:17). But it was only the beginning.

It is evident that Christianity in its early stages was not a threat to the Pharisees, who left the Christians alone because they observed the Law. Meanwhile, the Church was growing and many were being attracted by the miracles. But soon the differences in Christian doctrine and Pharisaism became apparent. This and the rapid growth of the Church brought persecution.

Stephen was one of the first to arouse conflict with the Pharisees. He was prominent among the Christians and was chosen as one of the first seven deacons. He was of Hellenist descent and education, which fitted him for appealing to the foreign Jews, was of good reputation, full of faith, wisdom and the Holy Spirit (Acts 6:3, 5).

He not only administered his secular post, he also performed great wonders and signs among the people (Acts 6:8). But some men from the Synagogue of the Freedmen, which included Hellenist Jews, rose up against him, being zealous for the ancestral law and customs. They incited the elders and scribes, presenting false witnesses who said that Stephen had blasphemed against Moses and God. The accusers had distorted Stephen's words, for if he had actually persisted in speaking against the Holy Place and the Law, he would have incurred the disfavor of his fellow Christians. He was not different enough from his peers to cause a split among the believers.

It is likely that opposition to his message resulted from his emphasis on the spiritual character of the future Messianic Kingdom, which to conservative witnesses would have appeared to neglect its physical and political aspects and threaten the stability of Jewish Law and custom. Stephen's high concept of the spirituality of Christianity thus gave a lower value to the Temple as the exclusive place of worship and a lower appreciation of the Law with its voluminous interpretations.

Stephen's design in the council was to show that not he, but his accusers and the unconverted Jews in general were the real criminals and violators of God's Law. He attempted to clarify the accusations. The topic and arrangement of his discourse were designed to prepare the council's minds for the main subject. He reviewed the history of Israel, showing that God worked with the Israelites in spite of their failings, and ended with the accusation that they were following in their father's footsteps (Acts 7:51-53). He then said, "Behold I see the heavens opened up and the Son of Man standing at the right hand of God" (Acts 7:56).

Stephen's words struck at the Pharisaic party. Consequently, the populace, even those under the Christians' influence, either abandoned

Stephen to his fate or joined in the ruthless vengeance. He was carried out of the city and stoned.

Blasphemy, according to Jewish Law, was punishable by death. As Stephen was formally accused and brought to trial before the Sanhedrin, it is probable that he was formally condemned by that body, and that his death was not the result of a mere riot. Death was the legal punishment for blasphemy, and he evidently was stoned at the behest of his *accusers,* not by the crowd. Because the Romans usually withheld the privilege of execution from their provinces, Arthur McGiffert, (McGiffert, 82-83) suggests that the Sanhedrin may have obtained the sanction of execution from the Romans. Otherwise, they could not have carried out their other persecutions of the Church. The Scripture, on the other hand, seems to imply a mad rush by the crowd due to their anger and frustration at Stephen's words (Acts 7:57, 58).

The date of Stephen's death is disputed among scholars. Michaelis (quoted by Milman) (Milman, 377) has said that these violent measures would scarcely have been ventured under Pilate's administration. Vitellius, on the other hand, who sent Pilate back to Rome in disgrace (A.D. 36), visited Jerusalem in A.D. 37, was received with honors, and seems to have treated the Jewish authorities with respect. On these grounds Michaelis dates this persecution as late as A.D. 37. Yet, although the government of Pilate was not systematically severe, it was capricious, and it may have been his policy at the close of his career to court the ruling authorities to the Jews. Merrill C. Tenney (Tenny, 189-90) says that a date after A.D. 36 is unlikely since it does not leave enough time for Pauls' conversion and early ministry. He suggests that Pilate was probably at Caesarea and knew nothing of the violence, which left no political effects.

Stephen's death brought about three important results. First, it triggered a violent persecution of the new church (Acts 8:1). This was severe and extensive because it involved the Pharisees, who were very powerful with the common people. Saul of Tarsus (Paul) was in hearty agreement with Stephen's execution (8:1) and it is possible that the general persecution was due in part to his influence.

Possibly because of Stephen's accusations, which struck at the vital principles of their religion, or because of alarm at the progress of Christianity, the Pharisaic party seems to have become enemies of the faith.

The persecution marked the first open conflict between Christianity and Judaism. Prior to this time the disciples had been a "sect" of Judaism, but after Stephen's conflict with the Pharisees they were denounced as heretics. Recognition of their existence independent of the Jews had begun. They still observed the Law, but a step had been taken toward ultimate separation of Christians and Jews. Neander described this step as a progressive development of the consciousness of independence and the intrinsic capability of Christianity as a doctrine to all men, all nations.

A third important result of the persecution was the spread of the Gospel beyond Jerusalem. "And on that day a great persecution arose against the Church in Jerusalem; and they were all scattered throughout the regions of Judea and Samaria, except the apostles" (Acts 8:2). The ministry of Philip among the Samaritans and the Ethiopians opened new areas to the gospel (Acts 8:5-40). Peter traveled along the costal plain of Philistia and Sharon to Caesarea, healing Aeneas at Lydda and raising Dorcas from the dead in Joppa. In Caesarea, the Lord began to work among the Gentiles when He sent Peter to the house of Cornelius (Acts 10). Another outreach to the Gentiles was led by men of Cyprus and Cyrene, who founded the church at Syrian Antioch (Acts 11:20). This city was fertile soil for Christ's message because there were many Jews and proselytes there, as well as Hellenists. In a short time the Christians' presence at Damascus was so important that Saul made a special journey to suppress it (Acts 9:1-1). The Church also found its way to Cyprus, Phoenicia and Corinth in the East.

Thus, in many cities, towns and villages inside and outside of Judea, the kind of Christian brotherhood was begun that had existed in Jerusalem, for the flight of the disciples from persecution meant formation of little companies wherever they made their homes.

This persecution illustrates that persecution short of extermination always advances the Church. It proved that the Christian faith was stronger than death, the last resort of human cruelty. To the heathen it was evidence of a determined assurance of immortality, for Christians met torture and death calmly, with strong confidence in their God.

Though the growth of the early church appeared to have been checked in the bud by the violent persecution that began with Stephen's martyrdom, it was only to flourish to a greater extent through the person of Paul, formerly Saul of Tarsus.

Saul was a Pharisee by birth and belief (Acts 23:5, 6; Phil. 3:5) and a freeborn citizen of Rome (Acts 22:25, 28). He had strict religious training and was considered to be "in the law blameless" (Phil. 3:6). He had a good education under the great philosopher Gamaliel (Acts 22:3) and was therefore well acquainted with Greek philosophy and literature. As a native of a foreign city, Tarsus, he would have felt at home in a Hellenistic synagogue, and he may have heard Stephen preach there.

When he first came in contact with Christians is not known; he may have arrived at Jerusalem only shortly before Stephen's execution. This could explain the outbreak of persecution that occurred at that time. We know that he was one of Stephen's chief accusers because Stephen's executioners laid his clothes at Saul's feet. This action suggests that Saul was the principal witness, showing his devotion and zeal for the religion of his fathers by witnessing against Stephen.

Saul did not rest with Stephen's death; he felt called to carry his persecutions beyond Jerusalem in an effort to destroy Christianity. This may have been due partly to his interest in the progress of Judaism in the heathen world. His persecutions at Damascus may well have been just the beginning of a planned wider attack against the Church, which he intended to pursue until his task was completed. His zeal in persecution showed that Stephen's death had made no decisive impression on him. Nevertheless, his mind may have been prepared by it to listen to the call of Jesus.

As Saul set forth for Damascus he was inveterate in prejudice, unshaken in his ardent attachment to Moses' religion, indignant and austere in his sense of duty, and fully authorized to exterminate all renegades from the severest Judaism. But God had other plans. Acts 9 records the conversion of Saul, through which he ceased to be Saul the persecutor and became Paul the persecuted. He eventually stood in the confines of both

Judaism and Christianity, qualified beyond all others to develop a system that would unite Jew and Gentile in one harmonious faith.

The extent and intensity of his persecution of the Christians is evident in Acts 9:31, which tells the effect on the Church of Paul's conversion: "So the church throughout all Judea and Galilee and Samaria *enjoyed peace, being built up....*"

Paul's conversion aroused the hostility of the Jewish community: Their chief "zealot" had been converted to the enemy's cause. They began to plot against him even while he was in Damascus, soon after his conversion, when he was preaching in the synagogues; "...The Jews plotted to do away with him" (Acts 9:23). But he escaped in a basket let down over a wall. They followed him, persecuting him or stirring up proselytes and the rabble against him.

On his first missionary journey, from Antioch of Syria (A.D. 46), Paul met opposition in almost every city to which he ministered. In Pisidian Antioch, because of their jealousy of the crowds he attracted, the Jews contradicted him and blasphemed (Acts 13:45). They then stirred up the prominent men and women, who drove Paul and Barnabas out of the city (Acts 13:50). Again, in Iconium, the Jews who disbelieved embittered the Gentiles against the brethren, provoking an attempt to stone them (Acts 14:2, 5). In Lystra he was favorably received, but Jews from Antioch and Iconium, hearing of it, came down, won the people over and stoned Paul leaving him for dead outside the city (Acts 14:19).

On Paul's second missionary journey (A.D. 51) he was imprisoned in Philippi because he had healed a demon-possessed girl who was the means of a profit for certain men (Acts 16:19-40). As he preached in Thessalonia, once again the Jews became jealous and set the city in an uproar (17:5). These Jews followed him to Berea and agitated the crowds there. In Corinth the Jews brought Paul before the proconsul Gallio with the accusation, "This man persuades men to worship God contrary to the Law" (Acts 18:13). But Gallio dismissed the case.

Most of these episodes were instigated by the Jews out of jealousy, but in Ephesus an uprising occurred among the pagan silversmiths because Paul was preaching against gods made with hands. They incited the crowd into shouting praise to Diana for two hours in opposition to Paul and his company (Acts 19:23-24).

In Jerusalem, Paul was accosted by a mob of Jews and accused of bringing Gentiles into the synagogue, but he was rescued by a company of soldiers (Acts 21:27-32). After his defense before the Jews, he was to be examined by whipping, but was spared by his Roman citizenship (Acts 22:24-29). Then he was sent to Felix the Governor in Casearea, where he was tried for sedition, heresy, "majestas," sacrilege, and profanation of the Temple (Acts 24). After he had been held in prison for two years, Festus, the new governor, offered to send him to Jerusalem to be tried there, but Paul appealed to Caesar in Rome (Acts 25:11). Soon he sailed for Rome and for two years preached and taught the Kingdom of God until his death in the persecution under Nero (A.D. 64) (Acts 28:30, 31).

In his epistles Paul often speaks of the severe persecutions that he suffered. He says that his and his companions' affliction or trouble, including persecution, came in Asia beyond their strength, causing them to despair even of life (II Cor. 1:8).

> We are afflicted in every way, but not crushed; perplexed, but not despairing; persecuted, but not forsaken; struck down, but not destroyed...For we who live are constantly being delivered over to death for Jesus' sake.... (II Cor. 4:8-11)

He relates exactly the number of times he was beaten, lashed, stoned, or put in danger from his countrymen, the Gentiles, the government or false brethren (II Cor. 11:23-33).

During Paul's ministry, which began about A.D. 37, relative peace prevailed among the apostles in Jerusalem. In about A.D. 44, however, there was a brief time for sharp persecution, during which James the son of Zebedee lost his life. Herod Agrippa seized James and Peter in an effort to show his dedication to the Jews and gain favor with the Pharisees (Acts 12:1-3). James was beheaded but Peter escaped martyrdom when he was released from prison by an angel. That this incident of sudden persecution was recorded by the author of Acts denotes that it was unusual and formed a contrast to the general situation during this period. It is probable that preceding Herod's ascendancy and during most of his reign Christians were left in peace, and even after his death they were not persecuted by the

Roman procurators. The sudden persecution by Agrippa indicates the determined rejection of Christianity by both the Jewish state and the Jewish religious leaders, for Acts 12:3 says that the death of James "pleased" the Jews.

In most of the persecutions recorded in Acts, especially those in Asia, the Jewish leaders played a key role. The synagogues were centers of persecution for several reasons. The Jews were numerous in the lands beyond Jerusalem, constituting about seven percent of the population of the Roman empire, enough to create problems for the Church. They were one of the most homogeneous of races. They possessed wealth, culture and an exclusive religion that had attracted proselytes from every land but was now being threatened by Christianity. One of the most important causes of Jewish persecution was the message being preached. The claim of Jesus' resurrection put the Jews in the position of having rejected the purpose of God and having murdered their Messiah. The Sadducees did not believe in bodily resurrection, yet found that many people were accepting the apostle's doctrine.

Furthermore, the signs and miracles of the apostles presented a stumbling block to the Jews because they were performed in the name of Jesus, not Jehovah. This reverence of Jesus, which also appeared in the apostle's preaching, seemed to endanger the monotheistic faith. Moreover, the apostle's ecstatic, dynamic conduct contrasted so sharply with the established religious conduct of the priests. Some of the Jewish persecution arose out of envy, when the Jews saw the multitudes that believed the message of the apostles (Acts 13:45). Perhaps, they were often convinced, yet were unwilling to believe.

Persecution by the Gentiles often involved economics. The demoniac girl of Philippi being cured could no longer bring profit, so her masters stirred up the crowd against Paul (Act 16:19). Again, in Ephesus, the silversmiths began an uprising because too many people were worshiping the true god rather than the idols they were selling (Acts 19:26).

The various persecutions produced several good effects on the first-century Church. They unified the Church in prayer and works: They caused Christians to depend more on God and each other. Christians of the early

Church learned that material things did not matter, that only what was done for Christ had eternal value. The Church began to carry the gospel to the uttermost parts of the earth under a new identity, "Christianity," completely separate from Judaism.

The persecutions began to convince the world that the faith of Christianity was stronger than all the torments of man. They showed the pagan world that Christianity offered much more than idol worship could ever give.

The Church stood firm and strong in persecution because its foundation was laid deep in Calvary. As Christ suffered and died to bring us life, so the early Christians gave their lives to tell others about the Kingdom of God.

CALIGULA, ONE OF *nine children, was the son of Germanicus, son of Tiberius' brother Drusus. His name, meaning "little boots," was given to him as an army joke.*

Caligula, from the beginning, was cruel and brutal. Suetonius says that he loved to watch tortures and executions, and disguised nightly would indulge in feasting and scandalous living. Tiberius encouraged him in his interest in singing and dancing, hoping it would provide a civilizing influence. He often remarked on the ruin of Rome which would undoubtedly result from Caligula: "I am nursing a viper in Rome's bosom. I am educating a Phaethon who will mishandle the fiery sun-chariot and scorch the whole world."

Caligula, however, was popular with the provincials and legions in his reign (A.D. 37-41); he lightened taxes and provided games, celebrations and public works.

Quite early in his career, possibly because of a disease that affected his mind, Caligula became a monster. He assassinated his brother, became the consort of his sister and caused his father-in-law to commit suicide. He took the power away from the senate, murdered anyone for not attending his games, spent money recklessly and became a devotee of the Roman "baths."

He adopted several titles, such as "Son of the Camp," "Father of the Army," "Pious," "Caesar, Greatest and Best of Men." Once when his guests were arguing about who were the most nobly descended, Caligula quoted a line from Homer, "Nay, let there be one master, and one king." He would have accepted the kingship then and there but when his courtiers reminded him that he already outranked any king or tribal chieftain, he insisted on being treated as a god. He went so far as to sever the heads of the famous statues of the Greek gods, as well as Jupiter, and to substitute his own. He furthermore established a shrine to himself as a god with priests and life-sized golden image.

Suetonius writes:

> The following instances will illustrate his bloodthirstiness. Having collected wild animals for one of his shows, he found butcher's meat too expensive and decided to feed them with criminals instead. He paid no attention to the charge-sheets, but simply stood in the middle of a colonnade, glanced at the prisoners lined up before him, and gave the order: 'Kill every man between that bald head and the other one over there!' Someone had sworn to fight in the arena if Gaius [Caligula] recovered

from his illness; Gaius forced him to fulfil this oath, and watched his swordplay closely, not letting him go until he had won the match and begged abjectedly to be released. Another fellow had pledged himself, on the same occasion, to commit suicide; Gaius finding that he was still alive, ordered him to be dressed in wreaths and fillets, and driven through Rome by the imperial slaves – who kept harping on his pledge and finally flung him over the embankment into the river. Many men of decent family were branded at his command, and sent down the mines, or put to work on the roads, or thrown to the wild beasts. Others were confined in narrow cages, where they had to crouch on all fours like animals; or were sawn in half – and not necessarily for major offences, but merely for criticizing his shows, or failing to swear by Gaius.

Gaius made parents attend their sons' executions, and when one father excused himself on the ground of ill-health, provided a litter for him. Having invited another father to dinner just after the son's execution, he overflowed with good fellowship in an attempt to make him laugh and joke. He watched the manager of his gladiatorial and wild-beast shows being flogged with chains for several days running, and had him killed only when the smell of suppurating brains became insupportable. A writer of Atellan farces was burned alive in the amphitheatre, because of a line which had an amusing double-entendre. *One knight, on the point of being thrown to the wild beasts, shouted that he was innocent; Gaius brought him back, removed his tongue, and then ordered the sentence to be carried out.*

Caligula reigned for about four years until he was assassinated at the age of 29. The terror he inspired was so great that everyone was reluctant to believe he was actually dead, suspecting that he himself had devised the story to find out what people really thought of him.

During Caligula's reign, a new procurator ruled in Judea, Pilate having been recalled by Tiberius in A.D. 36. Herod Agrippa I, a friend of Caligula, was placed on the throne in northern Galilee. Caligula eventually gave the procuratorship to Agrippa I, who as a matter of policy supported the Jews. When Caligula decided that he was a god, he provided images of himself for all the provincial temples in order that the people might worship him. Before this could be carried out in Judea, however, Caligula was dead. (For an account of the effect of the decree for the placement of the image in the Jewish temple, see Josephus, Antiquities, *xviii; viii.2.)*

After Stephen's death and Saul's persecution, which had occurred under Tiberius' reign, the Church spread beyond Jerusalem throughout Samaria and north to Antioch. Antioch became the center for Gentile outreach (Acts 11:19-26) and was the place that the disciples were first called "Christians."

Claudius (Tiberius Claudius Drusus), Caligula's uncle, was born at Lyons, on August 1, 10 B.C. It was suspected that he wasn't "all there" or at least that he was dim.

It is probable that Claudius suffered from infantile paralysis, but although he looked physically incapable, he was mentally sound and quite intelligent. He was well versed in political science and Roman history and was a student of religion.

Claudius became Emperor by a bizarre set of circumstances. Suetonius tells us:

> ...Claudius became Emperor, at the age of fifty, by an extraordinary accident. When the assassins of Gaius shut everyone out, pretending that he wished to be alone, Claudius went off with the rest and retired to a room called the Hermaeum; but presently heard about the murder and slipped away in alarm to a near-by balcony, where he hid trembling behind the door curtains. A guardsman, wandering vaguely through the Palace, noticed a pair of feet beneath the curtain, pulled their owner out for identification and recognized him. Claudius dropped on the floor and clasped the soldier's knees, but found himself acclaimed Emperor. The man took him to his fellow-soldiers who were angry, confused, and at a a loss what to do; however, they placed him in a litter and, because his own bearers had run off, took turns carrying him to the Praetorian Camp. Claudius was filled with terror and despair; in his passage through the streets everyone cast him pitying glances as if he were an innocent man being hurried to execution. Once safely inside the rampart of the camp, Claudius spent the night among the sentries, confident now that no immediate danger threatened, but feeling little hope for the future since the Consuls, with the approval of the Senate and the aid of city cohorts, had seized the Forum and Capitol, and were determined to maintain public liberty.
>
> When the tribunes of the people summoned him to visit the House and there advise on the situation, Claudius replied that he was being forcibly detained and could not come. The Senate, however, was dilatory in putting its plans into effect because of the tiresome recriminations of those who held opposing opinions. Meanwhile, crowds surrounded the building and demanded a monarchy, expressly calling for Claudius; so he allowed the Guards to acclaim him Emperor and to swear allegiance. He also promised every man 150 gold pieces, which made him the first of the Caesars to purchase the loyalty of his troops.

This incident has been said to mark the beginning of the Imperial government because the army could now elect or disannul emperors.

Claudius, in his reign (A.D. 41-54), created a more rational bureaucracy, restored power to the Senate, and provided a space of relative calm, productive works and sanity.

The atmosphere during Claudius' reign was generally peaceful for the Church but there were several notable conflicts.

Suetonius explains that "Because the Jews at Rome caused continuous disturbances at the instigation of Chrestus, he [Claudius] expelled them from the City." This is a fascinating reference, because in Greek ί and ε in Chrestus can both be translated as i. In other words, "Chrestus" probably refers to "Christ"; the Christians were "causing a disturbance." This is one of the secular references to the Christians' existence in Rome and therefore one of the earliest known imperial persecutions of the Christians. It indicates that under Claudius the Christians were still under the auspices of Judaism – the distinction had not yet been widely made. This problem could possibly have accounted for the increasingly hostile attitude of the Jews toward the Christians – the Jews were beginning to suffer because of the Christians.

Another episode is interesting. The "Nazareth Decree" was published under Claudius. It basically states that digging up graves is prohibited.

> *Ordinance of Caesar. It is my pleasure that graves and tombs remain undisturbed in perpetuity for those who have them for the cult of their ancestors or children or members of their house. If however any man lay information that another has either demolished them, or has in any other way extracted the buried, or has maliciously transferred them to other places in order to wrong them, or has displaced the sealing or other stones, against such a one I order that a trial be instituted, as in respect of the gods, so in regard to the cult of mortals. For it shall be much more obligatory to honour the buried. Let it be absolutely forbidden for any one to disturb them. In case of contravention I desire that the offended be sentenced to capital punishment on charge of violation of sepulture. (Quoted by Tenney, Times, 222)*

This indicates the widespread effect of the belief in the resurrection, which was prompting some people to disturb and inspect tombs and gravesites.

At this time, Agrippa I was still ruling in Judea. The Church had begun to grow and had come into conflict with the Jewish religious leaders. James had recently been killed and Peter had been imprisoned by Agrippa and released by an angel (Acts 5). The Church had begun to expand to Asia Minor and Greece with Paul's ministry to the Gentiles.

Claudius' rule provided a peaceful atmosphere for this expansion. Although Jews had been expelled from Rome and there was a local persecution in Jerusalem, the Church was generally free to expand into the Gentile regions of the Empire—Asia Minor, Corinth and Macedonia. During this time Paul conducted two of his three missionary journeys. The Church also officially broke with Judaism and felt the need to clarify the issues of the relation between Judaism and Christianity as seen in Galatians and Romans.

Nero was born on December 15, A.D. 37, nine months after Tiberius' death. Several signs of ill luck occurred at his birth, one of which was a comment made by his father, according to Suetonius, that "any child born to himself and Agrippina was bound to have a detestable nature and become a public danger."

During the first five years of his reign (A.D. 54-68), Nero was influenced greatly by Seneca, his tutor, and by Burrus, the head of the Praetorian Guard, both of whom were Stoics. The advice of both to Nero was based on the principles of equality, justice and humaneness.

Nero's follies began, however, at an early age, but were not obvious because of this good counsel. Because music had always been important to him, he established contests in which he himself would take part, of course winning the prize. He even went so far as to bar the gates during his recitals so that no one, for any reason, could leave. His cruel and insolent practices went beyond music, however.

> It might have been possible to excuse his insolent, lustful, extravagant, greedy, or cruel early practices (which were furtive and increased only gradually), by saying that boys will be boys; yet at the same time, this was clearly the true Nero, not merely Nero in his adolescence. As soon as night fell he would snatch a cap or a wig and make a round of the taverns, or prowl the streets in search of mischief—and not always innocent mischief either, because one of his games was to attack men on their way home from dinner, stab them if they offered resistance, and then drop their bodies down the sewers. He would also break into shops and rob them, afterwards opening a market at the Palace with the stolen goods, dividing them up into lots, auctioning them himself, and squandering the proceeds. During these escapades he often

> risked being blinded or killed—once he was beaten almost to death by a senator whose wife he had molested, which taught him never to go out after dark unless an escort of colonels was following him at an unobserved distance. He would even secretly visit the Theatre by day, in a sedan chair, and watch the quarrels among the pantomime actors, cheering them on from the top of the proscenium; then, when they came to blows and fought it out with stones and broken benches, he joined in by throwing things on the heads of the crowd. On one occasion he fractured a praetor's skull. (Suetonius, 227)

He held feasts which lasted from noon to midnight with various kinds of entertainments. He practiced every kind of perversion, inventing novel sexual games for excitement, according to both Suetonius and Tacitus.

About the eight year of his reign, his influence for good died. Burrus' death was possibly from natural causes but some said Nero poisoned him, and Seneca was banished from the palace. Eventually, however, an informer implicated Seneca in a treasonous plot, so Nero demanded his death by suicide. Without these two restraining influences Nero was free to vent the full extent of his cruelty and treachery.

His murderous career had actually begun with the slaying of the benign Claudius. If Nero did not personally murder him he knew all about the plot. He repeatedly tried to poison his cousin Britannicus and eventually succeeded. He attempted on several occasions to murder his mother Agrippina.

Nero's mercy also came to an end. Once in conversation a line attributed to him – "When I am dead, may fire consume the earth" was quoted to him. He said the line should read "While I yet live" (Suetonius, 235). Soon Rome was set afire—whether by Nero or by others is uncertain. Tacitus calls it

> ...the most terrible and destructive fire which Rome has ever experienced. It began in the circus, where it adjoins the Palatine and Caelin hills. Breaking out in shops selling inflammable goods, and fanned by the wind, the conflagration instantly grew and swept the whole length of the circus. There were no walled mansions or temples, or any other obstructions, which could arrest it. First, the fire swept violently over the level spaces. Then it climbed the hills—but returned to ravage the lower ground again. It outstripped every counter-measure. The ancient city's narrow winding streets and irregular blocks encouraged its progress.

Suetonius and Tacitus both report that people were seen throwing torches to encourage the flames and shouting that they had acted under orders. It is not true that Nero fiddled while Rome burned, though he reportedly did watch the fire from the Tower of Maecenas, put on his tragedian's costume and sang "The Fall of Ilium" from beginning to end. Nero erected his infamous Golden House on the burned-over ground. He eventually blamed the Christians for setting the fire.

The armies finally revolted against Nero. He committed suicide at the age of 32 when he realized there was no hope of escaping his fate.

Nero's attitude toward the Church, like his reign, can be divided into two contrasting parts. During the first part of Nero's reign, Paul encountered opposition by the Jewish religious leaders in Jerusalem and subsequently was sent to Caesarea to wait trial. There he appeared first before Felix and then Festus and finally King Agrippa II. Fearing release, which would put him again into the hands of the Jewish leaders, Paul appealed to Caesar (Nero). Once in Rome he was put under "house arrest" where he was able to preach and teach, although he was confined to his quarters. During this imprisonment Paul probably wrote Ephesians, Colossians, Phillippians and Philemon. After pleading his cause before Nero, he was released and returned to continue his ministry in Asia Minor. This indicates that Nero was not concerned with the Church or her leaders, and even on hearing a specific case, did not see it as a threat to Roman government.

At the same time, the Jews in Jerusalem rose up against James, the Lord's brother, who was head of the Church. They demanded that he renounce his faith; since he would not they threw him from a wing of the temple, then beat him to death with a club. In the account of the martyrdom given by Josephus, it is clear that when more moderate citizens complained to the Roman provincial authorities, the procurator Albinus influenced King Agrippa to replace the high priest responsible for the execution. Therefore, the persecution of the Church was still being led by the Jewish authorities rather than the Romans.

In the eighth year of Nero's reign, however, Roman policy toward the Christians changed. When Nero could not escape the accusations of setting Rome on fire, he blamed the Christians. Sulpicius Severus describes the situation:

> In the meantime, the number of the Christians being now very large, it happened that Rome was destroyed by fire, while Nero was stationed at Antium. But the opinion of all cast the odium of causing the fire upon the emperor, and he was believed in this

way to have sought for the glory of building a new city. And in fact Nero could not, by any means he tried, escape from the charge that the fire had been caused by his orders. He therefore turned the accusation against the Christians, and most cruel tortures were accordingly inflicted upon the innocent. Nay, even new kinds of deaths were invented so that, being covered in the skins of wild beasts, they perished by being devoured by dogs, while many were crucified or slain by fire, and not a few were set apart for this purpose, that, when the day came to a close, they should be consumed to serve for light during the night. In this way, cruelty first began to be manifested against the Christians. Afterwards, too, their religion was prohibited by laws which were enacted; and by edicts openly set forth it was proclaimed unlawful to be a Christian. At that time Paul and Peter were condemned to death, the former being beheaded with a sword, while Peter suffered crucifixion.

Several scripture references reflect the two aspects of Nero's rule. In Romans 13, Paul talks about relations between Christianity and the government. Although Romans cannot be dated with certainty, it most likely falls within the peaceful early years of Nero's reign. On the other hand, II Timothy 4 was most likely written during the latter years of Nero's rule and reflects the time of persecution. I Peter likewise encourages the Church to face the "fiery trials with joy and hope."

Chapter 3

THE JUDAIZERS

THE JUDAIZERS APPEAR to have been Jewish Christians who resisted the modification of legal tradition (Acts 11:2), and demanded that Gentile converts adhere to ceremonial Jewish customs (15:1).[*] They traveled from Jerusalem to the new churches in Gentile territory, preaching against Paul's teachings (Gal. 1:6-9) and demanding that Gentile converts accept the rite of circumcision in order to be saved (Gal. 5:3,12; 7:12,15; Acts 15:1). Paul called them "false brethren." Tenney says:

> In Romans 9:3 Paul applied 'brethren' to the Jewish people, his 'kinsmen according to the flesh.' 'False brethren,' however, implies a contrast with the 'true brethren' who shared his convictions, and who were consequently within the church. (Tenney, 239)

Conzelmann says they were not necessarily "consciously malicious," but that their preaching was in opposition to the act of salvation (Conzelmann, 84). They were probably Pharisees who were converted to Christianity and therefore had a high regard for the Law and its customs.

---

[*] The problem of the Judaizers has long been of scholarly concern. The Tübingen school of F. C. Baur described an extensive Judaizing movement which began in Galatia and was met by Paul later in Corinth and Rome. Hans Lietzmann and Edvard Meyer agreed with this finding in part, but current scholars have seen the opponents in Corinth and Rome as part of a Gnostic Judaism, quite different from the type described in Galatians and the Acts of the Apostles. This chapter will deal primarily with the Judaism represented by the latter books, rather then the problems of Corinth or Rome. We assume that Galatians was written prior to the Jerusalem Council which took place in A.D. 48/49, and reflects the Judaizing controversy that arose in Antioch and led to the Council (Acts 15).

Since the Pharisees believed in the doctrine of the resurrection, they could easily have become Christians without giving up their distinctive beliefs, and would merely have had to accept the belief that Jesus was the Messiah. Bruce says, "Christian Pharisees, then, were the leaders in insisting that Gentile converts should be instructed to submit to circumcision and the general obligation to keep the Mosaic law which that rite carried with it" (Bruce, 305).

The Jew-Gentile tension had been growing for some time (Acts 11:29, 30; Gal. 2:1-10). In fact, it began with Peter's witness to Cornelius (Acts 11:1-3). Tenney states that,

> Perhaps the dispersion of Jerusalem Christians, which began between A.D. 32 and 35 at the death of Stephen and was aggravated by the persecution of Herod in A.D. 44, had left in Jerusalem a majority of the stricter party of Jewish believers, who reacted against the more tolerant attitude of the Hellenistic Jews toward the Gentile brethren.... (Tenney, 246-47)

> The eminent success of the Gentile Church in Antioch and the enthusiastic reception given to Paul and Barnabas by the Gentile communities of Galatia evoked the jealousy of the synagogue adherents and the displeasure of the Jewish believers who had clung to the letter of the Mosaic Law. The resented the fact that Gentiles had received the blessings of the Messiah without submitting to the ceremonial restrictions which the Jews had so carefully observed. (Tenney, 240)

Christianity had not defined its relation to Judaism, and as more and more Gentiles were joining the Church, the situation was approaching a crisis. The issue lay in two dimensions: fellowship of Jews with Gentiles (such as in table-fellowship) and the way of salvation.

The problem of fellowship arose when Peter witnessed to Cornelius (Acts 10, 11). Word spread quickly that Gentiles also had received the gospel; and when Peter came to Jerusalem "those who were circumcised took issue with him, saying, 'You went to uncircumcised men and ate with them'" (Acts 11:3). The issue was not the preaching of the gospel itself, but the fact that Peter broke the Law forbidding Jews to have close association with Gentiles. It appears, however, that after Peter's explanation of the vision and the outpouring of the Holy Spirit, the group "quieted down, and glorified God, saying, 'Well then, God has granted to the Gentiles also the repentance that leads to life'" (Acts 11:18). Therefore, despite the acknowledgment that salvation was to be extended to the Gentiles, the problem of fellowship was not explicitly resolved.

In Antioch, the problem was more demanding. Certain men of Cyprus and Cyrene preached to Greeks, who then believed. Hearing of this, the Jerusalem church sent Barnabas to visit. He apparently found everything in order and so reported (Acts 11:20-24). But there were also Jews in the church (Acts 11:19; Gal. 2:13) who appear to have been allowed to fellowship with Gentiles in daily life and eating (Gal. 2:12,13). Even Peter took part in the table-fellowship (Gal. 2:11,12) until a group sent by James came from Jerusalem. They are described as "the party of the circumcision" (Gal. 2:12). The fact that they disagreed with such "freedom" is evident, for Peter and the other Jews returned to Jewish customs upon their arrival. Paul was very angry and even rebuked Peter for his vacillation. Bruce says:

> Paul saw quite clearly that the concession in the matter of table fellowship was bound in the long run to compromise the basic gospel principle that salvation was the gift of God's grace in Christ, to be received by faith alone. Refusal to have table fellowship with Gentiles would soon be followed by refusal to admit them to church membership or indeed to recognize them as Christians at all. (Bruce, 304)

Paul's rebuke apparently had an effect on Peter because at the Council which occurred soon after, Peter defended Paul's position.

The second point of conflict concerned the way of salvation. This issue also came to a head in Antioch, where certain men from Judea began teaching that circumcision was necessary for salvation (Acts 15:1). The rite of circumcision was essential in Judaism because it symbolized participation in God's Covenant (Gen. 17:9-14). Therefore, many Christian Jews saw it as a necessity for both Jews and Gentiles before salvation could be complete. The implications of this were unacceptable, however, for as Conzelmann says,

> ....the demand for the circumcision of the Gentiles also would mean that the salvation event was not the only condition of salvation, that for the reception of grace a human achievement was to be brought forward. And it would depend on this achievement whether God would fulfil his offer. Christianity would then be a radical Jewish sect. Thus the alternative is posed: salvation through God's act or through the fulfillment

> of certain rules. In this connection it is no longer important whether it is the fulfilling of the whole law or only of its most important parts that is demanded of the Gentiles. (Conzelmann, 83)

The necessity of circumcision for salvation was also preached by the Judaizers in the Galatian churches, for Paul says that "those who desire to make a good showing in the flesh try to compel you to be circumcised" (Gal. 6:12). Perhaps those "false brethren" saw the church as a branch of Judaism. As Coneybeare suggests, "Their great object was to turn the newly-converted Christians into Jewish proselytes, who should differ from other Jews only in the recognition of Jesus as the Messiah" (Coneybeare, 347).

The problem which the church faced was a great one because it involved the future relationship of the church to its Jewish heritage. How it was resolved would affect the nature of its beliefs and rituals. The answer would determine whether Christianity would be abandoned by Judaism or whether two schismatic bodies would be created, as Tenney describes:

> One would be the Judaistic church, differing from Judaism only by acknowledging Jesus of Nazareth to be the true Messiah, and the other would be the free Gentile church that would repudiate all the Judaic heritage and become rootless by discarding all previous revelation. (Tenney, 246)

The solution was too difficult to be made by any one person or church. Therefore, Paul and Barnabas went to Jerusalem to discuss the problem with the apostles and elders (Acts 15:2). In Acts, Luke implies that Paul was sent as a sort of representative from the Gentile community, but Galatians suggests much more. Paul's own personal calling was at stake. As Conzelmann explains,

> For himself, at least, he emphasizes that he received the commission from the Lord himself. It is his concern to avoid giving the Galatians any suggestion that he is dependent upon human agencies. He meets the Jerusalemites as equal with equals, while in the book of Acts he appears as representative of a community that is dependent upon Jerusalem, one who is seeking instruction.
>
> ...For him, not only outward recognition is at stake, but his very 'call' itself: he was called to the Gentiles by means of a revelation. If the Gentiles must come under the Law, his commission is frustrated (Gal. 2:2) – and he will have to give account to the Lord. (Conzelmann, 84)

When the Council convened, the former Pharisees represented one side while Peter, Paul and Barnabas stood for the other. The Pharisees stated the issue: "It is necessary to circumcize them, and to direct them to observe the Law of Moses" (Acts 15:5). It seems that there was general discussion and debate, and finally the witness of those who were involved in the Gentile missionary endeavor.

Peter, recounting the first Gentile conversion, said that God made "no distinction between us and them, cleansing their hearts by faith" (Acts 15:11). He then suggested the logical outcome. As Haenchen explains Acts 15:10, "'οὖν' introduces a deduction: since God has recognized the Gentiles, it would amount to defying him if one were to lay on the neck of the disciples the intolerable yoke of the Law" (Haenchen, 446).

In fact, Peter went on to point out that Jews are "saved through the grace of the Lord Jesus, in the same way as they also are" (Acts 15:11). Then Paul and Barnabas witnessed to the actual work that was being done among the Gentiles, which obviously pointed to God's approval.

Finally, James related the problem to Scripture: work among Gentiles was in fact prophesied (Amos 9:11). "Therefore it is my judgment that we do not trouble those who are turning to God from among the Gentiles: (Acts 15:19).

There were, however, four compromises suggested by the Council which would be helpful to fellowship between Jew and Gentile. These did not concern salvation, but the daily responsibilities that would avoid bringing offense to Jews.

The first requirement forbad the eating of meat sacrificed to idols. This would be offensive to Jews because it suggested fellowship with other gods and the breaking of the first Commandment (Ex. 20:3).

The second requirement was that they abstain from fornication, "a common Gentile sin," Tenney says, "that violated the Jewish standards of chastity and that often accompanied the ecstatic rites of heathen worship" (Tenney, 249).

Abstinence from "things strangled" and "blood," the third and fourth requirement, deferred to Jewish dietary laws. These were ceremonial rather than moral requirements, but observance of them would help to avoid conflict.

These compromises were agreed on by the apostles, elders, and the congregation and then sent out to the churches in letters.

Therefore, as Haenchen points out, "at the protest of the former Pharisees the Apostles and elders immediately take charge of the situation" (Haenchen, 444). Thus, the church as a body disowned a connection with the Judaizers. The verdict meant that there was freedom for all: freedom of salvation through faith for Gentiles, and freedom to keep the Law for Jewish Christians. As Conzelmann explains:

> The Jew is no more obliged to give up his Jewishness than is the Gentile to become a Jew. Of course the keeping of the law has now taken on a new meaning for him: it now is no longer a means of gaining salvation but precisely a sign that salvation is bestowed without condition. (Conzelmann, 85-86)

The controversy led by the Judaizers did not cease immediately. It seems that traces of it appeared in Paul's churches from to time. (See Phil. 3:2, 3: "Beware of those of the circumcision"; also see Acts 21:17.) But as Tenney says,

> ...the main objective of liberty for the Gentiles had been attained so that they were no longer under bondage to the Law and its ceremonies. With the growing separation of synagogue and church, the question became less important and ultimately ceased to be a major issue. (Tenney, 250)

The historic effects of the Council on the Judaizing issue were far-reaching, and of great importance, for as Goppelt says,

> The Apostolic Council...represents a decisive turning point in our picture of the history of primitive Christianity. The ever-widening schism in the Church between Hellenism on one hand and Judaism on the other, which began with the persecution of Stephen, was closed once again through attention being focused on the Church's centre. The men whose word was considered authoritative for each side had now mutually acknowledged the other's respective ministries. Paul and Barnabas continued to stand in the tradition of Jesus' earthly ministry which came from Jerusalem as well as in the confession of the earliest Church. Conversely, Jerusalem acknowledged the Gospel free from the Law as an expression of the one true Gospel. In this manner the two branches of Christianity current at that time were brought together into an ecclesiological fellowship in spite of all the differences in their

> way of life. This fellowship then expressed itself through an active interchange of emissaries, through which they avoided being absorbed by their religious environment. The Apostolic Council, which is probably to be set in the year 48, also stands chronologically as the decisive turning point of the period extending to 64-70. After the persecution of Stephen a part of the Church had emerged from the shell of Judaism which had protectively surrounded her during the initial stages, but now the turn had been taken which in the following twenty years would force the whole Church from the circle of Judaism, with the result that by the time of the Neronic persecution she would appear to the world as a religion separated from Judaism. (Goppelt, 77)

The Judaizing controversy reflects an internal struggle which the Church had to face. Fortunately, through the strong leadership of Paul, the Church became a united body preaching freedom for all. The book of Galatians served as a guide for the Gentile churches, for there Paul outlined the doctrine of salvation by faith rather than by works of the Law.

Paul responds to the problem of the Judaizers in Galatians in two ways—he gives a theological argument and a practical argument.

Paul contrasts the "works of the Law" with the "hearing by faith" (Gal. 3). He uses Abraham as an example of faith because the Judaizers would agree with him in regard to Abraham. Paul states that Abraham believed God and was reckoned as righteous (Gen. 15:6). Abraham lived before the Law was given, so it was not the *Law* but *faith* which was recognized by God as the basis of righteousness. Paul concludes, therefore, that the Sons of Abraham are those who live by faith.

On the other hand, he says that those who are "under the Law" or, in other words, live by the Law are under a curse because they are being led to believe that man can be justified before God by keeping the Law rather than living by faith. The Law itself is not of faith since it must be practiced (Gal. 3:13). Christ redeemed us from the curse of the Law by becoming cursed Himself, crucifixion being a curse since only the worst criminals died in such a manner. Thus, Gentiles also are able to receive the promise through faith.

Since the Law was given 430 years after the promise to Abraham, Paul poses the question—why was the Law given? He answers, "because of transgressions" (Gal. 3:19). Therefore, the Law was not the contrary to God or the purpose of God, but was merely inadequate in that it was unable to impart life. The Law was given merely as a tutor—to lead man to God. But through faith we are no longer pupils but *sons* of God, able to approach God directly through Christ. Paul concludes that in faith there are no distinctions:

> There is neither Jew nor Greek, there is neither slave nor freeman, there is neither male nor female; for you are all one in Christ Jesus. (Gal. 3:38)

We are "all one in Christ Jesus" and thus heirs of the promise to Abraham.

Paul later addresses the practical problem of circumcision. He points out that "if you receive circumcision, Christ will be of no benefit to you" (Gal. 5:2), and that every man who receives circumcision "is under obligation to keep the whole Law" (v. 3). By receiving circumcision one is again attempting to be justified by the Law rather than by faith, and salvation cannot be achieved in this way.

Paul concludes, "For in Christ Jesus, neither circumcision nor uncircumcision means anything, but faith working through love" (Gal. 5:6). "The whole Law is fulfilled in one word, in the statement, you shall love your neighbor as yourself" (Gal. 5:14).

AFTER THE DEATH *of Nero (A.D. 68), the line of the Caesars had become extinct and it was uncertain who would follow. The troops in Spain had taken upon themselves to appoint Galba, who ruled only about six months; the guard then set up Otho, who reigned for 95 days and was followed by Vitellius, who was appointed by the troops in Germany, and who ruled eight to nine months before being assassinated.*

It was not strange, then, that the legions of Moesia would decide to appoint their own emperor, their general, Vespasian. Vespasian was rather bewildered by his new role as emperor, but after consulting the auspices at the Temple of Serapis and being granted several other signs and soothsayers' favorable predictions, he assumed the high office.

Vespasian had risen from humble beginnings. Suetonius describes the first step in his progress, when Vespasian became commander of the forces to subdue the revolt in Judea:

> *An ancient superstition was current in the East, that out of Judea at this time would come the rulers of the world. This prediction, as the event later proved, referred to a Roman Emperor, but the rebellious Jews, who read it as referring to themselves, murdered their Governor, routed the Governor of Syria when he came down to restore order, and captured an Eagle. To crush this uprising the Romans needed a strong army under an energetic commander, who could be trusted not to abuse his considerable powers. The choice fell on Vespasian. He had given signal proof of energy and nothing, it seemed, need be feared from a man of such modest antecedents. Two legions, with eight cavalry squadrons and ten auxiliary cohorts, were therefore dispatched to join the forces already in Judaea; and Vespasian took his elder son, Titus, to serve on his staff. No sooner had they reached Judaea than he impressed the neighbouring provinces by his prompt tightening up of discipline and his audacious conduct in battle after battle. During the assault on one enemy fortress he was wounded on the knee by a stone and caught several arrows on his shield. (Cf. Suetonius, chap. on Vespasian)*

Vespasian found Rome chaotic and bankrupt and the Senate disorganized. He immediately began to set things in order by treating the Senate with respect, by removing the informers who had created an atmosphere of suspicion and tension, and by clearing the law courts of long-standing cases. He restored financial stability, declared regular salaries for teachers, revived entertainments and games.

Vespasian had many good traits. He is said to have never punished an innocent man. He grieved even over convicted criminals who were forced to pay the extreme penalty.

In relation to the Church, we know very little of the time of Vespasian. Peter and Paul were both dead, as were most of the other major apostles except John the Beloved; churches had been founded throughout the main parts of the Empire, e.g., Corinth, Ephesus, Galatia and Phillippi, as well as in Rome itself. The Church had survived persecutions, particularly under Nero. The period under Vespasian (A.D. 69-79) must have been one of rest and growth for the Church.

But a very significant event of this time was the fall of Jerusalem in A.D. 70, and the destruction of the Temple. Jesus had predicted this fall (Mark 13 and Luke 21). Fortunately, the Church was well established in other regions of the Empire and so continued in spite of the violent subjugation of Jerusalem.

Chapter 4

THE GREEK GODS

ZEUS, RULER OF the gods, supreme deity and also the god of the sky and of weather – Hera, wife of Zeus – Apollo, god of the sun and ideal of fair and manly youth – Artemis, moon goddess, huntress – Hermes, swift herald of the gods, always beautiful and forever young – Poseidon, god of the sea and of streams and rivers – Athena, who sprang fully-armed and warlike from Zeus' brain, a goddess of wisdom – Ares, god of war – Hephaestus, god of fire – Aphrodite, goddess of love – goddess of agriculture, Demeter – and Hestia, goddess of the home – these twelve deities so familiar to us in Greek mythology were still much worshiped by the Hellenic people at the time of Christ and during the ministry of the apostles.* Not only these but many lesser divinities as well as the muses, the fates, satyrs, nymphs and other spirits were important in the minds of the people. Nor was this true of the Greeks alone, for as Cicero said of the Romans:

> However good an opinion we may have of ourselves, yet we do not excel the Spaniards in number, the Gauls in strength, the Carthaginians in cunning, the Greeks in arts, nor the Italians and Latins in the inborn sense of home and soil. We do, however, excel all peoples in religiosity and in that unique wisdom that has brought us to the realization that everything is subordinate to the rule and direction of the gods. (*Cf.* Kerenyi, *The Religion of the Greeks & Romans*, 95)

---

*Roman equivalents are Jupiter (Zeus), Juno (Hera), Apollo (same name for the Greeks and Romans), Diana (Artemis), Mercury (Hermes), Neptune (Poseidon), Minerva (Athena), Mars (Ares), Vulcan (Hephaestus), Venus (Aphrodite), Ceres (Demeter), and Vesta (Hestia).

A remarkable aspect of Greek and then Roman religion was its blend of old and new. William Guthrie comments: "Not only was it capable of astonishingly rapid development to some of the highest forms of religious experience; it was also loath to let even the oldest and crudest forms of worship disappear without trace" (W. Guthrie, *The Greeks and Their Gods*, 28).

The gods of the Greeks and Romans grew out of an attempt to understand the phenomena of nature such as storms, sunshine, the seasons, light and darkness. They explained man's emotions, such as love, jealousy and hate as results of the favor, mischief, or treachery of the gods. The world was merely a place for the gods to play. It was necessary, then, for these gods to be placated by sacrifices to keep them from wreaking havoc or mischief on people's lives, animals, and property.

In classical times the twelve gods were conceived as a corporate body. Altars were built to them and the oath "By the Twelve!" can be found in writings of several ancient authors. Although the list varies among authors, "it is clear," Guthrie says, "that the corporate conception of the Twelve retained its significance throughout and beyond the classical period, so that this collective expression called up definite associations in the mind of a Greek" (Guthrie, 112).

The Greek gods were described in detail by Homer, and it is primarily from him that the Greeks drew the portraits of the gods. Hesiod, the earliest important Greek writer, also contributed some of their characteristics. The gods inhabited an entire world consisting of a heavenly realm (Olympus), the earth, the waters and the underworld. Each of these was ruled by gods and inhabited by many lesser divinities.

Martin Nilsson sums up the core of the religion of the Greek gods:

> What interests primitive man is not nature in itself but nature so far as it intervenes in human life and forms a necessary and obvious basis for it. In the foreground are the needs of man together with nature as a means of satisfying those needs, for upon the generosity of nature depends whether men shall starve or live in abundance. Therefore, in a scantily watered land such as Greece, the groves and meadows where the water produces a rich vegetation are the dwelling places of the nature spirits, and so are the forests and mountains where the wild beasts live. In the forests the nymphs dance; centaurs, satyrs,

and seilenoi roam about; and Pan protects the herds, though
he may also drive them away in a panic. The life of nature
becomes centered in Artemis, who loves hills and groves and
well-watered places and promotes that natural fertility which
does not depend upon the efforts of man.

> Anyone who wishes to understand the religion of
> antiquity should have before him a living picture of the ancient
> landscape as it is represented in certain Pompeian frescoes and
> in Strabo's description of the lowland at the mouth of the river
> Alpheus. 'The whole tract,' Strabo says, 'is full of shrines of
> Artemis, Aphrodite, and the nymphs, in flowery groves, due
> mainly to the abundance of water; there are numerous hermae
> on the roads and shrines of Poseidon on the headlands by the
> sea.' One could hardly have taken a step out of doors without
> meeting a little shrine, a sacred enclosure, an image, a sacred
> stone, or a sacred tree. Nymphs lived in every cave and
> fountain. This was the most persistent, though not the highest,
> form of Greek religion. It outlived the fall of the great gods.
> (Nilsson, *Folk Religions*, 17, 18)

Some of the early churches were in major centers of Greek worship. Ephesus was the center of the cult of Artemis; Corinth was the seat of the worship of Apollo, his oracle being nearby at Delphi. In these and other places the early church dealt with a pagan society and culture.

M. Ward Fowler remarks on the relation of Greek religion to Christianity:

> The essential difference, as it appears to me as a
> student of the history of religion, is this, that whereas the
> connection between religion and morality has so far been a
> loose one, – at Rome, indeed, so loose, that many have refused
> to believe in its existence – the new religion was itself morality,
> but morality consecrated and raised to a higher power than it
> had ever yet reached. It becomes active instead of passive;
> mere good nature is replaced by a doctrine of universal love;
> *pietās*, the sense of duty in outward things, becomes an
> enthusiasm embracing all humanity, consecrated by such an
> appeal to the conscience as never had been in the world
> before – the appeal to the life and death of the divine Master.
> (Fowler, 466)

Nilsson points out that the Greeks, although they had religious ideas, lacked a system of theology. He says that "what the Greeks called theology was either metaphysics, or the doctrine of the persons and works of the various gods" (Nilsson, 4).

Thus, the early church did not come into conflict with theological systems or doctrines. The conflict was on a different level, which we can perhaps begin to understand by looking at one of the problems faced by the Corinthian church, that of eating meat sacrificed to idols (I Cor. 8:10). Of course, this passage has some reference to problems of Jewish ritual, but particularly where Paul discusses the problem of eating (8:10) we can see a Greek problem. Hans Conzelmann says, "There were not only ample opportunities to take part in meals in temples, but it was also a matter of family and social duty." A sacrifice was central to every club party and marriage, and concern for the dead. It was therefore necessary for Paul to help the Corinthian Christians deal with this integral part of their lives.

The Corinthian church had to confront not only the cult of Apollo, but also the worship of Aphrodite in the cult of Astarte, the original goddess of fertility brought into Greece by Phoenician traders. "Her shrine," says Tenney, "was served by one thousand sacred prostitutes who ministered in the temple on the Acropolis." It is little wonder that the Corinthian church had such a problem with immorality.

Another interesting reflection of Greek religion can be seen in the account of Paul and Barnabas's visit to Lystra (Acts 14:8-18). When Paul healed a lame man, the astonished people began to call Barnabas "Zeus" and Paul "Hermes." "The priest of Zeus, whose temple was just outside the city, brought oxen and garland to the gates, and wanted to offer sacrifice with the crowds" (v.13). The people of Lystra associated Paul and Barnabas with Hermes and Zeus because of an ancient myth about a visit these two gods had paid to an elderly couple. Charles Gayley tells the story from Ovid:

> Once on a time Jupiter, in human shape, visited the land of Phyrgia, and with him Mercury, without his wings. They presented themselves as weary travelers at many a door, seeking rest and shelter, but found all closed; for it was late, and the inhospitable inhabitants would not rouse themselves to open for their reception. At last a small thatched cottage received them, where Baucis, a pious old dame, and her husband Philemon had grown old together. Not ashamed of their poverty, they made it endurable by moderate desires and kind dispositions. When the guests crossed the humble threshold and bowed their heads to pass under the low door, the old man placed a seat, on which Baucis, bustling and attentive, spread a cloth, and begged them to sit down. The she raked out the coals from the ashes, kindled a fire, and prepared some pot-herbs and bacon for them. A beechen bowl

was filled with warm water, that their guests might wash. While all was doing, they beguiled the time with conversation.

The old woman with trembling hand set the table. One leg was shorter than the rest, but a piece of slate put under restored the level. When it was steady she rubbed the table down with sweet-smelling herbs. Upon it she set some of chaste Minerva's olives, some cornel berries preserved in vinegar, and added radishes and cheese, with eggs lightly cooked in the ashes. The meal was served in earthen dishes; and an earthenware pitcher, with wooden cups, stood beside them. When all was ready the stew, smoking hot, was set on the table. Some wine, not of the oldest, was added, and for dessert, apples with wild honey.

Now while the repast proceeded, the old folks were astonished to see that the wine, as fast as it was poured out, renewed itself in the pitcher of its own accord. Struck with terror, Baucis and Philemon recognized their heavenly guests, fell on their knees, and with clasped hands implored forgiveness for their poor entertainment. There was an old goose, which they kept as the guardian of their humble cottage, and they bethought them to make this a sacrifice in honor of their guests. But the goose, too nimble for the old folk, with the aid of feet and wings eluded their pursuit and at last took shelter between the gods themselves. They forbade it to be slain, and spoke in these works: 'We are gods. This inhospitable village shall pay the penalty of its impiety; you alone shall go free from the chastisement. Quit your house and come with us to the top of yonder hill.' They hastened to obey. The country behind them was speedily sunk in a lake, only their house left standing. While they gazed with wonder at the sight that old house of theirs was changed. Columns took the place of the corner posts, the thatch grew yellow and appeared a gilded roof, the floors became marble, the doors were enriched with carving and ornaments of gold. Then spoke Jupiter in benignant accents: 'Excellent old man, and woman worthy of such a husband, speak, tell us your wishes. What favor have you to ask of us?' Philemon took counsel with Baucis a few moments, then declared to the gods with common wish. 'We ask to be priests and guardians of this thy temple, and that one and the same hour may take us both from life.' Their prayer was granted. When they had attained a great age, as they stood one day before the steps of the sacred edifice and were telling the story of the place, Baucis saw Philemon begin to put forth leaves, and Philemon saw Baucis changing in like manner. While still they exchanged parting words, a leafy crown grew over their heads. 'Farewell, dear spouse,' they said together, and at the same moment the bark closed over their mouth. The Tyanean shepherd still shows the two trees, – an oak and a linden, standing side by side. (Gayley, 77-79; *cf.* Ovid, *Metamorphosis,* 195-97).

Not only did the miracle suggest the myth but the appearance and actions of Paul and Barnabas did also. Barnabas was tall, stately and venerable, suggesting the characteristics of Zeus. Paul reminded them of Hermes "because he was the chief speaker" (Acts 14:12). Hermes generally bore the messages and did the speaking, even when accompanied by Zeus. The people brought oxen and garlands because these were often used in sacrifices to the gods.

In Ephesus, Paul again encountered a powerful cult—the worship of Artemis. The temple of this cult was one of the seven wonders of the world, 360 feet long and 180 feet wide, with ornate carvings, beautiful paintings and an image of Artemis which supposedly had fallen from heaven. Paul's preaching had such an effect in Ephesus that the sale of religious symbols of Artemis began to decline. Demetrius the silversmith gathered together other workmen of the area and incited them to riot against Paul, shouting, "Great is Artemis of the Ephesians!" (Acts 19:28) A great riot followed. The incident tells us in effect that Christianity was gradually replacing Greek temple worship. This is also evidenced by historical sources, such as when Pliny wrote to Trajan (A.D. 98-117), "The temples at least, which were once almost deserted, begin now to be frequented; and the sacred rites, after a long intermission are again revived" (*Letters of Pliny*, xcvii). Christianity had caused a noticeable decline in temple worship, in the interim.

The worship of gods who permeated all phases and aspects of ancient Greek life was confronted by the gospel message. It is this world that Paul indicated when he said in his speech in Athens, "I perceive that in every way you are very religious" (Acts 17:22). As Tenney remarks, "The entire religious culture of the past was represented by the buildings and rites of pagan worship; its legends and ethics were engrained into the people; and as Christianity slowly penetrated the fabric of society, it met the resistance of these antecedents" (Tenney, *Times*, 112).

When Christianity confronted the worship of the gods, it triumphed because though the gods dominated the lives and thoughts of the Greek and Roman people, their worship left a spiritual vacuum. They represented a state religion, one that was basically impersonal, without a redemptive plan or any idea of salvation. One could ask the oracle for advice in personal matters but there was no idea of being loved or cared about by the gods. Likewise, there was no love involved in the people's worship of the gods – they were placated or bribed so that the gods would not ruin the crops or cause a storm at sea.

In contrast, Christianity emphasizes love of God as well as love of one another (I John). Jesus emphasized a very personal and individual relationship with his followers when he talked about "abiding in the vine" (John 15). Jesus' final prayer to God for his disciples (John 17) shows the love and care that he felt – it was not cold and impersonal like the worship of the Greek gods, it was deep and living and intense. The worship of the Greek gods involved no moral code nor standard for living. Indeed, the worship itself in some cases involved rituals of immorality, although the worship of the Greek gods was not as immoral as that of the mystery cults. The moral weakness of Greek worship was yet another gap addressed by Christianity with its emphasis on the personal love for God, its moral living standards and its plan of salvation.

BECAUSE HE WAS *an efficient and active colonel in Germany and Britain, Titus, Vespasian's eldest son, became, according to Suetonius, "Vespasian's colleague, almost his guardian; sharing in the Judean triumph, in the censorship, in the exercise of tribunical power, and in the seven consulships."*

Three major catastrophies occurred during Titus' reign (A.D. 79-81) – the volcanic eruption of Mt. Vesuvius (A.D. 79), a fire in Rome (A.D. 80), and one of the worst outbreaks of plague n the history of the world (A.D. 81). The eruption of Vesuvius was a national disaster, not only for Pompeii, which it totally destroyed, but also for towns as far away as Herculaneum, on which it rained ashes for several days. Pliny describes the horror of the volcano in a letter to Tacitus. Titus sent money for relief for the families of those stricken by the eruption. When Rome burned (A.D. 80), the city was devastated and Titus sold his own possessions to help those in need. And then the plague was extremely severe. Suetonius says that "Titus attempted to control the plague by every imaginable means, human as well as divine, resorting to all sorts of sacrifices and medical remedies."

When Titus died at the age of 42, having reigned for two years, two months and twenty days, the people mourned as though for a personal loss.

We know little about the church at this time. During the siege of Jerusalem which fell under Vespasian in A.D. 70, the Christians probably fled to Pella for safety. After the war, it seems that they returned to Jerusalem.

Outside of Jerusalem it is not known for certain what the church was doing. It is quite certain that the Apostle John was still working, perhaps with a community reflected in John 20-21. There is also the influence of a community of Matthew in Syria (Gospel of Matthew). *Conzelmann mentions Ariston, a church father who came from Pella. Other Christian centers, Cochaba (in Hauren) and Beroea near Antioch (Aleppo), are also mentioned (Conzelmann, 138).*

The relation of Judaism to Christianity was hostile. As Goppelt says,

> According to rabbinic legends, the [Christian] group which returned after A.D. 70 made such an impression on the rabbinic students themselves by means of their active missionary witness that the Nazarenes were mentioned specifically in the curse formula against the minim. (Goppelt, 121)

Because of such opposition, by A.D. 80 the church was mainly concerned with her own members and outreach to Gentiles rather than conversion of Jews.

Chapter 5

THE MYSTERY RELIGIONS

CHRISTIANITY WAS NEITHER the first nor the only religious alternative for Hellenic and Roman peoples yearning for a more personal, intense form of worship, and for the promise of redemption. There were also the "mystery religions." Some scholars have suggested that Christianity was a mere branch of the mysteries, but the evidence does not support such a view.

The mystery religions owed their development in the West to Alexander the Great who, through conquest, fused the cultures of East and West. The mysteries which the armies of Alexander brought from the East offered a symbolism in which the initiate found religious truth, a doctrine of the ultimate unity of God and man, a response to sin, a sacramental cathartic, and an assurance of immortality. Franz Cumont states: "Those religions gave greater satisfaction first, to the senses and passions; secondly, to the intelligence; finally, and above all, to the conscience" (Cumont, x).

With the advent of the Roman empire, the mystery religions were sometimes threatened. The emperors, recognizing the mystic qualities and immoral functions of the cults, forbade the people to participate in them. However with the accession of Caligula (A.D. 37-41) a few of the mystery gods from the Near East were accepted into the Roman pantheon.

At the time of Paul, Roman religion was closely bound up with the life of the Roman City-State, and was concerned mostly with a system of auguries and religious ceremonies intended to guide the fortunes of the city and to inspire favor with the gods. There was no personal contact of the gods and their worshipers, and the people were open for something new, such as the mystery of religion.

The mystery religions appealed to the emotional rather than the doctrinal side of worship. They included pageantry, delirious dramas, music, physical mortifications, abstinence, silence, and in some instances a sacred drama that pictured the earthly sufferings, deaths and resurrections of their human-like deities in a manner analogous to medieval miracle plays. The mourning for the death of a god turned to rejoicing at his rebirth. These cults were generally kept secret and were supported by voluntary contributions.

At first these cults featured simple agrarian rites to increase fertility, but gradually, as they were drawn into the Greek orbit, they became activated by higher motives such as the relation of man to deity. For example, man would pray to Persephone, queen of the lower world, for assurance of protection. The Greek Dionysiac and Orphic elements modified the rites more in the sixth century B.C. when the mysteries became more concerned with a future life.

The oldest of the popular mysteries, originating before Alexander, was the cult of Eleusis, a town not far from Athens. It centered on the worship of Demeter, and people came from all over the known world to participate in its celebrations. The rites of the cult were kept secret, but we know that the preparation of a candidate for initiation occurred in three stages. First, the candidate was admitted to the lesser mysteries at Agrae; then into the first stage of the Great Mysteries of Eleusis; and finally, one year later at Eleusis, he received the mystic vision. The candidate for initiation then washed in the sea and, following a sacrifice, formed a processional to Eleusis. They sang on their way and arrived around midnight. The initiation took place in the darkness and involved sacrifices, banquets and a consecrated drink, after which they witnessed a sacred drama enacted by the priests of the shrine. The initiates were then led through a dark passageway to represent the wanderings of the dead in the underworld, and finally were brought back to the light, where they were shown the sacred objects of the cult. The vision of these objects was the culmination of the initiation, for they represented the personal revelation of the deity to the individual.

The cult goddesses Demeter and Persephone were thought of as living in the nether world, the abode of the dead. The mysteries valued this belief as providing a guarantee of a blessed immortality. Those in the mysteries were able to expect a better lot in a future life than other men.

The worship of Cybele was one of the first Oriental religions to invade Italy. She was the "mother of the gods," whose rites from immemorial antiquity had centered at Pessinus in the southwestern corner of Galatia on the frontier of Phrygia. On her way west, she became identified with Greek Rhea, another "mother of gods," of Cretan origin, whose shrine was located on mainland Greece. Cybele entered Rome about 204 B.C., when her black stone fetish was received at Ostia, carried to Rome, and ensconced in the Temple of Victory on the Palatine. In 202 B.C. she was accepted officially as a part of the Roman pantheon, and in 191 B.C. was given her own shrine. Bruce Metzger describes the rites of this cult:

> Celebrating her principal rites in the springtime, her devotees would work themselves into a frenzy of excitement, during the course of which they gashed their arms and sprinkled the blood on their altars, while her priests went so far as to emasculate themselves. (Metzger, 70)

The cult as developed in Rome included Attis as the male element. He was driven mad by Cybele, to whom he had been unfaithful. He mutilated himself under a pine tree, into which his spirit passed while his blood was transformed into violets. This led to a ritual in which a pine log wreathed with violets was carried in procession, along with images, to the music of cymbals and horns.

This cult ritual, which involved a wild, orgiastic worship, was held annually in Rome from March 15 to 27. The first stage, in which there was a processional, involved mourning for the dead Attis. A pine tree was felled; a log was prepared to represent the corpse and was carried to Cybele's temple. It was buried with great lamentations. Then the priests dedicated themselves to the service of the goddess by mutilating themselves. By this act they participated in the sorrow of the gods. Toward the end of the festival the resurrection of the god was celebrated by a carnival of license and merry-making. Worshipers also partook of a sacred meal.

The worship of Cybele spread over Italy, North Africa, Spain, Gaul and especially along the empire's Rhine and Danube frontiers. Claudius released restriction on her worship, and it came under supervision of the state. Worship continued through the fourth century A.D. with the last appearance of the procession in Rome occurring in A.D. 394 under Eugenus. In the beginning of the fifth century it still flourished in North Africa. In all, it lasted for six centuries in the West.

Another popular cult was that of Isis, from Egypt. This mystery actually involved three deities: Serapis, official god of Greek rulers whose worship was centered at Alexandria; Isis, a survival from an ancient Egyptian caste; and their son Harpocrates, god of peasant fellaheen. Metzger describes the essential elements of the myth upon which the cult is based:

> Osiris, a wise and beneficent king, fell victim to the plotting of his wicked brother Set...who hacked Osiris into fourteen pieces and dispatched them to different parts of Egypt. Isis, his wife and sister of Osiris, searched out and found all but one piece of the dismembered body, which she reassembled and carefully embalmed. After a ceremonial lament over the corpse, in which her sister Nephtys joined, by means of magical rites, Isis revivified Osiris, who then received the title 'Lord of the Underworld, Ruler of the Dead.' (Metzger, 68-69)

The initiation of the Isis cult is described by Lucius. First he is summoned by the goddess, Isis, taken into the temple, made acquainted with certain mysterious books and cleansed. He then fasts for ten days. Next, he is taken into the secret part of the temple, where he goes through a sort of vision or drama that marks his death, passes through the elements and rises to new life. The next day he is presented to the multitude and regarded as having partaken of divine nature.

In the November festival at Rome the drama of the finding of Osiris was enacted. It pictured Osiris' murder, Isis' grief and wanderings and the resurrection of Osiris. Banquets and games were a part of the festival. Osiris became the ideal of manhood. By reverencing the god, men could also live hereafter in possession of the mind and body in heaven. The cult also attracted women by the novelty of its impressionistic ritual, beautiful drama, rigorous rules, the tenderness of Isis, communion with deity, separation of clergy from the world, the final judgment and the promise of a blissful hereafter.

The earliest colloquium on the worship of Isis in Rome dates to 80 B.C. It remained obscure for half a century, checked by the Senate because of its immorality and emotionalism. But during the reign of Caligula (A.D. 37-41) it was revived and began to spread over the whole empire. It was one of the most serious rivals of Christianity and Book XI of the *Golden Age of Apuleius* relates the devotion to her cult.

Adonis of Phoenicia was another god, whose cult was found at Byblos where his death and resurrection were celebrated. Lucian tells us that his worshipers mourned over his death, which was caused by a wild boar. They offered sacrifices, then alleged he was alive again, exhibiting his effigy to the sky.

The Baals (Lords) from Syria were also popular. Every locality had its own Baal and his consort. But the best known was Atargatis, a goddess at Hieropolis described by Lucian. The cult was characterized by especially immoral features but was ennobled by the Babylonian worship of heavenly bodies. It therefore contributed to the formation of solar monotheism, which was the final form of the official pagan religion of the empire prior to adoption of Christianity.

Atargatis was the first mystery cult to reach Greece and Italy from Syria. Represented as a mermaid, she was worshiped as the founder of social and religious life, the goddess of generation and fertility, and the protector of communities. She became known as the goddess of nature and, according to Lucian, wild beasts were tamed in her presence. Her priests were eunuchs; her temples were defiled by sacred prostitution and the sacrifices of adults and children, until the practice was banned by Hadrian (A.D. 117-138).

Atargatis' symbol was the fish, a food which her worshipers were forbidden to eat because of the belief that it caused tumors. Some have suggested a connection between this cult's symbol and the Christian's fish symbol. But the Christian word for the symbol comes from the Greek "Ἰχθύς" which uses the first letters of "Jesus Christ Son of God, Saviour."

This cult was attractive to the Romans because of its scientific astrology. The priests were experts in astral lore and Chaldean fatalism. In contrast to the Greeks they believed that the Elysian fields of the blessed were above, and therefore they worshiped the sun.

The important cult of Mithra had its origin in Zoroastrianism, and became a serious rival of Christianity in the second and third centuries, A.D. Its appeals were its human qualities of fraternity, democracy, faith, antiquity and impressive ritual; its clerical organization; its ethics; and its doctrines of purification from sin, of good and evil powers on earth, of the final judgment and the blessed hereafter. It was also appealing because of its freedom from immoral sexual practices.

Mithra was demi-god created by the supreme deity Ahura-Mazda to help fight evil. Zoroaster had simplified the ancient faith by relating the gods to positions of "daemas" and teaching the purificatory qualities of fire. His evangel could be summed up: "good thoughts, good works, good acts"–man's choice of good or evil.

With the Persian conquest (500 B.C.) Zoroastrianism spread and was modified by contact with the Chaldean astrology. After the collapse of Persia, the cult lived in obscurity in Pontus and Cappadocia where the advant of a saviour-god was taught. It has been suggested that the biblical wise men who came to see the Christ Child were from this sect.

Rome came in contact with Mithraism through the Mithraic wars in Asia Minor (88-63 B.C.), where it became the religion of the soldiers. It lasted in Rome for 450 years.

The cult, made up of men only, was organized like a fraternity, and its members were bound by vows of secrecy. The priests were taken from the highest order of its members. Its theology held that behind all is "boundless time," the ultimate creator, represented by a human monster with a lion's head, circled by serpents and covered with zodiacal signs and emblems. It had four wings signifying the swiftness of time. It held the keys of heaven and a scepter in its hands. Its offering was heaven and earth, which begat ocean.

The chief deity of the cult was Mithra, who was born full grown from a rock and reigned as the god of all life. His first task was to show his strength in a struggle with the sun, then kill a bull, whose sacrificial death was viewed as the birth of life: as Mithra killed the bull, its blood brought forth useful plants and animals. Meanwhile, man was created and protected by Mithra. His labors over, Mithra went to heaven with the sun, and good and evil continued on the earth. His worshipers believed that after an allotted time a second bull would appear and would be destroyed by Mithra, who would then call the dead from their tombs, separate the good from the evil and take the good to dwell above. Evil would be annihilated. Also involved in the cult were the sacred elements: earth, water, air and fire. The sun, moon and planets were worshiped.

The Mithraic ritual itself was secret. There were six to seven stages of initiation, in which absolutions and ordeals accompanied successive grades testing the initiate's courage and faith. There was a baptism of immersion and a passing through flames blind-folded, both of which signified death. A "summus pontiflex" was in charge of the ritual, holding office for life.

Metzger describes the major initiation rite:

> The initiate, who was naked, crouched in a pit covered with a grating over which a bull, garlanded with flowers, was slaughtered. As the warm blood streamed over the devotee, he would eagerly drink in some of the life-giving fluid. Inscriptions dating from the early Christian period and commemorating the performance of this rite indicate that the initiate believed that he had been reborn for twenty years or, in some cases, for eternity. (Metzger, 68)

Drenched in the blood and coming up into the light, the initiate would hear the words: "Take courage, ye mystae, the god is saved; so shall salvation be ours, sometime, from all need."

In comparing Mithraism and Christianity, many parallels can be drawn. Both called their adherents "brothers," and both had legends of shepherds coming to adore the newborn. Justin says that a comet appeared to signal the birth of Mithradates, a clear parallel to the star mentioned by Matthew. He also says that Mithra was supposed to be unconquerable: some Persians tried but failed to kill him in infancy. This parallels the account of Herod failing to annihilate Christ (S. Eddy, *The King is Dead*, 179). (And yet Mithra was said to have been born as a full grown man.) Both religions had legends of a global flood with one family surviving in an ark, and final conflagration. Both taught that heaven was above the earth. Both taught that there were good and evil influences struggling together on earth. Both had a sacred meal and baptism. Both had an elevated system of ethics and a deity who mediated between this world and the next. Both Jesus and Mithra taught they would return, awaken the dead, and justify good and evil, giving immortality to one and annihilation to the other. Both reached the West simultaneously and so the message of each was diffused under similar conditions. Both drew members from the lower classes, and each felt the other's rivalry for religious leadership of the empire.

Edward Carpenter asserts:

> It is clear anyhow, that all these elements of the pagan religions—pouring down into the vast reservoir, or rather whirlpool, of the Roman Empire, and mixing among all these numerous brotherhoods, societies, *Collegia*, mystery-clubs, and groups which were at that time looking for some new revelation or inspiration—did more or less automatically act and react upon each other, and by the general conditions prevailing were modified, till they ultimately combined and took united shape in the movement which we call Christianity, but which only—as I have said—narrowly escaped being called Mithraism—so nearly related and closely allied were these cults with each other. (Carpenter, 208-09)

Carpenter suggests that Christ was an extension of the saviour-god concept which was familiar in Judaism. χριστός, meaning "the anointed one," was a common term.) Osiris from Egypt, then, assertedly gave color to the Christian teaching by its worship of Isis, the Christian form of the Virgin Mary. The Mediator concept came from Mithra in Persia. Thus, Carpenter says that Christianity was only an imitation of the popular pagan cult. He says: "History shows that as a Church progresses and expands it generally feels compelled to enlarge and fortify its own foundations by inserting material which was not here at first" (Carpenter, 198-201).

According to Carpenter, in the Hellenistic/Roman fusion of language, customs, philosophies, creeds and religions, a new religion was inevitable. It would combine elements of all the cults, though showing reactions against many practices. It would evolve an inner inspiration of its own, that of loving one's neighbor. Its sanction would not reside in external authorities, but in a sense of the soul's direct responsibility to God. This is to say, Christianity was a result of its environment, and perhaps this is feasible in a very particular sense – the sense that people were ready for a more personal, individual, meaningful approach to religion. But if we accept Carpenter's conclusions we are forced into the illogical position of asserting that because the world was ready for a movement such as Christianity, therefore the movement was merely a product of various influences in the world. The more one compares Christianity to the mysteries, the more telling their differences become. And the more sensitive one is to the spiritual appeal of Christianity, the clearer it becomes that Christianity prevailed *precisely because* it was *not* just an outgrowth of cultic traditions or social pressures. It is the unique, Divinely inspired integrity, independence and strength of Christ's ministry, we suggest, which endowed Christianity with the spark for which the world was waiting.

Walter Hyde points out that the church fathers believed that direct borrowing was insignificant, because of the open hostilities between Christianity and Hellenic cults. Therefore, if the mystery religions exercised any influence it must have been through the general atmosphere they diffused. Hyde further says that the Synoptic Gospels have nothing in common with the mysteries, since Jesus' work was done in public and confined to His historical locale Judaea, while the message of the mysteries was secret and immediately diffused all over Europe and Asia Minor. And in early Christianity there were no induction communications, purifications or other ceremonies, and little about life to come (Hyde, 68-69).

Another important difference is that in Christianity Jesus was not revered as a prophet or teacher, but as the Divine Lord who replaced the many gods and lords of the pagans.

Paul especially has prompted diversity of opinion about whether Christianity borrowed from the mysteries. Paul was reared in Tarsus, a Mithraic center. Thus, such terms as the "Rock," in I Corinthians 10:4 has been viewed as a possible borrowing from the Rock that was connected with Mithra. Bu "Rock" as used in this context is too common a metaphor on which to base such an opinion. Besides, Paul says relatively little of heaven or hell, rewards or penalties, which are so common in the mysteries.

Certain references made by Paul are worth noting. I Corinthians 2:6,7 speaks of the "secret and hidden wisdom of God." This could be likened to secrets of the mystery religions known only to the members. However, this is most likely a matter of terminology only and not an implication of secret rituals. For in Colossians 2:8-10 and 16-22, Paul warns against the introduction of Oriental mystic notions into the church. Paul himself said that he had to approach the "Greek as a Greek," that is, he had to speak to the culture he was in. But it does not follow that he was affiliated with the pagan religions.

The cardinal value later attached to the sacraments does seem to have been influenced by Hellenism. From this influence the observances were changed to salvation rites. For example, to the Corinthians, baptism for the dead (I Cor. 15:29) was an Orphic custom. Also, the Lord's Supper gradually came to be thought of as the act of partaking of the actual body and blood of Christ, which brought one into union with Him. This concept and practice was common to a number of the mystery cults.

The mystery religions observed sacraments such as "eating the gods." These were observed in an effort to establish a union with them. The apostles, however, never attributed magical efficacy to the Christian rites. Salvation was in believing, not in the rites themselves (Mark. 16:16). The Lord's Supper was not a meal, but an observance and a memorial with only symbolic representation of the body of Christ. It was not until later in church history that the Church developed this observance into a salvation rite.

On close examination of apparent similarities between Christianity and mystery religions, we encounter a key problem. Most of our sources of information about the mysteries are of a late date. One has to go to sources subsequent to Paul's day to reconstruct them. For example, the words of Firmius Maternus to the mystery initiate who was about to be "born again": "Be of good courage, ye initiates, since the god is saved; for to us shall there be salvation out of troubles." A connection is implied between the resurrection of the god that is the salvation of the believer and the death and resurrection of Christ. But Firmius Maternus lived in the fourth century A.D., 300 years later than Paul! Thus we must consider the very real possibility that the pagan religions by this time could have borrowed from Christianity, because of the latter's success.

Thus, the problem exists: How are we supposed to reconstruct the *pre-Christian* mystery religions? Attention has been brought to a complex of writings on these religions under the name Hermes Trismegistus. The problem with these is that they were compiled after A.D. 300 and have been reproduced at various times. None are dated before the founding of Christianity.

The differences between Christianity and its milieu of pagan and mystery religions are notable and in many cases basic.

The religions of the Greeks and Romans, as indicated by their epic literature, constituted a highly developed polytheism of the anthropomorphic kind. The Greek gods were men and women with human passions and sins. They were more powerful than humans, but certainly not more righteous. Anthropomorphism gave free course to the imagination of the poet and the sculptor, which resulted in good artistry, but less than exalted (or exemplary) morals. Moreover, with them there was little hope of personal communion; for the gods to be revered by direct and individual contact was mostly unattainable.

By contrast, Christianity was monotheistic. It was the only religion which represented God as seeking man, antecedent to any device on man's part. Christ said in Luke 19:10: "I have come to seek and to save that which was lost." Other religions such as the Greek and Roman show only man's toilsome search for God.

Hellenism had no clear and consistent view of the origin of the world; it was steeped in arbitrary irrationality. For example, Mithraism says that plants and animals sprang from the blood of a slaughtered bull. In Christianity, however, God called the world into being by a free act of creation. All things were created by Him and are dependent on and governed by Him. In Hellenism the world is created by various means and is governed by an impersonal fate.

In the Hellenistic religions sin is removed by magical purifications, while in Christianity it is removed by faith in a Redeemer who is revealed in its teachings.

The incarnation is peculiar to Christianity. It appears that the Mithra cult claimed their god came to earth as a human being, then returned to heaven. Mithra is probably the closest approximation to Christ among the pagan gods though he is not pictured as having been pre-existent and then being incarnated.

The mysteries and Christianity are similar in regard to miracles. Both report healing the sick and casting out demons. For example, Appollonius of Tayana, a leading reformer of the expiring paganism in the Augustinian Age, was said to have performed many miracles. But there are differences: The miracles of the mysteries seem to be romanticized as if they were "heathenizations" of the gospel. None of them were connected with salvation. In contrast, Christ's miracles were more to rescue and to succor as well as to accredit His mission.

Enthusiasm was a leading feature in the mystery cults. Induced by a frenzy, it was a permanent condition in which the soul identified with the god. For example, Mithra's liturgy states: "Thou art I, and I am thou." Christianity was enthusiastic but involved no frenzy. Paul's speaking of "being in Christ" (Rom. 6:4; Gal. 2:20) could have been influenced by the mysteries because it implies a mystical union of the believer with Christ. However, this could also be a relationship of spiritual communication, being in the fellowship of Christ rather than in physical unity with him as the mysteries imply.

Hellenism is traceable in the eschatological passage of Romans 8:19, where there is a yearning of creation for happier conditions, and in II Peter 3:10, which tells of the world's future destruction by fire. But there is a difference in the fundamental characteristics. Hellenism waited in expectation of a golden age while Christianity looked to the Second Coming of Christ (its God) and a final judgment. In general, the New Testament alludes to fellowship with the Lord (John 14:2).

Reconciliation is distinctive of Christianity. Salvation centers in Jesus, in His death as a sacrifice (II Cor. 5:18). But Hellenism offers sacrifices in order to propitiate the deity by gifts. A full equivalent of Christ's death, resurrection and final rule cannot be found in the mystery religions, although some similarities can be found in Mithraism. For example, Attis, Osiris and

Adonis all die and rise again but their resurrections are profoundly different from Christ's. There is no mention of any resurrection in the myths that the religions are built on. These seem to be "vegetation gods," whose dying resuscitation represent the annual withering and renewal of vegetation. They found expression in the gross symbols and often immoral practices which appeared with these gods.

Christ's resurrection, however, is based on an historical event that was witnessed by many and was contained in the belief from its beginning. William Tarn says,

> To Hellenism generally, immortality was only for certain benefactors of their kind or the initiates in some mystery-religion; it was not for the mass of men, as their epitaphs reveal, pathetically enough. And of all the Hellenistic creeds, none was based on love of humanity; none had any message for the poor and the wretched, the publican and the sinner. (Tarn, 360)

In relation to the state cults, we see another difference between the mysteries and Christianity. Mithraism, for example, compromised with the state, establishing its monotheism without combating the prevailing polytheism. In contrast, Christianity opposed all other religions and the imperial and civic cult of Rome.

Christianity was free from the nature worship which characterized many of the religions, including Mithraism. The objects of adoration in the mysteries were always mystical creations of the imagination, whereas Jesus was an historical figure, with human sympathies and a personality which was even greater than His teachings.

The moral aspect is also a distinguishing feature of Christianity, which held an ascetic attitude toward sex. While most pagan cults favored pleasures and the world of the senses, Christianity followed Judaism in renouncing the world and flesh. It advocated a withdrawal into the inner and more spiritual regions of the mind, and distangled "love" and "sex."

W. Fairweather feels that Hellenistic thought may have materially affected the structural form of early Christianity, but not necessarily its content. He states:

> In view of the evidence adduced, it can scarcely be disputed that Hellenistic thought and religion materially affected the

structural form of early Christianity. To say this, however, is not to say that it affected its essential content. On the contrary, we have only to compare Hellenism and Christianity with reference to some of the more obvious directions in which they might be expected to present points of contact, or even to occupy common ground, in order to see that the religion of Jesus is no mere product of the age which witnessed its rise, but an absolutely independent revelation of spiritual truth, carrying with it an altogether unique conception of life and morals. (Fairweather, 354)

As Samuel Angus comments: "Christianity offered a more profound and spiritual message than the mysteries to the theosophic mind of the Orient, the speculative mind of Greece, and the legislative mind of Rome" (Hyde, 67-68).

It offered a personal communication with God who was not just a mythical concoction, but who was a reality both in history and in the experience of men. Those who labored and were heavy laden were to welcome a hope radically different from any which Hellenism could ever offer.

Chapter 6

STOICISM

WITH ALEXANDER'S CONQUESTS came the fall of two traditional guides for living: concern for one's city-state, and belief in the traditions and laws of the ancestors. When the city-states no longer functioned independently, man found himself in the larger scope of the Greek Empire attempting to hold on to religious traditions which had already proven ineffectual not only against Alexander's phalanx but also against the onslaught of Greek intellectual criticism.

With the fall of tradition came the fall of the set code of values and standards. "Desire," Edwyn Bevan writes, "was the propelling force, and action was spasmodic, furious, vain – a misery of craving forever disappointed and forever renewed" (Bevan, 28). The Hellenists also brought unparalleled development of the quality of human nature known as rationalism. The skepticism which accompanied the Greek cultural advance, with its questions and doubting, applied the final blows to dying religious traditions, and reason rose as superior in life. Thus, man had lost his public spirit (the city-state) and his belief in the gods, and was in a state of uncertainty and unrest. The basic questions of life needed to be answered: How do I live? What do I believe in?

This is the atmosphere into which Zeno, the founder of Stoicism, came. He was a Semite-Phoenician, born in the Cyprian town of Citium about 336 B.C. Although Cyprus was a center of Hellenism, the young Zeno was not drawn into Socratic philosophy until he had visited Athens, where he read Xenophon's *Memorabilia* and Plato's *Apology*. For a while, Zeno visited the different "schools" of philosophy—the Platonic, the Cynic and others, and studied under the Cynic Crates, and Stilpo (c. 329 B.C.) who opposed Plato's theory of ideas.

Zeno felt that none of these schools answered adequately the need of the people for guidance in how to live and what to believe, so he founded his own "school." He lectured in the Stoa Poikele, a colonnade near the Agora, and his followers became known as Stoics, or men of the porch. Zeno sought to give man a philosophy that would meet his needs. Man in the Hellenistic world had been left to fortune and the unknowns of the future—even possible torture or slavery—and was plagued by an ever-present fear. Zeno promised deliverance from fear and an answer to the bewildering uncertainty produced by skepticism. He realized that his philosophy must stand on a physical and metaphysical base and that his system of ethical conduct must be consistent with this base and must stand against the backdrop of the universe.

It has been debated whether Zeno's philosophy was purely Hellenistic or was influenced by the Phoenicians. In some ways Zeno differed from the Greek philosophers, but since we have so little knowledge of the wisdom of the Phoenicians, the questions may never be definitely answered. However, there are some points of similarity between Zeno's philosophy and those of the Near Eastern prophets outside the Hellenistic sphere, such as Pythagoras and Empedocles. These Near Eastern teachers seem to have discovered truth not by reason but by an "intent gaze." They "announced their conclusions in the voice of a herald, using the name of God and giving no reasons," Bevan says (Bevan, 20-22), whereas Greek philosophers such as Plato believed that truth was in the mind and could be brought forward by conversation in rational argument. Zeno seems to have combined the two. His message is Hellenistic, being in Hellenistic syllogistic form, though these forms served only as a means of conveying his intense convictions. His teaching was dogmatic and authoritative, in the voice of a prophet: "Thus saith Reason."

He earnestly declared his message in blunt speech borrowed from the Cynics, using many gestures and short syllogistic arguments: "It is reasonable to honor the gods: it would not be reasonable to honor beings which did not exist: therefore the gods exist." Bevan comments that Stoicism owed its success to the tenor of the time but just as much to a "human person of singular individuality and force." This seems quite evident, since Zeno's arguments are not always without inconsistencies or questionable implications.

In appearance, Zeno was not Hellenic. He was dark, tall and ungainly. He renounced the pleasure of the Hellenistic spirit, and was known for his integrity of character and frugality of life as well as his individualism. It is no wonder that the phrase grew up in Athens: "More self-restrained than Zeno."

This then, is an indistinct picture of the founder of Stoicism and the atmosphere in which Stoicism grew. Its principles were not entirely original with Zeno. There were several contributors: Heraclitus of Ephesus was the father of Stoic physics, having developed the concepts of the individual being subject to the λόγος, or Law of Nature, and of reason being a fire in man and in the universe; the Megarians contributed the Stoic logic, developing elaborate techniques of refutation, uses of paradox, and rigorous inference; the Cynics created much of the Stoic ethic such as cosmopolitanism, the love of nature above local convention or political power, and the belief in the autonomy of the virtuous man; and Socrates contributed the concepts of life and death being the symbols of rational self-control. Zeno synthesized these concepts and others of his own into a system of philosophy for the oppressed people of 320 B.C. Thus began what Gilbert Murray calls, "the greatest system of organized thought which the mind of man had built up for itself in the Graeco-Roman world before the coming of Christianity with its inspired book and its authoritative revelation" (Murray, 22).

Stoicism underwent important changes in the centuries following 320 B.C. Zeno's successor, Cleanthes of Assos in Asia Minor (c. 331 B.C.-c. 232 B.C.), a poet and religious visionary, carried on the Stoic tradition. Chrysippus of Soli in southeast Asia (c. 280 B.C.-c. 206 B.C.) known as the "second founder of Stoicism" succeeded Cleanthes and developed Stoicism into an intricate system. These three "Early Stoa" formed in effect a creative team, each contributing to a certain aspect of Stoicism.

The "Middle Stoa" (156 B.C.-c. 51 B.C.) were also important: Diogenes of Seleucia (156 B.C.) became the leader of the Athenian Stoa; Panaetius of Rhodes (185 B.C.-c. 110 B.C.) looked forward to the involvement of Stoics in the military, social and political life in Rome. Panaetius influenced Scipio and thus reached the Roman intellectuals. He softened the asceticism of Stoicism, laid more value on eternal goods and emphasized the gradual moral progress of discipleship rather than the pure ideal of the wise man. Posidonius of Apamea (c. 135 B.C.-c. 51 B.C.), like Chrysippus of the "Middle Stoa," brought more rigor and detail to the system and developed the golden-age theory of history–that the wise man ruled originally and men found happiness by seeking after and following nature.

The "Late Stoa" (first and second centuries A.D.) were Roman: Epictetus (A.D. c. 50-A.D. c. 138) was a freed slave of Nero's bodyguard and a pupil of Musonius. He developed distinctions between things in one's power, such as giving or withholding assent, and things not in one's power, such as one's impressions. He taught that innate moral predispositions could be actualized by education or left to decay. Seneca (c. 4 B.C.-A.D. 65), never trusting logical theory completely, developed the Stoic ethics of inward tranquility and social duty. He was advisor to the young Emperor Nero during the first five years of his reign and seemed to exert integrity and a wise influence. However, Nero suspected him of conspiring with the Senate against him and ordered him to commit suicide. Marcus Aurelius (A.D. 121-180), the last great Stoic, was emperor from 161 until his death. He also emphasized the Stoic ethics of inward self-control and useful citizenship in the universe.

As mentioned, Zeno faced a two-fold problem which his philosophy set out to solve: how to live and what to believe. In order to answer these, Zeno first had to define what he saw as true and untrue, real and unreal.

Zeno's position in regard to the real world was that the real is solid and material; he even once asserted that God, the soul and virtue were solid matter and therefore real. This position was later modified by his successors, who maintained that Zeno did not really mean that concepts such as virtue or justice were solid matter, but that the mutual relation or "tension" that existed between material objects was justice or virtue. Zeno held that we have knowledge of the real world through the evidence of our senses. The real, imprinted on our mind, is called a sense-impression.

In answer to the skeptic's question about our senses deceiving us, Zeno says that our senses have not deceived us; rather, our interpretation of the sense impression may be incorrect. When we have a "comprehensive sense-impression" (one which "grasps" its object so that there is no doubt of its interpretation), we have gotten the real sense imprint of the object. Zeno says that the real imprint "takes hold of us by the hair and drags us to assent." Not all impressions are this clear, however; they differ in clearness and sharpness of outline. Hence, when a man makes a mistake, his reasoning is fallacious, not the Laws of Reason; man simply uses the Laws of Reason inexactly. If the impression leaves an alternative open, then the wise man will withhold his assent; he will only assent to those "comprehensive sense-impressions," or *Kataleptike*, "phantasia."

With this basis for knowledge Zeno went on to found his ideas of the universe. He held that the eternal reality was a fiery ether or vapor of which a part, in the beginning, lost its divinity and changed into the other elements – air, water, and earth. This "passive principle" was acted upon by the remaining divine element of fire, or fiery ether, which had retained its form as "active principle" or Divine Reason (*logos spermatikos*). This active principle caused organic things to grow by being a formula of life in them; as divine fire and pure essence, this Divine Reason dwells in each soul. This Reason, or the Stoic God, is body, a living being with intelligence, which is in everything that lives and moves and has its being. He is the rational purpose in the universe, the universal law of reason which all nature obeys. R. D. Hicks comments: "As Logos, He brings all things to pass, for He is the Wisdom which steers all things; as Fire, He is the substance which creates, sustains, and in the end, perhaps, reabsorbs into itself the world" (Hicks, 12).

Seneca says of God:

> We understand Jove to be ruler and guardian of the whole mind and breath of the universe, lord and artificer of this fabric...He it is whose thought provides for the universe that it may move on its course unhurt and do its part...He it is of whom all things are born, by whose breath we live...He himself is this whole that you see, fills his own parts, sustains himself and what is his. (Seneca, *Nat. Quaest.*, ii.45)

Thus the λόγος knows best, makes the laws of the universe and obeys them himself. All events are directed by Reason to realize a certain purpose, the Good.

Zeno says that this Good consists of a state of inner tranquility which can be obtained by not being blinded by passion or desire, and by performing one's function well. To keep from being blinded by passion or desire means that no desire should accompany any action, and the success or failure of the action must be indifferent, since to desire the success of an action is to risk disappointment or upset which would disturb the impenetrable inner calm. Thus, the Stoic was to risk his health, possessions or life to serve his brother, but was never to risk his inner tranquility; he was to be detached from the desire for the outcome of the action; love or emotion could not be involved. To perform one's function well meant to Zeno "to live according to nature." In the world the Purpose, or Phusis, is God's mind, which guides all things that grow in the direction of God's will. Thus the whole world is working together to fulfill this Phusis.

This, however, does not disannul man's free will – God prefers free men, not slaves – "Man's soul," Murray explains, "being actually a portion of the divine fire, has the same freedom that God Himself has" (Murray, 28). It is man's duty to coincide his will with the Divine Will. Therefore, the free use of man's will will bring him into the will of God: "Thy will be done." By using his free will a man can find happiness since the good is "this or that which leaves the will satisfied"; man is happy when he does not want things to be any other than they are; hence by willing what exists, man becomes independent of fear, desire, fortune, pain. For example, Posidonius while suffering from a painful disease would cry at each spasm: "Do your worst, pain: do your worst. You will never compel me to acknowledge that you are an evil!" If one holds that the sovereign Reason knows best, and that he wills what exists, then he accepts whatever happens as God's will and therefore the best. Thus he obtains independence from fear or pain since he does not will things to be other than they are (Seneca, "On Providence").

Stoics were not definite on the end of the universe. Some held that perfection would be reached, and then there would be no falling back. The whole world would be brought to the level of the divine soul, which is fire.

This fire would cleanse existence of its earthly nature by burning it away. Then there would be only ecstasy and triumph, no more growth, decay, pleasure, pain or disturbance; the soul would have reached its fiery union with God. This view is not totally accepted by all of the Stoics: Some see the absorption by fire as only an interlude before the whole world process begins again; since if God's essence is to do something and to achieve an end, and if goodness is to exist, then the world process must begin again or Phusis, God's Purpose, would not be Phusis. Thus, some Stoics say that when the earth, air and water are absorbed into the fiery vapors, they will again emerge to continue the evergoing cycle of cause and effect.

In summary, the Stoics held that everyone should work toward the Good which is inner tranquility. This is obtained by living according to nature and desiring what God wills, since unhappiness comes form wanting what cannot be acquired. Gilbert Murray summarizes:

> You possess already, if you only knew it, all that is worth desiring. The good is yours if you but will it. You need fear nothing...no earthly power can make you good or bad except yourself, and to be good or bad is the only thing that matters. (Murray, 21-22)

In this way, Stoicism gave people purpose and a way to live independently of fear and pain. And by asserting a single Divine Purpose, λόγος, in the affairs of man, Stoicism prepared the way of Christianity.

Since Stoicism was one of the major philosophic schools at the time of Christ and in the following two centuries, it is likely that Stoics and Christians came into dialogue with each other. During the reign of Vespasian (A.D. 69-79) the Stoic was probably acquainted with the oral gospel as it was before the writing of the Four Gospels.

The Stoic would have known a little about Christ's background – that He was a Jew from Nazareth (Matt. 13:55; Luke 2:48) who had sat under the philosophical rabbis of Jerusalem (Luke 2:46,47) and learned how to interpret the Hebrew documents in the light of world religions. He would also have heard about Christ's rejecting the Pharisaic hypocrisy and coming forward as a teacher in His own name. He would probably have been impressed by the strength and force of character in Christ's preaching and most likely would have ranked Him with Socrates and Zeno. He would have recognized in Christ's teachings some similarities to those of Zeno's *Republic*: Christ's Kingdom of Heaven as a counterpart to Zeno's model state; the equality of all men in the state; the irrelevance of ceremonies, sacrifices and sabbaths (Matt. 12:1-13; Mark 2:23-28; Luke 6:1-10). Seneca believed that gods should be worshiped "not by sacrifice and ceremonies, but by purity of life; not in temples of stone, but in the shrine of the heart. He believed in the reformation of the social and economic system, which compares with Matthew 5:5: The poor will inherit the earth; the rich will be swept away.

Christ's teaching of future rewards for the good and the wicked would probably hold less interest for the Stoic than for the Christian, but it would not contradict his own tradition. What would interest him more would be that Jesus did not always maintain the imperturbable calm strived for by the wise man: His spirit was troubled (John 13:21); in righteous anger He denounced the Pharisees, Scribes and traders in the temple; He wept in pity over Jerusalem and grieved over Lazarus' death (John 11); He agonized in the Garden of Gethsemane (Luke 22:44) and attended festivities such as the wedding at Cana (John 2).

Cicero and Seneca describe the wise man as "dignified, magnificent, consistent; since reason declared that moral good is the only good, he alone must be happy" (Seneca). "Only the wise are free, beautiful, and rich; only they are kings and generals, orators and poets; only they are perfectly happy." Many of these ideals are embodied in Christ, but He did not teach that the Christian should suppress emotion in order to obtain virtue. The Stoic believed that the perfect wise man is in reality only an Ideal, and actually unattainable, and would have suspected that Christ's disciples minimized His weaknesses by attributing them to the body and not to the soul (Matt. 26:41; Mark 14:38) while accepting Him as their Lord and God (John 20:28). What would have shocked the Stoic would have been the divisions in the body of Christ's followers after His death, their return to the Hebrew traditions, and their forgetfulness of His teachings despite the fact that they held allegiance to His Person and the hope of His return. The poverty that the early Christians willingly fell into and their contentment with love and visions rather than the intellectual system of Christ's teachings the Stoic would have seen as suggestive of the idol-worshipers and the ignorant fanatics of Rome who were a danger to the Empire.

On the other hand, the Stoic would probably have recognized many aspects of his own doctrines in the fiery preachers of Acts, the Epistles of Paul, I Peter and Hebrews. These preachers emphasized the transmutation of Hebraism into a world religion: the presentation of Christ to the Roman world in intellectual form and the fusion of Judaism and Hellenism with Christ's teaching to present Him as the world's solution.

It is interesting to note the similarities in the backgrounds of Zeno and Paul. They both came from centers of Hellenism (Zeno-Cyprus, Paul-Tarsus), both were Semitic, and both came to Athens declaring, as did the Stoic, that

> ...the Deity was One Power, pervading the universe, and dwelling in all men everywhere, without distinction of race, and that in the ideal city there would be no temples because no temple, the work of builders and artificers, could be worthy of God. (See Acts 17)

This, of course, does not suggest that Paul was a Stoic, or that when he uses Stoic terms he is in accord with Stoic philosophy; rather Paul seems to parallel some Stoic terms and methods of thinking while giving them different and sometimes fuller meanings.

Paul, like the Stoics, accepted the evidence of the senses for knowledge and was not overly concerned about the possibility of illusion. He uses Stoic terms to explain the Christian idea of human nature: To the Stoics, man is a unity of body, soul and mind. He substitutes spirit πνεῦμα, for mind νους, and includes the mind with the soul ψυχη; he says that neither the *natural* or *intellectual* soul of man can receive the "things of the Spirit of God." It is only the spirit of man that can do so. Also, like the Stoics, Paul speaks of the opposition of the spirit and body/soul (Gal. 15:17); only in the end will the *spirit* ever triumph, when it will be rid of its earthly body. The Christian Trinity-the Father, the Word and the Spirit take the place of the four aspects of the Stoic divine unit-God, Word, Spirit and destiny. Also, when John says "these three are one," he is using familiar Stoic terms, while giving them a new dimension of significance.

When the Stoics said that Reason is imminent in all things, they brought together the ideal world of Plato and the material world; and when they asserted the unity of the final cause, they prepared the way for the recognition by the world of a single divine principle. Epictetus says that man is a "fragment of God, even a son of God" (D Ben, 1, 9; ii.9); and Virgil says: "What God we know not, yet a God there dwells" (Seneca, Ep. 41,2). Paul echoes these thoughts in Athens and other places: "For we are his offspring" (Acts 17:20); "For of him and through him and to him are all things..." (Rom. 11:36); "Yet for us there is one God, the Father from whom are all things and for whom we exist..." (I Cor. 8:6; see also Col. 1:15, 16). Aurelius said, "εκ σου πάντα, εισ σὲ πάντα, εν σοὶ πάντα."

However, though the terms used by Stoics and Christians are similar, their concepts of God are really quite different. By Epictetus' time (A.D. c. 50-130) God was not so often held to be a pure metaphysical abstraction as in Plato's day, but was more widely seen as an experiential reality:

> In thyself thou hearest Him and art unaware that thou art defiling Him with unclean thoughts and foul actions. If an image of God were present, thou wouldst not dare to behave so; but now God Himself is present within thee, seeing all things, hearing all things, yet thou art not ashamed of thy thoughts and deeds. (Epistetus quoted by More, 164)

This God, however, to the Stoic is only Providence, an impersonal Reason with no personality or being. Justin Martyr says: "I put myself in the hands of a Stoic, and I stayed a long time with him, but when I got no further in the matter of God—for he did not know himself and he used to say that this knowledge was not necessary—I left Him" (Dial. c. Tryph, 2).

Paul denied the Stoic fusion of God and man, teaching that man is wholly other than God. He went beyond the Stoic philosophy by stressing that repentance and worship of the true God form the basis of true ethics (Acts 17); whereas the Stoic held that God is a principle in man, and that the universe emanated from Him. Paul's God is the Creator of man—a personality who designed and created the universe. Though John (Rev. 1) uses the Stoic term λόγος for Christ, he also uses the term "Son of God." These terms together imply that Christ is not only the Divine Reason and Purpose of the universe, but also a personal Being who came to earth in the flesh and died for us. Thus, John gives much fuller significance and meaning to the Stoic term.

One of the main emphases in both Stoicism and Christianity is the brotherhood of man, which includes implications of both the equality of men and cosmopolitanism. Paul says that in Christ there is no Jew nor Gentile, no male nor female (Gal. 3:28; Col. 3:11). Zeno calls the world "one flock feeding in one pasture," and Marcus Aurelius says: "I cannot find it in my heart to be angry with any man, for we are all made for mutual help, as the feet, the hands, the eyelids...to me, Antonius, my city is Rome, but as a man it is the universe" (Aureluis, vi.44). So by both the Stoic and the Christian, men were considered equal and the world was cosmopolitan. But Paul makes a distinction: All those *in Christ* are equal; thus, the equality is not in human nature, rather, we can *become* brothers through Christ.

Similarly, the ethics of the Stoic and the Christian are very similar in terminology, although different in application. They both regard the way to virtue as a life of progress in which the utmost effort, vigilance and insight, as well as courage, patience and endurance are required to insure attainment of the goal. They both battle against the same enemies: the outward world of appearance, the treacherous inward self, the works of the flesh. They both seek inner freedom as opposed to outward freedom. One can see similarities between Paul's concept in I Corinthians 7:21-23 and (Seneca's) Stoic concept: "It (slavery) effects the body alone; the mind of the slave is free" (*cf.* Hicks, 143).

But the means of attaining virtue are different. The Stoics said the way to attain virtue was through self-control, serenity of mind, and freedom from fear or anxiety. This inner tranquility could only come by living in harmony with the divine will or purpose of the universe, and by being indifferent to the outcome of actions. The result was detachment from the affairs of the world and, even further, detachment from fear or pain: "Whatever the world did to you, in one sphere the world had no power; you could withdraw into your own soul, and there find peace; for none could harm you there but yourself" (Tarn, 300). Even human relations, relatives, were considered fleeting and uncontrollable, but inner peace, steadfastness of content, and compliance with God's will were the main and important things (Epictetus). This concept of reaching virtue is unlike Christianity's; though Christians are detached from the "cares of the world," such as riches, they are not indifferent to the success or failure of actions. Whereas the Stoic service of man is motivated by duty, Christian service is motivated by love.

William Fairweather comments: "The (Stoic) ideal of detachment and of the preservation at all costs of inner calm is irreconcilable with the ideal of love" (Fairweather, 242). To some measure, the Christian accepts the will of God in resignation, but whereas the Stoic does not share in another's suffering, the Christian is told to "bear one another's burdens," to serve one another with love (Gal. 6:2). The difference is between the Stoic sense of duty in life's relations and the Christian motivation to love others. Yet they point in the same direction by saying that man's obligations to God have priority over those of flesh and blood.

The Stoics believed that the world will end by being absorbed into the fiery ether from which it came, and then will emerge to begin again. In a similar way Paul speaks of being joined with Christ when once we are rid of the burden of flesh (Ph. 1:23; I Thess. 4:17: Heb. 11:16). But the Christian has the hope of a new life extending beyond the union with Christ: Instead of beginning the world process over again, the Christian looks forward to eternal life in the perfection of Christ. Peter, like the Stoic, speaks of the destruction of the world by fire (II Peter 3:7,10), but the world he speaks of does not begin again. Rather, a perfect universe comes forth. Although the Stoic does not fear death – Paul More says that for the Stoic "the Door is open," – emptiness lies beyond it.

> When God fails to provide for you, then He is giving the signal of retreat. He has opened the door, and says to you 'Come – where? – to nothing fearful, but thither whence you were born, to things friendly, and akin to you, to the elements.' (More, 169)

But for the Christian, this gate of death is the beginning of true life.

The question is, was Christianity influenced by Stoicism or vice versa? R. M. Wenley says that in the early church, philosophies of cosmology and metaphysics had not been worked out, and there was as yet no written gospel; so that when the Roman Christians faced philosophical questions concerning

God's relationship with man and the universe, he naturally turned to Stoicism, in which he found many principles similar to those of his own faith (Wenley, 118-20). Through Philo, a Stoic, "natural religion" was implanted in Christianity by Christianity's absorbing of the λόγος and Stoic moralism and the Stoic allegorical method, along with Plato's metaphysics and dualism, which were applied to interpret Jesus' sayings. The Christian "faith" had become Christian "philosophy," so that Justin Martyr even refers to Jesus as a "teacher" no less than a "Saviour." Thus, Wenley says that the Christian system was "impossible without Stoicism." By Trajan's time (A.D. 98-117) Christians regarded the Stoic λόγος as an "anticipation" of the Christian doctrine of the λόγος of John 1:1-3. Justin Martyr goes so far as to say that "all believers in the (Greek word) were (by anticipation) Christians."

Tertullian called the Roman Stoic Seneca "our Seneca" (in terms of Christianity) and Calvin commented on his (Seneca's) *On Clemency*. Jerome considered Seneca to have been a disciple of Paul, and the Council of Trent even cited him as one of the Church Fathers. From an examination of the evidence one can conclude that Seneca himself not improbably had a vague and partial acquaintance with Christianity, though he was certainly anything but a Christian himself; and that his personal intercourse with the Apostle of the Gentiles, though not substantiated, is at least not an impossibility. Possibly Seneca had some knowledge of Christianity but he was certainly not a Christian.

Paul, who had studied in Tarsus, one of the centers of Stoicism, was undoubtedly familiar with the Stoic philosophy and uses terms of its moral vocabulary to explain the Christian life. This is not unreasonable, since in the cities where the Christians preached and taught the gospel lived men and women who were educated in the Stoic concepts. Thus, although Paul used terms familiar to the people, he gave them a "new and higher significance"; for example, he taught that God was a personal Being and Father of the world, whereas to the Stoics, He was Nature, Fate, Fortune, the Universe, the all-pervading mind. As Lightfoot comments, "A living soul has been breathed into the marble statue by Christianity" (Fairweather, 300). When Paul quotes the Stoic poet Aratus or Cleanthes of Soli (Acts 17) he uses the Stoic doctrine as embodying an elementary truth and as *a starting point* for fuller knowledge. He brings forcibly to their recognition that though they had knowledge, they had in vain searched after truth. Now their altars to unknown gods "stood," in Ben Cochenet's phrase, "as mutely eloquent refutations, mocking their centuries of intellectual groping" (Cochenet, 33).

Parallel usages of concepts by Stoicism and Christianity (in Paul's writings) are seen in the following: "Good men toil, they spend and are spent" (Seneca and II Cor. 12:15); "Gather up and preserve the time: (Seneca and Eph. 5:16); "The evil man turns all things to evil" (Seneca and Titus 1:15); "I reflect how many exercise their bodies, how few their minds" (Seneca and I Tim. 4:3); and "They live ill who are always learning to live" (Seneca and II Tim. 3:7). However, it is not conclusive that either source is dependent upon the other, since it is unknown which is earlier. As Fairweather concludes:

> ...that is not, however, to say that the influence of Hellenism or primitive Christianity either vitally affected the substance of the faith or detracted from the essential independence of Christianity as an original and fresh revelation of religious truth. (Fairweather, *Jesus and the Greeks*, 296)

Both Stoicism and Christianity were born at a time when men needed something to believe in, and a guide for living. Stoicism answered some of these needs. It armed men against fear; it enabled brave and courageous spirits to face life's hardships; it encouraged endurance by its stern discipline; it taught the Providence of god and the brotherhood of man, made duty the paramount concern of life, and in many ways prepared the way for Christianity. Christianity then went beyond the Stoic principles. It brought a real and living personal God into contact with man; it taught the service of men out of love instead of cold duty; it gave a hope for the laborer and the heavy laden instead of admonitions to self-control. Finally, it gave a hope for the future, the promise of eternal life.

Chapter 7
EPICUREANISM

THE EPICUREANS WERE a philosophical school founded by Epicurus around 307-306 B.C. They were a rival to Platonism and Stoicism in the ancient Hellenistic world of the New Testament times. Epicureanism is not as important to the New Testament as is Stoicism, yet a knowledge of its beliefs helps to form the backdrop of the early church.

Epicurus was said to be a man of blameless character and amiable disposition. He purchased a garden in Athens where his group met to live and to discuss philosophy. Hence they became known as Epicureans or "philosophers of the Garden."

The major source of Epicurean doctrines is the *Life of Epicurus* by Diogenes Laertius which summarizes the philosophies. There are also three letters which Epicurus wrote to friends which reflect his principles: to Herodotus on atomic theory, to Pythocles on astronomy and meteorology, and to Menoeceus on ethics. In addition to these, Diogenes preserved a collection of forty *Kuriai Doxai (Cardinal Tenets)* – thought to have been formulated by Epicurus for the guidance of his followers.

Unfortunately, there seem to be several writings of Epicurus which are now lost: *Symposium* (a dialogue), *On the Gods, On the Highest Good,* and *Canon* (on the criterion of truth). The most important one is *Peri Physeos* (on nature) which consisted of 37 volumes. Fragments of nine of these were found in the charred remains of an Epicurean library at Herculaneum, which was buried by the eruption of Vesuvius in A.D. 79.

The mode of life of the "Garden philosophers" was plain; Water was the general drink and barley bread was the basic food. A half-pint of wine was considered an abundant allowance. Epicurus once wrote to a friend, "Send me some Cynthian (or potted) cheese, so that, should I choose, I may fare sumptuously" (Frag., 182).

Although the followers lived together, property was not in common. Epicurus felt that such commonality would imply distrust of their own and others' good resolutions.

The community was held together and functioned in unity because of Epicurus' own charming personality and the free society which he inculcated and exemplified. He treated all members as human beings rather than as political members or even as inferior students.

As for public life, Epicurus never entered it. Slaves and women belonged freely to his community—a fact which contributed to some of the scandalous opinions of his opponents. Not only free women belonged to this community, but female slaves with names like Leontion, Nikidion and Mammarion. Murray explains about these hetairae or courtesans:

> They were *hetairae*; perhaps victims of war, like many of the unfortunate heroines in the New Comedy; free women from conquered cities, who had been sold in the slave market or reduced to misery as refugees, and to whom now the Garden afforded a true and spiritual refuge. For, almost as much as Diogenes, Epicurus had obliterated the stamp on the conventional currency. The values of the world no longer held good after you had passed the wicket gate of the Garden, and spoken with the Deliverer. (Murray, 103)

Epicurus was born to Athenian parents on the Island of Samos. His father was a schoolmaster and his mother, Archestrata, was thought to have practiced witchcraft. While he was still young, the family was forced to become refugees and during this difficult time of his life, Epicurus began formulating philosophy in order to help his parents and brothers. "The problem," Gilbert Murray says, "was how to make the life of their little colony tolerable, and he somehow solved it" (Murray, 97).

When Epicurus was eighteen years old, he went to Athens to fulfill his year of military service, and from there he studied on the Island of the Aegean and coast of Asia Minor where he met followers of Plato and

Democritus. During these early studies Epicurus' mature philosophical awakening began. As he studied Hesiod about how chaos was the first of all things, it is said that he asked, "What then preceded chaos?" From this point he began formulating his own doctrines.

Epicurus first taught at Mytilene on Lesbos (c. 33 B.C.), and from there moved to Lampsacus, a city on the Hellespont, where he began to recruit followers.

Even in his early studies Epicurus protested against the inhuman superiority to natural sorrow which was so prized by the other ancient schools. He regarded such "apathy" as evidence of either a hard heart or a morbid vanity.

His letters are full of affectionate expressions. He waits for one friend's "heavenly presence'" he "melts with a peculiar joy mingled with tears in remembering the last words" of one who is dead; he enthuses over one who has walked five miles to help a barbarian prisoner. This often caused opposition from others but Diogenes Laertius says that the stories told by the Stoics (Epicurus' opponents) who sought to refute him by an appeal to his antecedents and habits are the stories of maniacs. In fact, they were simply attempting to undermine his rather different outlook on life.

In his later years, Epicurus had poor health. "But he had super-human courage," Murray says, "and – what does not always go with such courage – a very affectionate and gentle nature" (Murray, 98).

Epicurus eventually died painfully of stones in 270 B.C. It is interesting and characteristic that he spent his final moments remembering the happy hours spent in reasoning on questions of philosophy. The following are the words written to friends on his deathbed:

> I write to you on this blissful day which is the last of my life. The obstruction of my bladder and internal pains have reached the extreme point, but there is marshalled against them the delight of my mind in thinking over our talks together. Take care of the children of Metrodorus in a way worthy of your life-long devotion to me and to philosophy. (Frag., 138)

After his death, the school which Epicurus had founded celebrated his memory at a monthly feast. In the meantime his teaching spread through the Greek-speaking world. As for his philosophy, there were no further developments after his death. Two hundred and fifty years later, Lucretius varies little in detail from the master. Five hundred years later, Diogenes of Oenoanda actually repeats Epicurus' letters saying word for word.

Epicurus was primarily concerned with ethics, and physics and logic found a place only as a basis for his theory of life. For the purpose of our study, only his ethics will be discussed.

Epicurus believed that gods did exist and were immortal. They could be known by men by "clear vision" but many misunderstand them or misrepresent them. In his *Epistle to Menoeceus*, he says:

> The things which I used unceasingly to commend to you, these do and practice, considering them to be the first principles of the good life. First of all believe that god is a being immortal and blessed, even as the common idea of a god is engraved on men's minds, and do not assign to him anything alien to his immortality or ill-suited to his blessedness: but believe about him everything that can uphold his blessedness and immortality. For gods there are, since the knowledge of them is by clear vision. But they are not such as the many believe them to be: for indeed they do not consistently represent them as they believe them to be. And the impious man is not he who denies the gods of the many, but he who attaches to the gods the beliefs of the many. For the statements of the many about the gods are not conceptions derived from sensation, but false suppositions, according to which the greatest misfortunes befall the wicked and the greatest blessings (the good) by the gift of the gods. For men being accustomed always to their own virtues welcome those like themselves, but regard all that is not of their nature as alien. (*Ep. to Menoeceus*, 123ff.)

Epicurus reviews the moral principles which he has taught Menoeceus: Some desires are good while others are not; the right understanding of these facts enables one to choose in regard to the health of the body and freedom from disturbance which is ultimately the aim of the life of blessedness. Epicurus' own words:

> We must consider that of desires some are natural, others vain, and of the natural some are necessary and others merely natural; and of the necessary some are necessary for happiness, others for the repose of the body, and others for very life. The right understanding of these facts enables us to refer all choice and avoidance to the health of the body and [the soul's] freedom from disturbance, since this is the aim of the life of blessedness. For it is to obtain this end that we always act, namely, to avoid pain and fear. And when this is once secured

for us, all the tempest of the soul is dispersed.... (*Ep. to Menoeceus*, 128, 129)

One needs pleasure, Epicurus explains. On this issue, Epicurus seems to be often misunderstood. He explains what kind of pleasure he means when he says that it is the aim of the blessed life:

> For it is then that we have need of pleasure, when we feel pain owing to the absence of pleasure; [but when we do not feel pain], we no longer need pleasure. And for this cause we call pleasure the beginning and end of the blessed life. For we recognize pleasure as the first good innate in us, and from pleasure we begin every act of choice and avoidance, and to pleasure we return again, using the feeling as the standard by which we judge every good.
>
> And since pleasure is the first good and natural to us, for this reason we do not choose every pleasure, but sometimes we pass over many pleasures, when greater discomfort accrues to us as the result of them: and similarly we think many pains better than pleasures, since a greater pleasure comes to us when we have endured pains for a long time. Every pleasure then because of its natural kinship to us is good, yet not every pleasure is to be chosen: even as every pain also is an evil, yet not all are always of a nature to be avoided. Yet by a scale of comparison and by the consideration of advantages and disadvantages we must form our judgment on all these matters. For the good on certain occasions we treat as bad, and conversely the bad as good.
>
> And again independence of desire we think a great good—not that we may at all times enjoy but a few things, but that, if we do not possess many, we may enjoy the few in the genuine persuasion that those have the sweetest pleasure in luxury who least need it, and that all that is natural is easy to be obtained, but that which is superfluous is hard. And so plain savours bring us a pleasure equal to a luxurious diet, when all the pain due to want is removed; and bread and water produce the highest pleasure, when one who needs them puts them to his lips. To grow accustomed therefore to simple and not luxurious diet gives us health to the full, and makes a man alert for the needful employments of life, and when after long intervals we approach luxuries disposes us better toward them, and fits us to be fearless of fortune.
>
> When, therefore, we maintain that pleasure is the end, we do not mean the pleasures of profligates and those that consist in sensuality, as is supposed by some who are either ignorant or disagree with us or do not understand, but freedom from pain in the body and from trouble in the mind. For it is not continuous drinkings and revellings, nor the satisfaction of lusts, nor the enjoyment of fish and other luxuries of the

> wealthy table, which produce a pleasant life, but sober reasoning, searching out the motives for all choice and avoidance, and banishing mere opinions, to which are due the greatest disturbance of the spirit. (*Ep. to Menoeceus*, 129-32)

Epicurus further explains that,

> ...the beginning of all these [achievements of philosophy] and the greatest good [of all] is prudence....From it the other virtues are born, since it teaches [us] that it is impossible to live happily unless we live prudently, honestly, and justly; or to live prudently, honorably, and justly without living happily. For the virtues are one in origin with the life of happiness, and the life of happiness is inseparable from the virtues. (*Ep. to Menoeceus*, 132ff.)

Epicurus sees the future as "neither ours nor yet altogether not ours, so that we may not look forward to it as absolutely sure to come nor give up hope of it as if it will certainly not come" (*Ep. to Menoeceus*, 127).

Epicurus was often accused of encouraging sensuality and pleasure in a lustful sense, but his own words deny this. He says, "The wise man will not fall in love," and again, "Physical union of the sexes never did good; it is much if it does not do harm." Murray comments that Epicurus was not necessarily selfish but rather was aiming at the deliverance of mankind. He bases happiness on φιλιά (friendship) or affection rather than ἔρος (sensual love) (Murray, 104).

Epicurus had a very practical way of considering death.

> Get accustomed to the idea that death means nothing to us. For all good and evil consist in sensation, and death is only the deprivation of sensation. Hence a real understanding that death means nothing to us makes the mortality of [our] life enjoyable, not by adding to it an unlimited length of time, but by taking away the desire for immortality. For there is nothing dreadful in life for the man who has really grasped the idea that there is nothing dreadful in *not* living. So that anyone is foolish who says that he is afraid of death, not because it will be painful when it comes, but because it is painful in prospect. For what gives [us] no trouble when it comes is only an empty pain as we look forward to it. So death, the most terrifying of evils, is nothing to us; for as long as we exist death is not present with us, and when death comes then we no longer exist. It is no concern, therefore, either of the living or the dead; for the former it does not exist, while the latter themselves no longer exist.

> But the majority at one time flee from death as the greatest of all evils, but at another time [they yearn for it] as a rest from the [evils] in life. (*Ep. to Menoeceus*, 125, 126)

Epicurus' closing words to Menoeceus indicate to us the high regard he had for philosophy and companionship with others.

> Cherish these things and those like them day and night, by yourself and with someone [a companion] like yourself, and you will never be upset, but will live like a god among men. For the man who lives among the eternal values has lost all likeness to the beasts that perish. (*Ep. to Menoeceus*, 126)

The latter Epicureans seem to have held closely to their founder's teaching, as we can see by the writings of an Epicurean named Diogenes (c. A.D. 200). He wrote this inscription on a portico beside the road near Oenoanda in Lycia:

> Having arrived by our years at the sunset of life, and expecting at any time now to depart out of the world with a glad song and a heart filled with happiness, we have decided, lest we be snatched away too soon, to offer some help to the rightly disposed.
>
> For if even one person, or perhaps two or three or four or five or six, or any large number you choose – but not everyone – were in trouble, O fellow mortal, and I were called upon to help them one after another, I would do everything I could to give them good advice. But now, as I have said, the majority of mankind are everywhere sick as with a pestilence, by reason of their false beliefs about things. And the number of the diseased grows steadily; for they imitate one another, and catch the illness from each other like an epidemic in a flock of sheep.
>
> Furthermore, it is only right to help those who are to come after us, since they too belong to us, though not yet born. And finally, love for mankind bids us render aid to strangers passing by.
>
> Since, therefore, the help provided in writing [or from *the* writings, i.e., of Epicurus] is more certain, I have decided to use this wall [literally, stoa] to set forth the medicine needed for the healing [of mankind]....
>
> > Nothing to fear in God;
> > Nothing to feel in Death;
> > Good can be attained;
> > Evil can be endured.
>
> (F. C. Grant, *Hellenistic Religions*, 161)

The most significant follower of Epicurus was the Roman poet Lucretius (c. 99-55 B.C.) who found in the teaching of Epicurus such a great relief from pain and fear he expressed it in religious terms:

> When Man's life upon earth in base dismay,
> Crushed by the burthen of Religion lay,
> Whose face, from all the regions of the sky,
> Hung, glaring hate upon mortality,
> First one Greek man against her dared to raise
> His eyes, against her strive through all his days;
> Him noise of gods nor lightnings nor the roar
> Of raging heaven subdued, but pricked the more
> His spirit's valiance, till he longed the Gate
> To burst of this low prison of man's fate.
> And thus the living ardour of his mind
> Conquered, and clove its way; he passed behind
> The world's last flaming wall, and through the whole
> Of Space uncharted ranged his mind and soul.
> Whence, conquering, he returned to make Man see
> At last what can, what cannot, come to be:
> By what law to each Thing its power hath been
> Assigned, and what deep boundary set between;
> Till underfoot is tamed religion trod,
> And, by his victory, Man ascends to God.
> (Lucretius, *On the Nature of Things*, 1, 62-79)

The Epicureans are reflected very little in the New Testament literature. Unlike the Stoics, their terminology was not used by Paul to explain Christian concepts. Neither do they seem to have created any problem of heresy in the early Church. Nevertheless, there are a few passages upon which the Epicureans can shed light.

They are actually mentioned by name in Acts when Paul visited Mars Hill in Athens (Acts 17:18). They, along with the Stoics, listened to Paul talk about the one true God who created the world. They probably did not adamantly disagree with this since they did believe that God existed. They probably did not understand the reason for limiting the gods to one. The real issues of conflict would have been twofold: the resurrection and the idea of judgment. Since the Epicureans believed that one ceased to exist at death, they probably felt that Paul's emphasis on the resurrection of the dead was not only ridiculous but unnecessary. The idea of repentance, judgment and rewards would have been totally foreign. Since the Epicureans held that there was no afterlife, they would have had no use for repentance, judgment or rewards. There were undoubtedly Epicureans among the group which began to sneer at Paul, although it would have been characteristic had some suggested hearing him again (Acts 17:32).

There is an issue on which the Epicureans would have agreed with Christianity: love for our fellow man. Diogenes in his philosophical inscription bids the Epicurean to love mankind by helping the passing stranger. They would have responded warmly to Jesus' parable on the Good Samaritan (Luke 10:30-37). Along these same lines, they would have readily agreed with Paul's statements on the equality of men and women, slaves and free, rich and poor (Gal. 3:28). There is also a similarity between the communal living of the early Church and that of Epicurus and his followers who lived and met together in his Garden in Athens.

Epicurus would have agreed with the early Christians on the subject of love. He based happiness on φιλιά (friendship) or affection rather than ἔρος (sensual love) just as the early Christians based it on ἀγάπη (divine love).

Finally, there is one phrase quoted in the New Testament which is often attributed to or related to the Epicureans, "...let us eat and drink; for tomorrow we die" (I Cor. 15:32). In view of Epicurus' own words quoted above, this is not indicative of Epicurean philosophy, but could have reflected a popular view of Epicurus fostered by his opponents.

Chapter 8

GNOSTICISM

GNOSTICS, OR THE "knowing ones"—sects which claimed an esoteric, intuitive knowledge or spiritual truth—present a special problem for study of the world of the New Testament. Their origins seem to have been a synthesis of oriental and Hellenistic influence which cannot be accurately traced. But by the second century A.D. they emerge as a philosophy claiming to adhere to Christianity, or rather, as a Christian heresy. The question which has most occupied scholars is whether Gnosticism had an appreciable influence on the Christianity established by the Apostles.

In Gnosticism, a radical dualism governs the relation between God and the world. The Deity is pure abstraction, unknown and unknowable, an antithesis to the universe. He neither created it nor governs it. Montefoire and Turner comment: "We look in vain for any trace of the robust personalism of the New Testament religion despite all references to the living Jesus, the Living One, the living Father and sons of the living Father..." (van Groningen, 176). There is a type of spirituality present, but no personal relationship between God and man. The Divine realm is characterized by light, it is self-contained and remote. The cosmos is opposed as the realm of darkness.

The world is the work of the lowly powers, Archons (rulers) who obstruct any knowledge of God, though they descended from God. Because of them, knowledge of God requires supernatural illumination and revelation.

The universe is the domain of the Archons, or the great demon in some writings, and is a vast prison. Seven spheres of planets surround the earth, and an eighth sphere of fixed stars surrounds them. All these lie between God and man and by a demonic force keep man from God. The Archon's power the Gnostics call "Heimarmene," or Universal Fate (or the Law of Nature). After death, souls are kept from reaching God by the Archons ("Asclepius," The Nag Hammadi Library, VI. 8. 76-78). "As guardian of his sphere," Hans Jonas summarizes, "each Archon bars the passage to the souls that seek to ascend after death, in order to prevent their escape from the world and their return to God." The leader of the Archons is the Demiurge (from Plato's *Timaeus*), and is sometimes pictured similar to the Old Testament God (*cf.* Plato, *Timaeus*, 41a-d).

Man is predominantly involved in the evil aspects of the cosmos. He originated from the cosmic powers and is made up of three parts: flesh, soul and spirit (pneuma). Through the body and soul man is subjected to the power of the Archons; only the spirit can be awakened by knowledge.

> In its unredeemed state the pneuma thus immersed in soul and flesh is unconscious of itself, benumbed, asleep, or intoxicated by the prison of the world (i.e., it is ignorant). Its awakening and liberation is effected through knowledge. (Jonas, 44)

Not everyone is able to attain salvation through knowledge. There are three types of men: the purely material; the "soulish" or animal; and the "gnostic" or spiritual. Only this last type has the "spark" which enables him to attain salvation.

Because of the concept that the cosmos is generally evil, Gnostic morality was determined by contempt for the mundane world. This produced two contrasting systems of ethics. In one, the Ascetics held that redemption was release from the material world itself. Asceticism prevents defilement from the evil, material world. To Gnostics such as Marcion, Tatian and Saturinus any violation of a rigid asceticism was "sinful." To Marcion even marriage was an evil and unchaste thing. But in a second system the Libertines held that redemption was release from convention. They defiled the body by indulging in sensuality to prove the exaltation of spirit over matter. They felt that the Old Testament Law should be disobeyed out of regard for the true God; disobedience to the Ten Commandments constituted morality.

Gnosis refers to the *means* of redemption. Men must take this means, this "knowing," and use it to free themselves from the cosmic prison. The Holy Spirit gives men the power to use the means. But this power (Holy Spirit) is already in the man who has the seed (Father) or the revelation (Logos). Sometimes the power in man is called the "spark." Gnosis then made man capable of redemption (van Groningen, 181).

The function of Christ was to redeem the world out of the evil realm and to bring Gnostics to the spiritual realm. Details differ on Christ's connection with the Demiurge, but basically Gnostics held that,

> From the supreme God, a spiritual power came forth (Logos or Christos), descended to earth, and helped the kindred spirit in mankind to break from the prison of the body. This is close to Christianity, but their dualism would not permit the Word to become flesh. (More, 58-59)

This led to Docetism, which held if Christ was divine, He could not have come in the flesh. Gnostics held that Christ took up His human abode in the man Jesus at His baptism and departed before His crucifixion. They held that Jesus' life was only a temporary and seeming union of two natures. Since Christ was not actually crucified (only the man Jesus), redemption comes not through Christ's death but through His impartation of the true gnosis to the disciples. This gnosis enabled one to attain freedom from the evil material world.

The Anti-Judaistic Gnostics rejected the Old Testament. The Judaistic Gnostics accepted the Old Testament but interpreted it allegorically. Jonas says that "Gnostic allegory is not always conventional, that is, adapting myth to philosophy, but proves the deeper knowledge by reversing the roles of good and evil, sublime and base, blest and original" (Jonas, 91-92). Tertullian wrote:

> One man perverts the Scriptures with his hand, another with their meaning by his exposition. For although Valentinus [a prominent Gnostic] seems to use the entire volume, he has nonetheless laid violent hands on the truth, only with a more cunning mind and skill than Marcion [another Gnostic]. Marcion expressly and openly used the knife, not the pen, since he made such an excision of the Scriptures as suited his own

subject matter. (Tertullian, "The Prescription Against Heresies," XXXVIII)

The goal for the Gnostic was to release the captive "inner man" from the world and return to the realm of light. Knowledge made freedom possible. The Valentinian formula is: "What liberates is the knowledge of who we were; what we became; where we were; whereinto we have been thrown; whereto we speed; wherefrom we are redeemed; what birth is and what rebirth."

Although details differed among various Gnostic sects, the foregoing tenets above were generally basic to all Gnostics. Robert Grant summarizes Gnostic beliefs.

> ...that the world is bad; it is under the control of evil or ignorance or nothingness. It cannot be redeemed; indeed, for some Gnostics the world is the equivalent of hell. Only the divine spark, which somehow is imprisoned in some men, is capable of salvation. It is saved when, by divine grace, it comes to know itself, its origin, and its destiny. (Grant, 15)

Although Gnosticism was a developed and organized system by A.D. 100, not much is known about its earlier development, or about its pre-Christian (sometimes called pre-Gnostic) origins. There is much controversy and discussion concerning these origins.

It is thought that Gnosticism could have come from Greek philosophy, especially Platonism. Scholars today generally agree that Gnosticism is not *pure* Hellenic Platonism, but rather an orientalized version of it. Thomas Lindsay suggests that Philo, from the Graeco-Jewish school at Alexandria, falsely interpreted Plato's ideas such as those of the Absolute, the contrast of real and ideal, and the material nature of evil, and that these modified ideas were used by the Gnostics. Paul More points out that though Gnosticism carries some ideas from Plato's *Phaedrus* and *Timaeus*, it is radically different from Platonism. Plato considered evil to be a necessity which lurks in creation, but creation itself is good, while the Gnostics held that creation itself is evil in origin and essence. Any stray element of good has been captured from the realm of light by the realm of darkness (More, 54).

More suggests that Gnosticism was originally connected with the Persian myth of two hostile kingdoms of light and darkness and the Assyrian conflict of Marduk and Tiamat (More, 53). From each of these kingdoms came a series of emanations. Gnosticism differs from the Persian religion, however, in its view of the original evil: Gnosticism regards it as material while the Persian religion regards it as spiritual. Possibly the Persian Parseeism was mediated by the Jewish Essenes who, like the Gnostics, emphasize asceticism, despisal of the body, denial of bodily resurrection, intellectual exclusivism and angelology (Lindsay, 17-18).

Gnosticism could also have originated from Palestinian and Syrian sources. Some scholars hold that Simon Magus, a magician in Samaria (Acts 8:9), and his successors, Menander and Saturninus, were the originators of Gnosticism (van Groningen, 10-11).

It could have originated from Judaism, even though Judaism did not have within it the basic motifs for gnostic thinking. In fact, the Gnostics generally denounced the Old Testament Scriptures. But there is the possibility that it could have sprung from Hellenestic Judaism through Philo and the Diaspora, as several scholars, such as R. M. Wilson, Rudolf Bultmann and Robert Grant, maintain. The Gnostics seemed to have borrowed some Old Testament ideas from Genesis for their cosmology, despite their stated disdain for Scripture (van Groningen, 10).

Some early Church Fathers can be interpreted to indicate that Gnosticism grew either into or from Christianity, that is, that Christianity incorporated Gnostic elements or Gnosticism adapted Christianity. We will examine this debate later in this chapter (van Groningen, 10-11).

It has been suggested that Gnosticism could have originated from the Buddhism of India, but most scholars agree that it probably did not (*cf.* Lindsay, 14). Grant suggests a broader view: "I should be inclined, in view of 1) the nonphilosophical nature of Gnosticism, and 2) the relative rarity of this kind of dualism among Hellenistic philosophers, to claim that it originates from historical experience" (Grant, 38).

Many scholars in fact hold that Gnosticism was syncretistic, that is, it did not originate from any single source; rather, it was a synthesis of many influences. More says that it is possibly found "in the imposition of the Zoroastrian religion of Ormazd and Ahriman on the astrological science of Babylon....Then there entered in a Syrian belief in the Great Mother, fragments of the Jewish Law and story of creation, the confusion of

Platonism and Pythagoreanism and other myths from Egypt and the far corners of the world. Various proportions of each of these, along with the Christian concept of salvation and a pagan background, would have mixed to form Gnosticism" (More, 52-53).

Otto Pfleiderer holds that Gnosticism was Jewish-Babylonian and originally rose in the Jewish Diaspora of the East, apart from the Christian influence and prior to Christianity. It then came in contact with Christianity and mingled with it because they had much in common; for example, the doctrine of redemption: the Redeemer coming to earth and returning to heaven as victor (Pfleiderer, 126).

W. C. van Unnik lists the probable spheres of influence in Gnosticism: dualism from Iran; astrology from Babylon; worship of sun-god from Syria; Greek philosophy; reaction against Judaic Scriptures; and the Egyptian mystery cult of Isis-Osiris (van Groningen, 13).

The evidence, obviously, for any one or all of these is not conclusive. Hans Jonas observes that because Gnosticism is syncretistic, each theory can be substantiated (Jonas, 33). The problem is obscure because it is not even clear what the early Gnosticism of the first century actually was. Only inferences can be made from the evidence of later Gnostic forms, from what the Church Fathers say from their impressions or acquaintances, or from the few available writings of the Gnostics themselves (Grant, 3-6).

The definition of Gnosis presents another problem: Does this include all the sects and trends which emphasized a special knowledge or only the later developed systems like that of Valentinus?

> Gnosis denotes in general all more profound and philosophical or religious knowledge, in distinction from superficial opinion or blind belief. (Thomas P. Lindsay, 1)

> The emphasis is on knowledge as the means for attainment for salvation, or salvation itself, and the claim of this knowledge in one's own articulate doctrine. (Jonas, 32)

Gnostic knowledge, in this general sense, was different than philosophical knowledge, which points to rational objects and natural reason. Gnostic knowledge meant that knowledge of God, and its objects such as salvation were heavenly and from above.

The Valentinians defined gnosis as "redemption of the inner, spiritual man, not of the body or the soul" (Grant, 7). Gnosis was subjective and involved knowing oneself: Monomius, a first century Gnostic, said:

> Abandon the search for God and the creation and other matters of a similar sort. Look for him taking *yourself* as the starting point. Learn who it is who *within you* makes everything his own and says, 'My God, *my* mind, *my* thought, *my* soul, *my* body.' Learn the sources of sorrow, joy, love, hate. Learn how it happens that one watches without willing, rests without willing, becomes angry without willing, loves without willing. If you carefully investigate these matters you will find him in *yourself*. (Hippolytus, *Ref.* VIII, 15.1-2)

Thus, Gnosis in the broad sense is pre-Christian, and includes all those trends which emphasized knowledge. There are indications that an incipient Gnosticism in the narrow sense existed in the New Testament period and developed into the systems of the second century. R. M. Wilson discerns three possible stages: first, "pre-Gnosticism," including the various trends seen in Hellenistic syncretism, Philo and the Dead Sea Scrolls, an incipient form opposed by the New Testament; second, "Gnosticism-proper," represented by the sects of the second century; and third, later developments such as Manicheism, Mandeism and others (Wilson, 98).

Many scholars say that Simon Magnus began Gnosticism and that his successors Menander, Saturninus and Basilides were responsible for the Christian turn. With Saturninus came also asceticism. Otto Pfleiderer says, "Thus the libertinism of the Cainite-Simonian Gnosis is here transmuted into asceticism, a transformation which materially aided the propagation of this gnosis in Christian circles (Pfleiderer, 144).

Gnosticism and the New Testament

Although there is almost nothing in the Synoptic Gospels resembling Gnosticism, some Gnostics supported their views by allegorical interpretation of Jesus' saying or noncontextual literal exegesis.

Matthew 11:25 (Luke 10:21, 22): "At that time Jesus answered and said, 'I praise Thee, O Father, Lord of heaven and earth, that Thou didst hide these things from the wise and intelligent and didst reveal them to babes.'" The Son is presented as the sole instrument of revelation, as in Gnosticism.

Matthew 11:28-30: "Come to Me, all who are weary and heavy-laden, and I will give you rest. Take My yoke upon you, and learn from Me, for I am gentle and humble in heart: and you shall find rest for your souls. For My yoke is easy, and My load is light." The wisdom-Christology points to the Gnostic speculation, but there is no reason that these words should not be original to Christ, rather than influenced by Gnosticism. R. M. Wilson comments:

> What is beyond question is that the Synoptic Gospels later provided the material for much Gnostic speculation, and also that Thomas (the Gospel of) at times shows a special affinity for Luke; but this of course does not make the Synoptics themselves 'Gnostic,' or prove that they were subject to Gnostic influence. (Wilson, 44)

G. Quespel points out the significance of the discovery of the Gnostic *Gospel of Truth* a few years ago. Among other things, it challenges G. A. Van den Bergh van Eysinga's theory that the Four Gospels were an historical development from the Gnostic Alexandrian Gospel. The codex seems to have been written around A.D. 150 and the writer seems to have been familiar with the Gospels and the Epistles of John, as well as the Synoptic Gospels and the Epistles of Paul. According to Quespel, this shows that Gnosticism rests on the Gospels, not vice versa (Frank Cross, *The Jung Codex*, 49-50).

Some say that John's Gospel was Gnostic. Robert Grant, however, says that the Gospel was probably "used" by Gnostics but that the author himself was not a Gnostic: "The Gospel thus belongs to the history of Gnosticism only in the sense that it was used by Gnostics, who read into it speculations from a thought-world not altogether alien to that of the Evangelist himself. He himself, however, was no Gnostic" (Grant, 45-46).

Several themes in the Gospel could be interpreted to suggest a Gnostic relationship. For example, John indicated a definite dualism of light and darkness, the world above and this world, spirit and flesh, but this is more of an ethical dualism than that of the Gnostics and seems closer to Judaism (8:23; 17:6, 16; 12:46; 8:12). John also speaks of the mystery surrounding Christ—no one knew whence He came or where He was going (4:14; 8:14; 9:29). He gave that which no one knew about—the Spirit (3:8) and living water (4:11). Jesus imparted this knowledge to the disciples (13:36; 14:5).

But even though some of John's terminology is Gnostic, most of his concepts are decidedly not, and many stand in direct opposition to Gnostic teaching. "The Word became flesh" (1:4) – the Gnostics developed Docetism in opposition to this claim.

"Its own did not receive It" (1:11) – the Gnostics held that only those who had the divine "spark" could receive the Logos. This idea of rejection was foreign to the Gnostics.

John wrote of a future resurrection and of water in connection with rebirth, neither of which is a Gnostic concept. In comparison with the Valentinian *Gospel of Truth*, John alone includes an eschatological motif; and Gnosticism shows the human situation in terms of ignorance rather than sin. Andrew Hembold comments that "the Nag Hammadi" texts, along with those from Qumran, make it impossible to regard the Gospel of John as a Hellenistically informed Gospel (Hembold, 89-90).

R. M. Wilson observes however that the relationship between John's Gospel and Gnosticism is problematical. Is it called Gnostic because it was used in the later Gnostic systems, or was it already Gnostic and in what sense? The later Gnostics may have borrowed from John or John may have used their own language to combat them, or he may simply have used the language of his period which was broadly characterized by Gnosis (Wilson, 47-48).

I John contains probably the clearest and most distinct examples of New Testament writings against the Gnostic heresy. He combatted some of the main concepts of the Gnostics: those who say "we have no sin," those who deny that Christ came in the flesh (4:2; 5:6), those who are indifferent to moral conduct ("do not walk as he walked").

The heretics of I John evidently have a problem with Christ himself. The question now arises, in what sense do the heretical teachers deny that Jesus is the Christ? Since they belong, or claim to belong, to the Christian congregation, they must have believed in Christ in some sense, must have understood him as the revealer or bringer of salvation, indeed, even as the preexistent one. In what sense they believed can only become clear when one perceived in what sense they denied his divine sonship.

According to 4:2f and 2 Jn 7 they dispute that Jesus Christ 'came in the flesh,' and when in 5:6 it is claimed, in opposition to them, that Jesus came 'by water and blood,' then everything points to the fact that they deny that Christ is identical with the earthly, historical Jesus. This can only be understood from the standpoint that the doctrine of the heretics is rooted in the dualism of Gnosticism, which asserts the exclusive antithesis between God and the sensible world. It is a secondary question whether we can determine more precisely the specific Gnostic tendency or sect that the author has in mind. The decisive point is that Gnostic thought cannot comprehend the offense which the Christian idea of revelation offers, namely the paradox that a historical event (or historical form) is the eschatological event (or form).

Several theories state that Paul's writings were influenced by Gnosticism or that Paul himself was a Gnostic (Wilson, 71). One theory holds that Paul took the Gnostic motifs and used them without understanding their meaning. Later Gnostics then allegedly adapted Paul and restored the "real" and "original" meaning to the terms. But Wilson observes that this interpretation is based on many mere assumptions. There are, however, several terms used by Paul which sounds Gnostic

In Galatians, Paul says that we are not to serve gods who are "weak and impoverished *stoicheia*" (principles). Possibly these *stoicheia* could be identified with the angels through whom the Mosaic Law was ordained (3:19). They were "weak and impoverished" because of Christ's triumph. In Colossians, he said that we have "died with Christ and are separated from the *stoicheia* of the world" (2:20).

Ephesians contains several conceivably Gnostic concepts. Christians live in "heavenly regions"; the Church ascended to heaven to make the wisdom of God known to the principalities and powers (3:10); our warfare is against principalities, powers and spiritual beings (6:12). These could conceivably reflect the daemons of the seven planets which kept man from reaching God.

I and II Corinthians contain even more elements that could reflect Gnosticism: the contrast of ψυχικοί (souls) and πνευματικοί (spirits) (I Cor. 2:14f.; 15:21, 44-49), the demonic rulers of the age (I Cor. 2:6-8; II Cor. 4:4), the dangers of marriage (I Cor. 7:32-34, 38), the "archons of this aeon" who crucified the Lord of Glory because they did not know God's hidden wisdom (I Cor. 2:8), the wisdom section (I Cor. 1-2) indicating a reflection of the pre-Christian Sophia myth prominent in the Gnostic systems, figures of speech such as Satan as an angel of light, and the third heaven (both in II Cor. 11-12).

Some scholars suggests that Paul's opponents in Corinth were Gnostic or a combination of Judaizers and Gnostics (see Schmithal's *Gnosticism in Corinth* for a discussion of the problem). It is probable that in some way they were connected with Gnostics because of Paul's emphasis on knowledge, e.g., the wisdom of God versus the wisdom of the world (I Cor. 2:4), etc. In II Corinthians 11:22, however, the opponents are described by Paul as Jewish, so the problem is not a simple one. There is the possibility that they may have been Jewish Gnostics, but the problem is too complicated to discuss in detail here.

The Pastoral Epistles can be read to suggest several Gnostic doctrines and practices that are anti-Christian: the resurrection being already past (II Tim. 2:18), Docetic Christology (II Tim. 2:8; I Tim. 2:5f.; 3:16), myths and genealogies possibly referring to the Gnostic sequence of powers (I Tim. 1:4), prohibitions against marriage and certain foods (I Tim. 4:3), Paul warning Timothy to guard against the false gnosis (I Tim. 6:20). Paul seems simply to be using Gnostic vocabulary to explain Christian concepts.

In II Peter and Jude those referred to as opponents of Christian doctrine and conduct also seem to be Gnostics. Readers are warned against those who deny the *Parousia* and the Lord himself, and those who practice immorality.

Dr. M. C. Tenney explains in relation to II Peter, that "the peril confronting the churches was that of doubt and error arising from the false teachings of those who professed to be leaders. 'There shall be false teachers, who shall privily bring in destructive heresies, denying even the Master that bought them' (II Peter 2:1). The nature of this departure from the norm of faith was not outlined completely. It seems to have involved a denial of the redemption and lordship of Christ (2:1) adding a complete abandonment of all moral standards and a bold self-assertiveness which was the accompaniment of spiritual ignorance" (Tenney, *Survey*, 386).

Peter appears to look ahead to the problem, whereas the community of Jude is actually experiencing the problem: "For certain persons have crept in unnoticed, those who were long beforehand marked out for this condemnation, ungodly persons who turn the grace of our God into licentiousness and deny our only Master and Lord, Jesus Christ" (Jude 4; *cf.* also vv. 8, 12, 16ff., which also denote a present situation).

The problem in II Peter's community seems to involve knowledge – the words *know* and *knowledge* appear sixteen times, six of which refer to the knowledge of Christ. Tenney comments, "If the errorists were magnifying their knowledge as the basis of their superiority, Peter wanted to show that the answer to false knowledge is true knowledge" (Tenney, *Survey*, 386). This emphasis on knowledge combined with the issue of "denying the Master" (II Peter 2:1; Jude 4) suggests the Gnostics with their emphasis on gnosis and their problem about Jesus coming in the flesh.

We can observe several contrasts in Paul's theology and Gnostic teaching. The Gnostic gift of salvation frees man from responsibility while Paul emphasizes responsibility to God and man. To the Gnostics, the heavenly gift was an end in itself while Paul stressed that the gifts were to be used for the good of the community. McGiffert observes that though Marcion and other Gnostics found elements for their systems in Paul's writings (dualism, salvation as a gift, etc.), they perverted and distorted Paul's concepts.

> All have their points of contact in the system of Paul, and may be recognized as more or less perverted and distorted reproductions of his views touching the relation of law and Gospel, the origin and nature of the Christian life, and the person and work of Christ. (McGiffert, 503)

Was Christianity, then, influenced by Gnosticism, or was Gnosticism influenced by Christianity? Was Gnosticism a heresy rising from within Christianity or was it a separate system of its own? Because so little is known conclusively about the origins of Gnosticism, these questions cannot be answered definitely. Scholars, however, have given their opinions on the matter.

Irenaeus says it was a false religion that may have borrowed some Christian concepts, but it was not a Christian heresy. Rudolf Bultmann, Hans Jonas and others say that Christianity and Gnosticism were two simultaneously emerging movements which influenced each other (van Groningen, 16). R. M. Wilson comments: "...on its entry upon the stage of the wider world Christianity had to be 'translated' from its original Palestinian thought-forms and terms of reference into those comprehensible in its new environment" (Wilson, 51). Hence, Paul, used Hellenistic terms for the proclamation of the gospel while opposing the attempt to make it another form of Judaism or to merge it with the general syncretism of the age. Wilson also says that there is nothing to indicate whether Gnosticism was a false teaching within Christianity, or whether it was a system developed outside.

W. C. van Unnik from studying the Valentinian *Gospel of Truth* said, "It is clear that the *Gospel of Truth* seeks to build on the foundation of the New Testament, but with a plan of its own which was not that outlined in the New Testament." Wilson states:

> ...'Christianity attracted the attention of thinkers who stood in the line of development of which the Poimandres is a representative,' and who introduced the figure of Christ with a varying measure of other Christian elements, into the speculations to produce the Gnostic systems.

In consideration of the Gnostic problem in the first century, its place and date of origin, and its relation to the New Testament, one must be cautious from which angle one approaches. If one were to look from the side of the second century and interpret the evidence in the light of the later systems, one would probably conclude that much of the New Testament was influenced by Gnosticism. But when one begins at the New Testament end, the so-called "Gnostic" features admit of a different interpretation – they seldom demand a truly Gnostic interpretation. One must ask if these elements are interpreted as "Gnostic" only in the context of the later developed systems of the second century.

The recent discoveries at Nag Hammadi and Egypt have shed some light on these questions, but not all of the finds have been studied fully yet. With the publication of the *Nag Hammadi Library*, a collection of the Gnostic tractites found at Nag Hammadi, these important documents are now available to all scholars. Work is still in progress, however, on the significance of these Gnostic texts. Perhaps in the near future these discoveries of Gnostic writings will lead to definitive answers to our questions.

WHEN VESPASIAN DIED, *Domitian constantly plotted secretly or openly against his brother Titus. As an example of Domitian's perverted and cruel nature, Suetonius says the following:* "At the beginning of his reign Domitian would spend hours every day catching flies – believe it or not! – and stabbing them with a needle-sharp pen."

During the early part of his reign (A.D. 81-96), Domitian fostered games, music and displays; he restored public buildings, some which had been ruined in the fire of A.D. 80. At this time, though he was cruel, he hated bloodshed and even forbad the sacrificing of oxen.

His cruel streak soon surfaced, however. He executed anyone on the least suspicion, devised cruel and inhuman tortures and put many senators to death on extremely trivial charges. Suetonius describes an episode which indicates Domitian's tendency toward insanity:

> He summoned a Palace steward to his bedroom, invited him to share his couch, made him feel perfectly secure and happy, condescended to share a dinner with him – yet had already given orders for his crucifixion on the following day!

At his ascension to the throne, Domitian began to voice thoughts about his divinity. He once wrote a letter and forced his procurator to circulate it, with the preface "Our Lord God instructs you to do this." *The title* "Lord God" *became his regular title both in writing and conversation.*

Everyone eventually hated and feared Domitian. A conspiracy arose to murder him and he was killed in A.D. 96, after he had reigned for fourteen years.

During Domitian's reign the Church again experienced persecution. Eusebius says:

> Domitian, having exercised his cruelty against many, and unjustly slain no small number of noble and illustrious men at Rome, and having, without cause, punished vast numbers of honourable men with exile and the confiscation of their property, at length established himself as the successor of Nero, in his hatred and hostility to God. He was the second that raised a persecution against us, although his father Vespasian had attempted nothing to our prejudice.

Probably during Domitian's persecution John the Apostle was banished to Patmos, and Flavia Domitilla, niece of Flavius Clemens, a consul of Rome was sent to Pontia. Hegesippus says that Domitian also persecuted Jews. He recounts an episode in which Christians, when asked about their belief, said, that it was not a temporal nor an earthly kingdom, but celestial and angelic; that it would appear at the end of the world, when coming in glory he would judge the quick and the dead, and give to everyone according to his works (Hegesippus, quoted in Conzelmann, 167).

Hegesippus goes on to say that though Domitian despised Christians and treated them with contempt, he dismissed them and ordered an end to the persecution. Tertullian comments on this:

> *Domitian had also once attempted the same against him, who was, in fact, a limb of Nero for cruelty; but I think, because he had yet some remains of reason, he very soon suppressed the persecution, even recalling those whom he had exiled.*

Therefore, the persecution, though severe, did not last very long, and many of those who were punished by banishment were returned. John, the apostle, however, was not released from Patmos until Trajan's time (A.D. 98-117).

CONCLUSION

CONCLUSION

THE CHURCH WAS not born alone and it did not develop alone. It confronted an often hostile environment, and the way it faced the conflicts and questions that arose around it not only determined its survival, but further defined its own meaning for mankind. It had to deal internally with struggles of doctrine as well as externally with struggles and persecution.

The Church was triumphant. It did not succumb to persecutions, or to zealous Judaizers who attempted to force traditions of the Law on new converts. It did not fall to competitive mystery cults which copied its practices and doctrines, nor did it compromise with the gods of State which were promoted by the emperors and worshiped perfunctorily. Neither did it waver or retreat when "false prophets" of Gnosticism "crept in secretly" to undermine the belief in the nature of Jesus.

One might ask why the Church stood so strong in the face of such conflicts while other religious groups, such as the Mithra cult, blended into the whirlpool of syncretistic religions. Dr. Tenney states it well:

> The collapse of the second Jewish Commonwealth and the slow spiritual decay of the Western world left a vacuum which only the creation of a regenerate church could fill. Ceremonialism and political formalism were not satisfying to the spirit; a new life was demanded. On the foundation of the Old Testament revelation the Christian message was built, and its appeal to the Gentiles offered them personal faith in a living Sovereign greater and more permanent than the Caesars. As Rome declined, Christianity increased, until it was able to provide the light for dark ages and the stabilizing force in a world made chaotic by Rome's fall. (Tenney, *Times*, 359)

The Church was an answer to the needs of the world, in spite of all opposition. It was, and is, the Church Triumphant.

BIBLIOGRAPHY

Abbott, Jacob. *Alexander the Great.* New York: Circle Publishing Co., n. d.

Allegro, John M. *The Dead Sea Scrolls; A Reappraisal.* Hammondsworth, Middlesex: Penguin Books, 1956

Allen, Willoughby Charles.
A Critical and Exegetical Commentary on the Gospel According to St. Matthew. (The International Critical Commentary.) New York: Charles Scribner's Sons, 1957.

Angus, Samuel. *The Mystery Religions and Christianity.* London: Murray, 1928.

Arndt, William and Gingrich, F. Wilbur.
A Greek-English Lexicon of the New Testament. Chicago: University of Chicago Press, 4th ed., 1952.

Arnold, E. Vernon. *Roman Stoicism.* New York: The Humanities Press, 1958.

Bainton, Roland Herbert.
Early Christianity. Princeton: Van Nastrand, 1960.

Barrett, C. K. *The New Testament Background: Selected Documents.* New York: Harper and Row, 1961.

Barthelemy, D. and Milik, Josef T.
Qumran Cave I (Discoveries in the Judean Desert I). Oxford: Clarendon Press, 1955.

Baumbach, Günther.
Das Sadduzäerverständnis bei Josephus Flavius und im Neuen Testament. Kairos 13 (1971): 27.

Bevan, Edwyn. *Stoics and Skeptics.* London: W. Heffer and Sons, Ltd., 1959.

Bible. *The Holy Bible Containing the Old and New Testament.* KJV. New York: American Bible Society, 1970.

_____. *New American Standard Bible.* Carol Stream, Ill.: Creation House, 1973.

_____. *The New Oxford Annotated Bible with the Aprocrypha.* Edited by Herbert G. May and Bruce M. Metzger. RVS. New York: Oxford University Press, 1973.

Bickerman, Elias. *From Ezra to the Last of the Maccabees.* New York: Schocken Books, 1962.

⸻. *The Maccabees: An Account of Their History from the Beginnings to the Fall of the House of the Hasmoneans.* New York: Schocken Books, 1947.

Brandon, Samuel G. H. *Jesus and the Zealots: A Study of the Political Factor in Primitive Christianity.* New York: Charles Scribner's Sons, 1967.

Bright, John. *A History of Israel*, 2nd edition. Philadelphia: Westminster Press, 1972.

Bruce, Frederick F. *Commentary on the Books of Acts.* Grand Rapids: Wm. B. Eerdmans Publishing Co., 1954.

⸻. *New Testament History.* Garden City, NY: Anchor Books, Doubleday, 1972.

⸻, ed. *Second Thoughts on the Dead Sea Scrolls.* Grand Rapids: Wm. B. Eerdmans Publishing Co., 1956.

Buhl, Frantz Peder William. *Det Israelitiske Folkes Historie.* Copenhagen: Gyldendalske Boghandel, Nordisk Forlag, 1922.

Bultmann, Rudolph. *The Johannine Epistles.* Translated by R. Philip O'Hara. Philadelphia: Fortress Press, 1967.

⸻. *The Theology of the New Testament.* Vol. I. London: S. C. M. Press, 1955.

Burns, Edward McNall. *Western Civilizations.* 6th ed. New York: W. W. Norton, 1963.

Burrows, Millar. *Burrows on the Dead Sea Scrolls.* Grand Rapids: Baker Book House, 1978.

⸻. *Dead Sea Scrolls.* New York: Viking Press, 1958.

⸻. *More Light on the Dead Sea Scrolls.* New York: Viking Press, 1958.

Burrows, Millar; Trever, John C. and Brownlee, William H., editors. *The Dead Sea Scrolls of St. Mark's Monastery. Vol. I: The Isaiah Manuscript, and the Habakkuk Commentary.* New Haven: The American Schools of Oriental Research, 1950.

Carpenter, Edward. *Pagan and Christian Creeds, Their Origin and Meaning.* New York: Harcourt, Brace and Howe, 1920.

Case, Shirley Jackson. *The Evolution of Early Christianity.* Chicago: The University of Chicago Press, 1914.

Charles, Robert H., ed. and trans. *The Apocrypha and Pseudepigrapha of the Old Testament.* 2 vols. Oxford, 1913.

Coggins, R. J.　　　*Samaritans and Jews*. Atlanta GA.: John Knox Press, 1975.

Coneybeare, Rev. W. J.
　　　The Life and Epistles of St. Paul. New York: Fleming H. Revell Co., 1916.

Conzelmann, Hans.　*History of Primitive Christianity*. Translated by John E. Steely. Nashville: Abingdon Press, 1973.

_____.　　　*I Corinthians*. Translated by J. Leitch. Philadelphia: Fortress Press, 1969.

Cook, Arthur Bernard.
　　　Zeus: A Study in Ancient Religion. Vols. I and II. New York: Biblo and Tanner, 1964.

Coss, Thurman L.　*Secrets from the Caves*. New York: Abingdon Press, 1963.

Craig, Asa Hollister. *Christian Persecutions*. Burlington: Burlington Publishing Co., 1899.

Cross, Frank Leslie, ed.
　　　The Jung Codex. London: Morehouse, Gotham Co., 1955.

Cross, Frank M., Jr. *The Ancient Library of Qumran and Modern Biblical Studies* (The Haskell Lectures 1956-57). New York: Doubleday, 1958.

Cullman, Oscar.　　*The Christology of the New Testament*. Rev. ed. Translated by Shirley C. Guthrie and Charles A. M. Hall. Philadelphia: Westminster Press, 1963.

Cumont, Franz.　　*Oriental Religions in Roman Paganism*. New York: Dover Publications, 1956.

Delling, Gerhard.　"Josephus und das Wunderbare." *NT2* (1958): 305.

The Delphian Course: World's Progress.
　　　Vol. I. Chicago: The Delphian Society, 1913.

Dimont, Max I.　　*Jews, God and History*. New York: New American Library, 1962.

Dupont-Sommer, André.
　　　The Dead Sea Scrolls: A Preliminary Survey. Translated by E. Margaret Rowley. New York: Macmillan Co., 1952.

_____.　　　*The Essene Writing From Qumran*. Gloucester, Mass.: Peter Smith, 1973.

Eddy, Samuel K.　　*The King Is Dead*. Lincoln: University of Nebraska Press, 1961.

Encyclopaedia Judaica.
　　　11th ed. S. v. "Music," by Yohanan Boehn.

Epicurus. *The Extant Remains, With Short Critical Apparatus.* Trans. by C. Bailey. Oxford: Clarendon Press, 1926.

Eusebius. *Greek Ecclesiastical History.* 4th ed. London: Samuel Bagster & Sons, M.DCCC. XLVII.

Fairweather, William.
The Background of the Epistles. New York: Charles Scribner's Sons, 1935.

_____. *Jesus and the Greeks.* Edinburgh: T. & T. Clark, 1924.

Farmer, William Reuben.
The Maccabees, Zealots and Josephus. New York: Columbia University Press, 1956.

Farnell, Lewis Richard.
The Cults of the Greek States. Vol. IV. Oxford: Clarendon Press, 1907.

Fitzmyer, Joseph A. *Essays on the Semitic Background of the New Testament.* London: Scholar's Press, 1974.

Foakes-Jackson, Frederick John.
A Brief Biblical History, New Testament. New York: George H. Doran Co., 1923.

Foerster, Werner *From the Exile to Christ.* Philadelphia: Fortress Press, 1964.

Fowler, W. Ward. *The Religious Experience of the Roman People.* London: Macmillan Co., Ltd., 1922.

Freudenthal, J. *Hellenistische Studien. Haft 1 and 2: Alexander Polyhistor.* Breslau: Verlag von H. Skutsch, 1875.

Gager, John G. "The Figure of Moses in Greek and Roman Pagan Literature." Ph.D. dissertation, Harvard University, 1968.

Galpin, Francis William.
The Music of the Sumerians and Their Immediate Successors, the Babylonians and Assyrians. New York: Da Capo Press, 1970.

Gaster, Theodor Herzl.
Dead Sea Scriptures. Garden City, New York: Doubleday, 1956.

Gayley, Charles Mills.
The Classic Myths. New rev. ed. Boston: Ginn & Co., 1939.

Georgi, Dieter. *Die Gegner des Paulus im 2. Korintherbrief: Studien zur Religiösen Propaganda in der Spätantike.* (Wissenschaftliche Monographien zum Alten and Neuen Testament, 11.) Neukirchen-Vluyn: Neukirchener Verlag, 1964.

Ginzberg, Louis. *Eine unbekannte jüdische Sekte.* E. T. *The Legends of the Jews.* Philadelphia: The Jewish Publication Society of America, 1911.

Goodman, Paul. *History of the Jews.* Rev. and enl. by Israel Cohen. New York: E. P. Dutton, 1953.

Goppelt, Leonhard. *Apostolic and Post-Apostolic Times.* Trans. by Robert A. Guelich. Grand Rapids: Baker Book House, 1962.

Grant, Robert M. *A Historical Introduction to the New Testament.* New York: Simon & Schuster, 1972.

————. *Gnosticism and Early Christianity.* New York: Columbia University Press, 1966.

Groningen, G. van. *First Century Gnosticism.* Leiden: E. J. Brill, 1967.

Guthrie, W. K. C. *The Greeks and Their Gods.* Boston: Beacon Press, 1955.

Haenchen, Ernst. *The Acts of the Apostles.* Philadelphia: The Westminster Press, 1971. (English translation).

Hahn, Ferdinand. *The Titles of Jesus in Christology.* New York: World Publishing Co., 1969.

Harrison, Everett F. *A Short Life of Christ.* Grand Rapids: Wm. B. Eerdmans Publishing Co., 1968.

Harrison, R. K. *The Dead Sea Scrolls.* New York: Harper & Bros., 1961.

Hicks, Robert Drew.
Stoic and Epicurean. New York: Russell and Russell, Inc., 1962.

Hippolytus. *Refutation of All Heresies* or *Philosophumena.* Trans. by F. Legge. London, New York: The Macmillan Co., 1921.

Hodas, Moses. *Stoic Philosophy of Seneca.* Trans. by M. Hodas. Gloucester: P. Smith, 1965.

Hyde, Walter W. *Paganism to Christianity in the Roman Empire.* Philadelphia: University of Pennsylvania Press, 1946.

Idelsohn, Abraham. *Jewish Music in Its Historical Development.* New York: Schocken Books, 1967.

Ishak, Priest Amram.
The History of Religion of the Samaritans. Jerusalem: Greek Convent Press, n. d.

Jackson, F. J. Foakes.
    Josephus and the Jews. Grand Rapids: Baker Book House, 1977.

Jacoby, Felix.   *Die Fragmente der Griechischen Historiker.* Leiden: E. J. Brill, 1957.

Jeremias, Joachim.   "Ἠλίας." *TWNT* II:930-35. E. T. *TDNT* 2:928-41. Grand Rapids: Wm. B. Eerdmans Publishing Co., 1964.

The Jewish Encylopedia.
    Vol. V, 1907 ed. S. v. "Elijah."

_____. Vol. VIII, 1907 ed. S. v. "Pesikta Rabbati" and "Yalkut Shimoni," by J. Theodor.

_____. Vol. IX, 1905 ed. S. v. "Pharisees," by Kaufmann Kohler.

Jonas, Hans.   *The Gnostic Religion.* Boston: Beacon Press, 1972.

Josephus, Flavius.   *The Complete Works of Flavius Josephus.* Chicago: Thompson & Thomas, 1901.

Kahen, Hasanein Wasef.
    The Samaritans: Their History, Religion, Customs. Nablus, Israel: 1974.

Kerenyi, Kzroly.   *The Religion of the Greeks and Romans.* London: Thomas & Hudson, 1962.

Klausner, Joseph.   *The Messianic Idea in Israel: From Its Beginning to the Completion of the Mishnah.* New York: Macmillan Co., 1955.

Kuhn, Karl Georg.   "Die beiden Messias Aarons und Israels." *NTS* 1, (1954-55): 178.

Landman, Isaac.   *The Universal Jewish Encyclopedia.* New York: KTAV Publishing House, 1969.

Lamb, Harold.   *Alexander of Macedon.* Garden City, NY: Doubleday & Co., Inc., 1946.

LaSor, William Sanford.
    The Dead Sea Scrolls and the Christian Faith. Chicago: Moody Press, 1962.

_____. *The Dead Sea Scrolls and the New Testament.* Grand Rapids: Wm. B. Eerdmans Publishing Co., 1972.

Levinger, Elma Ehrlich and Levinger, Rabbi Lee J.
    The Story of the Jews. New York: Behrman's Jewish Book Shop, 1928.

Lightfoot, Joseph Barber.
    St. Paul's Epistle to Philemon. London: Macmillan Co., Ltd., 1891.

Lohse, Edward.	*The New Testament Environment.* Translated by John E. Steely. Nashville: Abingdon Press, 1976.
Lucian.	*The Loeb Classical Library,* Vols. I-VIII. Cambridge: Cambridge University Press, 1967.
Lucius.	*True History and Lucius or the Ass.* Trans. by P. Turner. Bloomington, Indiana: University Press, 1958.
MacDonald, John.	*The Theology of the Samaritans.* Philadelphia: Westminster Press, 1964.

MacGregor, George Hogarth.
    Jew and Greek: Tutors Unto Christ. London: Nicholson and Watson, Limited, 1936.

MacRae, George W.
    "Miracle in the Antiquities of Josephus" in Charles F. D. Moule, ed., *Miracles: Cambridge Studies in Their Philosophy and History.* London: A. R. Mowbray, 1965.

Machen, John G.	*The Origin of Paul's Religion.* New York: Macmillan Co., 1923.

Manson, Thomas William.
    The Servant-Messiah: A Study of the Public Ministry of Jesus. Grand Rapids: Baker Book House, 1977.

Marsden. E. W.	*Greek and Roman Artillery.* Oxford: Clarendon Press, 1969.
Martyr, Justin.	*Dialogue With Trypho.* Trans. by Lukyn Williams. London, New York, and Toronto: Macmillan Co., 1930.

McGiffert, Arthur C.
    The Apostolic Age. New York: Charles Scribner's Sons, 1906.

McNeill, William H. *History of Western Civilization: A Handbook.* Rev. and enl. Chicago: University of Chicago Press, 1969.

Menzies, Allen, ed.	*The Ante-Nicene Fathers.* Vol. X. Grand Rapids: Wm. B. Eerdmans Publishing Co., 1969.
Merx, Adalbert.	*Der Messias oder Ta'eb der Samaritaner.* Giessen: A. Töpelmann, 1909.
Metzger, Bruce M.	*The New Testament: Its Background, Growth, and Content.* Nashville: Abingdon Press, 1965.
Meyer, Eduard.	*Ursprung und Anfänge des Christentums,* i-iii. Stuttgart und Berlin: J. G. Cotta, 1921.
Meyer, R.	*Der Prophet aus Galiläa.* Buchges: Darmstadt, Wissenschaftliche, 1970.

Milik, Josef T. *Ten Years of Discovery in the Wilderness of Judaea.* Translated by J. Strugnell. Naperville, Ill.: A. R. Allenson, 1959.

Milman, Henry. *The History of Christianity.* New York: W. J. Widdleton, 1871.

Montgomery, James A. *The Samaritans.* Rev. ed., 1968, repr. of 1907 ed. New York: KTAV Publishing House, 1968.

Moore, George Foot. *Judaism in the First Centuries of the Christian Era: The Age of the Tannaim,* Vol. I. New York: Schocken Books, 1971.

More, Paul. *Christ The Word.* Princeton: Princeton University Press, 1927.

_____. *Hellenistic Philosophy.* Princeton: Princeton University Press, 1923.

Mowinckel, Sigmund Olaf. *He That Cometh.* Translated by G. W. Anderson. New York: Abingdon Press, 1954.

Murray, Gilbert. *The Five Stages of Greek Religion.* Garden City: Doubleday & Co., Inc., 1951.

_____. *The Stoic Philosophy.* New York and London: G. P. Putnam's Sons, 1915.

Neander, August. *History of the Christian Church.* Vol. I. London: G. Bell and Sons, 1876.

Neusner, Jacob. *A Life of Yahanan Ben Zakkai: Ca. 1-80 C. E.* Leiden: E. J. Brill, 1970.

Nilsson, Martin P. *Greek Folk Religion.* Philadelphia: University of Pennsylvania Press, 1972.

Norwood, Frederick Abbott. *Strangers and Exiles.* Vol. I. New York: Abingdon Press, 1969.

Pearlman, Moshe. *The Macabees.* London: Weidenfeld and Nicolson, 1973.

Pfeiffer, Charles F. *Between the Testaments.* Grand Rapids: Baker Book House, 1959.

_____. *The Dead Sea Scrolls.* Grand Rapids: Baker Book House, 1962.

Pfleiderer, Otto. *Primitive Christianity.* Translated by W. Montgomery. Clifton, NJ: Reference Book Publishers, 1965.

Pliny. *Letters and Pangyricus.* Loeb Classical Library. Translated by Betty Radice. Cambridge: Harvard University Press, 1969.

Poland, Franz. *Geschichte des Griechischen, Vereinsuiesens.* Leipzig: Teubner, 1909.

Polybius. *The Histories of Polybius.* Trans. by E. Shuckburgh. London and New York: Macmillan Co., 1889.

Pseudo-Clementine. Berlin: Akademie-Verlag, 1953.

Purnes, George Tyhout.
Christianity in the Apostolic Age. New York: Charles Scribner's Sons, 1902.

Purvis, James D. *The Samaritan Pentateuch and the Origin of the Samaritan Sect.* Cambridge, Mass.: Harvard University Press, 1968.

Quispel, Gilles. *Vigiliae Christianae.* (Amsterdam), I. (1947), 48-73.

Raskin, P. M. "The Eternal Riddle," quoted by Levinger, Elma. *The Story of The Jew.* New York: Behrmen's Jewish Book House, 1938.

Reicke, Bo Ivar. *The New Testament Era.* Philadelphia: Fortress Press, 1976.

Rhoads, David M. *Israel in Revolution: 6-74 C.E.* Philadelphia: Fortress Press, 1976.

Ropes, James. *The Apostolic Age.* New York: Charles Scribner's Sons, 1906.

Roth, Cecil. *A History of the Jews.* New York: Schocken Books, 1961.

Rothmüller, Aron Marko.
The Music of the Jews. New and rev. ed. Cranbury, NJ: A. S. Barnes, 1975.

Russell, David S. *The Jews from Alexander to Herod.* London: Oxford University Press, 1967.

Schermerhorn, William.
Beginnings of the Christian Church. New York: Methodist Book Concern, 1929.

Schure, Edward. *From Sphinx To Christ.* San Francisco: Harper & Row, 1982, ©1970.

Scott, R. B. Y. "The Expectation of Elijah." *The Canadian Journal of Religious Thought.* Vol. 3, No. 6 (Nov.-Dec. 1929): 490-502.

Sendrey, Alfred. *Music in Ancient Israel.* New York: Philosophical Library, 1969.

Sendrey, Alfred and Norton, Mildred.
　　　　　　　　David's Harp: The Story of Music in Biblical Times. New York: The New American Library, 1964.

Smith, Morton.　"Palestinian Judaism in the First Century," in Moshe Davis, ed., *Israel, Its Role in Civilization*, Part II, Ch. 4. New York: Arno Press, 1977.

Strack, Herman L. and Billerback, Paul.
　　　　　　　　Kommentar zum Neuen Testament aus Talmud Midrasch. Vol. IV. Munich: Beck Verlag, 1922-65.

Suetonius.　　　*The Twleve Caesars.* Translated by Robert Graves. Baltimore: Penguin Classics, 1957.

Tactitus.　　　*The Annals of Imperial Rome.* Rev. ed. Translated by Michael Grant. Great Britain: Penguin Classics, 1975.

Tarn, William Woodthorpe.
　　　　　　　　Hellenistic Civilization. New York: New American Library, 1952.

Tcherikover, Victor. *Hellenistic Civilization and the Jews.* New York: Atheneum, 1970.

Tedesche, Sidney. *The First Book of Maccabees* (Jewish Apocryphal Literature, Vol. 1). New York: Harper & Bros., 1950.

Teeple, Howard M. *The Mosaic Eschatological Prophet.* Philadelphia: Society of Biblical Literature, 1957.

Tenney, Merrill C. *New Testament Survey.* Grand Rapids: Wm. B,. Eerdmans Publishing Co., 1974.

_____.　　　*New Testament Times.* Grand Rapids: Wm. B. Eerdmans Publishing Co., 1965.

_____, ed.　*The Zondervan Bible Pictoral Dictionary.* Grand Rapids: Zondervan Publishing House, 1963.

Tertullian.　　　*Against the Valentinians.* Venice: Opera Omnia Ed. Alliricius, 1701, pp. 150ff.

Thackeray, H. St. John.
　　　　　　　　Josephus: The Man and the Historian. New York: Jewish Institute of Religion Press, 1929.

_____.　　　*The Relation of St. Paul to Contemporary Jewish Thought.* New York: Macmillan Co., 1900.

The Gospel According To Thomas.
　　　　　　　　Leiden: E. J. Brill, 1959.

The Interpreter's Dictionary of the Bible.
　　　　　　　　Vol. 4. Edited by George Arthur Buttrick. Nashville: Abingdon Press, 1962.

The Nag Hammadi Library.
        Trans. by Members of the Coptic Gnostic Library Project, dir. by James Robinson. Leiden: E. J. Brill, 1977.

Theophrastus. *Enquiry Into Plants.* Trans. by Sir Arthur Hort. London: W. Heinemann; Cambridge, Mass.: Harvard University Press, 1948-49.

Tiede, David Lenz. *The Charismatic Figure as Miracle Worker.* SBL Dissertation Series, Number 1. University of Montana: Missoula, Montana, 1972.

Toynbee, Arnold J. *Hellenism, The History of A Civilization.* London: Oxford University Press, 1959.

Trever, John C. *The Dead Sea Scrolls, A Personal Account.* Grand Rapids: Wm. B. Eerdmans Publishing Co., 1977.

_____. *The Untold Story of Qumran.* Westwood, NJ: Fleming Revell, 1965.

Vaux, Roland de (Père).
        L'Archéologie et les mánuscrits de la Mer Morte (Schweich Lectures of the British Academy, 1959). London: Oxford University Press, 1961.

Valentinus. *Gospel of Truth.* Trans. by Kendrick Grobel. New York and Nashville: Abingdon Press, 1960.

Van Unnik, W. C. "The Gospel of Truth and The New Testament," *The Jung Codex.* Ed. F. C. Cross. London: Mowbray & Co., 1955.

Volz, Paul. *Die Eschatologie der Jüdischen Gemeinde in neutestamentlicher Zeitalter.* Tübingen: J. C. B. Mohr (Paul Siebeck), 1934.

Ward, John. *A History of the Early Church to A.D. 500.* London: Methuen & Co., Ltd., 1963.

Weber, Ferdinand Wilhem.
        Jüdische Theologie auf Grund des Talmud un verwandter Schriften gemeinfasslich dargestellt. 2nd ed. Leipzig: Dorffling & Franke, 1897.

Weeden, Theodore J.
        Mark: Traditions in Conflict. Philadelphia: Fortress Press, 1971.

Wernle, Paul. *The Beginnings of Christianity,* Vol. 1. New York: Williams and Norgate, 1914.

Wesley, Robert Mark.
        Stoicism and Its Influence. New York: Cooper Square Publishers, 1963.

Wilson, Robert McLachlan.
    Gnosis and the New Testament. Philadelphia: Fortress Press, 1968.

_____. *The Gnostic Problem.* London: A. R. Mowbray, 1958.

Workman, Herbert. *Persecution in the Early Church.* London: Charles Kelly, 1906.

Yadin, Yigael. *The Message of the Scrolls.* New York: Simon & Schuster, 1957.

Zeller, Dr. Edward. *Stoics, Epicureans and Sceptics.* New and rev. ed. New York: Russell and Russell, Inc., 1962.

INDEX

A

Acts 1:13-14, 116, 141
  1:21, 142
  2:14, 142
  2:38, 142
  2:41, 141
  2:42, 142
  2:44, 143
  2:46, 142, 143
  3:1, 84
  4:4, 141
  4:18, 149
  4:23-31, 149
  4:35, 142
  5:1-11, 142
  5:14, 141
  5:14-16, 149
  5:17, 65
  5:34-40, 54
  6:2, 142
  6:3, 151
  6:4, 142
  6:5, 151
  6:7, 141
  6:8, 151
  7:51-53, 151
  7:56, 151
  7:57, 152
  7:58, 152
  8:1, 152
  8:5 141
  8:5-40, 153
  9:1-1, 153
  9:23, 155
  9:31, 114, 155
  10, 153, 168
  11, 168
  11:1-3, 168
  11:2, 167
  11:3, 168
  11:18, 169
  11:19, 169
  11:20, 153, 142
  11:20-24, 169
  11:22, 142
  11:26, 141, 143
  11:27, 143
  11:29, 168

Acts (cont'd)
  11:30, 168
  12:3, 157
  12:13, 156
  13:1-3, 143
  13:45, 155
  13:50, 155
  14:2, 155
  14:5, 155
  14:8-18, 180
    v. 13, 180
  14:12, 182
  14:19, 155
  14:45, 155
  15, 142
  15:1, 167, 169
  15:2, 170
  15:19, 171
  16:19, 157
  16:19-40, 155
  17, 210, 213
  17:5, 155
  17:18, 222
  17:20, 210
  17:22, 182
  17:32, 223
  18:13, 155
  19:23-24, 156
  19:26, 157
  19:28, 182
  21:17, 172
  21:18, 142
  21:27-32, 156
  22-3, 154
  22-25, 154
  22-28, 154
  22:24-29, 156
  23-5, 154
  23-6, 154
  23:6-8, 54
  23:8, 58
  24, 156
  25:11, 156
  28:30, 156
  28:31, 156
Acts, chapter 8, 114
Agrippa, 40
  Herod I, 160
  King, II, 165

Alexandra, 36
Amos 9:11, 171
Annas, 65
Antigonus, 36
Antiochus, 16, 18-20, 22
   I, 3
   III, 16
   IV (Epiphanes), iv, 15-17, 22-24
   IV, 17, 23, 24
   V (Eupator), 23
   VI, 26
   VII, 27
Antipater, 34, 35, 39
Antony, Mark, 36
apocalyptic, 128
Apostolic Council, 172
Appollonius of Tayana, 198
Archelaus, 40, 80
Aristobulus,
   I, 80
   II, 33, 34
Aristotle, 6-8
Augustus, 146
Aurelius, Marcus, 211

B

Bar Kochba War, 56
Bar Kochba, 43, 97
Ben-Gurion, 90
Brutus, 36
Burrus, 163

C

Caesar, Augustus, 134, 135
Caesar, Julias, 35, 134
Caligula, 159, 187
Cassius, 36
Cave I of Qumran, 86, 96
   II, 98
   III, 98
   IV, 98
   V, 98
   VI, 98
   XI, 99
II Chron. 15:14, 105
   29:25, 116
II Chronicles 34:9, 111

Church Fathers, 43, 63
Cicero, 208
Claudius, 161
Cleopatra, 37
Col. 1:15, 210
   1:16, 210
   3:11, 211
Colossians 2:8-10, 196
   2:16-22, 196
Cor. 12:15, 214
   8:10, 180
   15:21, 235
   15:29, 196
   15:32, 223
   15:44-49, 235
I Cor. 1-2, 235
   2:4, 235
   2:6-8, 235
   2:8, 235
   2:14f, 235
   7:32-34, 235
   7:38, 235
   8:10, 180
   8:6, 210
   15:21, 235
   15:29,
   15:32, 223
   15-44-49, 235
II Cor. 11:23-33, 156
   1:8, 156
   4:4, 235
   4:8-11, 156
   5:18, 198
   11-12, 235
   11:22, 235
Corinthians 7:21-23, 211
I Corinthians, 2:6, 196
   2:7, 196
   7:21-23. 211
   10:4, 195
II Corinthians, 12:15, 214
Cynics, 203

D

Damascus Document, 78
Dan. 3:5, 103
   3:7, 103
   3:10, 103
   3:15, 103

Daniel 3:5, 68, 69
   7, 68, 69
   10, 68, 69
   15, 68, 69
Dead Sea, 36, 82, 89
Demetrius, 24-26
Deuteronomy 18:18, 112
   25:5-6, 65
   32:34, 113
   32:35, 113
Diaspora, 42
Domitian, 239

E

Egypt, 30
Eleazar, 20
Elijah, 124
Enoch I, 79
Eph. 5:16, 214
Ephesians, 234
   3:10, 234
   6:12, 234
Epictetus, 210
Epicurus, 9
Epiphanes, 17
   Antiochus, 15, 16-17, 22
Eusebius, 85
Ex. 20:3, 171
Exod. 3:14, 111
   19:13, 105
   19:16, 105
   19:19, 105
Exodus 15:1-19, 13
   15:20-21, 13
   16:33, 128
   28:33, 116
   28:34, 116
   39:25, 116
   39:26, 116
Ezek, 40:46, 61
   43:19, 61
   44:15, 61
   48:11, 61
Ezekiel 40-48, 61
Ezra, 109

F

Felix, 165
Festus, 123, 165

G

Gal. 1:6-9, 167
   2:1-10, 168
   2:9, 142
   2:11, 169
   2:12, 169
   2:13, 169
   2:20, 198
   3, 173
   3:13, 173
   3:19, 173
   3:28, 211, 223
   5:2, 174
      v.3, 174
   5:3, 167
   5:6, 174
   5-14, 174
   5:12, 167
   6:2, 212
   6:12, 170
   7:12, 167
   7:15, 167
Galatians, 234
   3:19, 234
   2:20, 234
Gamaliel, 60, 149
   I, 54
Gen. 4:21, 102
   15:6, 173
   17:12, 112
   17:9-14, 169
Gophna, 21
Greek Seleucid, 15

H

Hadrian, 191
Hamoneans, 66
Hanukkah, 27, 28
Hasidim, 47
Hasmonean Kingdom, 33, 37
Hasmonean, 51, 61

Heb. 11:16, 212
    24:6-Eng., 117
Heliodorus, 16
Herod, 150
Herod the Great, 40-41, 135
Herodians, 146
Hillel, 52-54, 58
Hippolytus, 72, 78, 79
Hyrcanus II, 33-35
Hyrcanus, John, 48

I

Isaiah 5:12, 102
    30:29, 102
    38:20, 69

J

Jason, 18
Jeremiah 48:36, 102
Jerusalem, 184
Jewish Diaspora, 230
Jewish music, 43
Job 21:12, 102
    21:30-31, 102
    30:9, 69
John 1:1-3, 213
    1:4, 233
    1:11, 233
    1:23, 84
    2, 208
    2:7, 234
    3:8, 232
    4:7-26, 114
    4:11, 233
    4:14, 232
    8:12, 232
    8:14, 232
    8:23, 232
    9:29, 232
    10:22, 28
    11:47-57, 60
    12:46, 232
    13:36, 233
    14:2, 198
    14:5, 233
    15, 183
    16, 232

John (*cont'd*)
    17, 183
    17:6, 232
    20-21, 184
    20:28, 208
John, Chapter 9, 60
I John 183, 233
    4:2, 233
    4:2f, 234
    5:6, 233
    5:6, 234
John the Baptist, 60, 84, 140, 146
Jonathan, 24, 26
Judaizers, 167, 167n, 170
Judas, 22-24
Jude 12, 236
    4, 236
    8, 236
    12, 236

K

Khirbet Qumran, 72, 81, 99
Khirbet Mird, 85
Kings 18:26-28, 31
I Kings 1:34, 105
    1:40, 102
    2:35, 61
    6:7, 38
II Kings 2:11, 125
    2:35, 61
    9:13, 105
    15:19, 111
    17:24, 110
    24:24, 111
Kinnor, 67

L

Laertius, Diogenes, 215
Lamentations 3:14, 69
    5:14, 69
Lev. 27:30-33, 58
Leviticus 25:9-54, 105
Logos, 205, 227
Lucian, 191
Lucretius, 222

Luke 2:46-47, 207
  2:48, 207
  3:3, 84
  6:1-10, 208
  6:6-11, 84
  7:34, 84
  9:9, 58
  10:21, 231
  10:22, 231
  10:25-37, 113
  10:30-37, 223
  11:39-40, 56
  11:42, 58
  13:31, 60
  14:1-6, 84
  15:2, 56
  19:10, 197
  21, 176
  22:44, 208
  24:49, 141

M

Magus, Simon, 229
Malachi, 4:5, 125
Malachi, 4:6, 125
Manahem, 80
Manual of Discipline, 82, 119
Marcion, 227
Mariamne, 39
Mark 1:4, 84
  1:5, 84
  2:14-17, 56
  2:15, 59
  2:23-28, 84, 208
  2:23-3:6, 59
  2:27, 59
  3:6, 60
  6:16, 58
  7:1-5, 59
  7:3-4, 56
  8:27, 132
  8:33, 132
  12:18-27, 65
  12:37, 84
  13, 176
  14:26, 133
  14:38, 208
  16:15, 141
  16:16, 196

Masada, 83
Mat. 5-7, 140
Matt. 3:5, 84
  3:6, 84
  7:29, 60
  10:1ff., 140
  10:16-18, 148
  10:17, 150
  10:22-23, 148
  10:23, 148
  10:28, 148
  11:19, 84
  12:1-2, 84
  12:1-13, 208
  12:13f., 60
  13:55, 207
  23:2-31, 60
  23:16, 59
  23:23, 58
  23:25-26, 56
  26:41, 208
  28:19, 140
  28:20, 140
Mattathias, 19-21, 26
Matthew 5:5, 208
  11:25,, 231
  11:28-30, 232
  16:18, 139
Megiddo, 44-45
Menelaus, 18-19
Messiah, 58, 114, 117, 157
Messianic, 107
Metropolitan, 94
Midrashic, 128
Moses, 118
Mount Gerizim, 111
Mystery religions, 10

N

Nag Hammadi Library, 226
Nash Papyrus, 92
Nebuchadnezzar (King), 67
Neh. 10:29-30
Nero, 163
Num. 10:2, 104
  10:8, 104
  10:10, 104
  18:21-24, 58

O

Octavian, 37
Onias, 17, 18

P

Paul, 209
persecution, 153
II Peter 2:1, 235-236
    3:7, 212
    3:10, 212
Ph. 1:23, 212
phalanx, 201
Phil. 3:2, 172
    3:3, 172
    3:5, 154
    3:6, 154
Philip of Macedon, 1, 2
Philo, 71, 73, 125
Pilate, 122
Plato, 226
Pliny, 71
polis, 4
Poluibus, 17
Pompey, 33, 35
Ps. 2:7, 118
    81:3,, 105
    98:6, 105
Psalms 4, 69
    5, 103
    6, 69
    8, 68
    33:2, 68
    45, 69
    53, 103
    54, 69
    55, 69
    60, 69
    61, 69
    67, 69
    69, 69
    76, 69
    77:7, 69
    80, 69
    81, 68
    84, 68

Psalms, (*cont'd*)
    88, 103
    92:3, 68
    144:9, 68
    150:4, 102
Ptolemies, 4, 37
Ptolemy I, 3, 8
Ptolemy II, 3, 10

Q

Qumran, 48, 61, 72, 79, 84, 119
Qumran caves, 97
Qumran literature, 125

R

rabbinic literature, 117
Rev. 1, 210
Rom. 6:3f, 142
    6:4, 198
    11:36, 210
Romans 9:3, 167
    13, 166

S

Salome, 39
Samaritan, 122, 141
I Sam. 18:6, 116
    24:7, 117
II Sam. 6:15, 105
    15:30, 105
Samuel 10:5, 102
I Samuel 10:5, 102
II Samuel 6:5, 116
Sanhedrin, 39, 49, 148, 150
Second Temple, 133
Seleucid, 4, 17, 20, 21, 24, 26, 27, 37, 62
Seleucid army, 25
Seleucid Empire, 16
Seleucus, 3,
    IV, 16
Seneca, 163, 206
Shammai, 52-54, 58
shofar, 104

Shrine of the Book, 95
Sicari, 123
Simon and Jonathan, 23
Simon, 26, 27
Son of David, 119
Son of Man, 122
Stoics, 9-10
Straton's Tower, 38
Suetonius, 164
Sumeria, 30
Syrian Metropolitan, 87

T

Tacitus, 164
Talmud, 117
Teacher of Righteousness, 119, 125, 140
Temple, 148, 151, 176
I Thess. 4:17, 212
Theudas, 131
Tiberius, 145
I Tim, 143
    1:4, 235
    2:5f, 235
    3:16, 235
    4:3, 214
    4:3, 235
II Tim, 143
    2:18, 235
    2:8, 235
    3:7, 214
II Timothy 4, 166
Titus, 143, 184
    1:15, 214
Torah, 52, 57, 63, 112, 129

V

Vespasian, 175
Vexuvius, 71

W

Wadi Murabba'ât, 85, 97
Wadi Qumran, 85, 86
Wumran literature, 125

Y

Yohanan, 55
Yohanan, ben Zakkai, 54

Z

Zakkai, Ben, 55, 59
Zakkai, Rabbi ben, 59
Zealots, 51
Zealots, 54
Zealots, 78
Zechariah 14:20, 116
Zeno, 201
Zoroastrian, 49

www.ingramcontent.com/pod-product-compliance
Lightning Source LLC
Chambersburg PA
CBHW050435240426
43661CB00055B/2386